Continuity and Discontinuity in Learning Careers

Research on the Education and Learning of Adults

Series Editors

(*On behalf of the European Society for Research on the Education of Adults*)
Emilio Lucio-Villegas (*University of Seville, Spain*)
Barbara Merrill (*University of Warwick, United Kingdom*)
Marcella Milana (*Aarhus University, Denmark*)
Henning Salling Olesen (*Roskilde University, Denmark*)

Editorial Advisory Board

Michal Bron Jr. (*Södertörn University College, Sweden*)
Anja Heikkinen (*University of Tampere, Finland*)
Françoise F. Laot (*University Paris-Descartes, France*)
Linda Morrice (*University of Sussex, United Kingdom*)
Joanna Ostrouch-Kamińska (*University of Warmia and Mazury, Poland*)
Angela Pilch-Ortega (*Graz University, Austria*)
Andreas Wallo (*Linköping University, Sweden*)
Georgios Zarifis (*Aristotle University of Thessaloniki, Greece*)

VOLUME 6

The titles published in this series are listed at *brill.com/esra*

Continuity and Discontinuity in Learning Careers

Potentials for a Learning Space in a Changing World

Edited by

Barbara Merrill, Andrea Galimberti, Adrianna Nizinska
and José González-Monteagudo

BRILL
SENSE

LEIDEN | BOSTON

This is an open access title distributed under the terms of the prevailing CC-BY-NC License at the time of publication, which permits any non-commercial use, distribution, and reproduction in any medium, provided the original author(s) and source are credited.

All chapters in this book have undergone peer review.

The Library of Congress Cataloging-in-Publication Data is available online at http://catalog.loc.gov

ISSN 2542-9345
ISBN 978-90-04-37545-1 (paperback)
ISBN 978-90-04-37546-8 (hardback)
ISBN 978-90-04-37547-5 (e-book)

Copyright 2018 Koninklijke Brill NV, Leiden, The Netherlands.
Koninklijke Brill NV incorporates the imprints Brill, Brill Hes & De Graaf, Brill Nijhoff, Brill Rodopi, Brill Sense and Hotei Publishing.
All rights reserved. No part of this publication may be reproduced, translated, stored in a retrieval system, or transmitted in any form or by any means, electronic, mechanical, photocopying, recording or otherwise, without prior written permission from the publisher.
Authorization to photocopy items for internal or personal use is granted by Koninklijke Brill NV provided that the appropriate fees are paid directly to The Copyright Clearance Center, 222 Rosewood Drive, Suite 910, Danvers, MA 01923, USA. Fees are subject to change.

This book is printed on acid-free paper and produced in a sustainable manner.

CONTENTS

The European Society for Research on the Education of Adults (ESREA)   vii

Introduction   ix
   Barbara Merrill, Adrianna Nizinska, Andrea Galimberti and José González-Monteagudo

1. Learning Careers and Transformative Learning: Challenges of Learning and Work in Neoliberal Spaces   1
   Ted Fleming

Part 1: Continuity and Discontinuity in Formal Education

2. Friendship, Discourse and Belonging in the Studio: The Experiences of 'Non-Traditional' Students in Design Higher Education   17
   Samantha Broadhead

3. English Language Book Club and Transformative Learning: Developing Critical Consciousness in the English Language Classroom in a UK Further Education (FE) College and in a South African Township   29
   Ida Leal

4. Participation and Persistence: An Analysis of Underserved Students at UOIT   45
   Alyson E. King, Allyson Eamer and Nawal Ammar

Part 2: Continuity and Discontinuity in Social Institutions

5. Education Interrupted: Learning Careers of Adults Living with Mental Illness   61
   Shanti Irene Fernando and Alyson E. King

6. Inmates in Higher Education in Italy and Spain: Legal, Cultural and Technological Issues in a Complex Network of Continuity and Discontinuity   73
   Giuseppe Pillera

Part 3: Continuity and Discontinuity around the Job Market

7. Continuity and Discontinuity around Academia: The "Find Your Doctor" Project as a Space for Researching and Facilitating Learning Careers   91
   Andrea Galimberti and Eva Ratti

CONTENTS

8. Stimulating Empowerment and Supporting Access to Learning for Formally Low-Qualified Adults: Potentials of Work-Related Competency Assessment in Social Enterprises   107
   Monika Kastner

9. Policies for Equality and Employability: Consequences for Non-Traditional Students in Sweden   125
   Camilla Thunborg and Agnieszka Bron

10. Learning Careers of Non-Traditional Students on Employability Skills   133
    María A. Tenorio-Rodríguez, Teresa Padilla-Carmona and José González-Monteagudo

11. Literacy Practices in Adult Learning Biographies: Possibilities and Constraints   143
    Ana Silva, Maria de Lourdes Dionísio and Juliana Cunha

Part 4: Continuity and Discontinuity in Professional Contexts

12. Adults' Learning and Career Temporalities in the Analysis of Professionalisation and Professional Identity Construction   155
    Pascal Roquet

13. Ways of Learning of Adult Educators in Uncertain Professional Contexts   169
    Catarina Paulos

14. No More Superheroes … Only Avatars? Survival Role Play in English Post Compulsory Education   181
    Carol A. Thompson and Peter J. Wolstencroft

Conclusions   195
Andrea Galimberti, Barbara Merrill, Adrianna Nizinska and Jose González-Monteagudo

THE EUROPEAN SOCIETY FOR RESEARCH ON THE EDUCATION OF ADULTS (ESREA)

ESREA is a European scientific society. It was established in 1991 to provide a European-wide forum for all researchers engaged in research on adult education and learning and to promote and disseminate theoretical and empirical research in the field. Since 1991 the landscape of adult education and learning has changed to include more diverse learning contexts at formal and informal levels. At the same time, there has been a policy push by the European Union, OECD, UNESCO and national governments to promote a policy of lifelong learning. ESREA provides an important space for these changes and (re)definition of adult education and learning in relation to research, theory, policy and practice to be reflected upon and discussed. This takes place at the triennial conference, network conferences and through the publication of books and a journal.

ESREA RESEARCH NETWORKS

The major priority of ESREA is the encouragement of co-operation between active researchers in the form of thematic research networks which encourage inter-disciplinary research drawing on a broad range of the social sciences. These research networks hold annual/biennial seminars and conferences for the exchange of research results and to encourage publications.

The current active ESREA networks are:

- Access, Learning Careers and Identities
- Active Democratic Citizenship and Adult Learning
- Adult Educators, Trainers and their and Professional Development
- Between Global and Local: Adult Learning and Development
- Education and Learning of Older Adults
- Gender and Adult Learning
- History of Adult Education and Training in Europe
- Interrogating transformative processes in learning: An international exchange
- Life-history and Biographical Research
- Migration, Ethnicity, Racism and Xenophobia
- Policy Studies in Adult Education
- Working Life and Learning

ESREA TRIENNIAL EUROPEAN RESEARCH CONFERENCE

In order to encourage the widest possible forum for the exchange of ongoing research activities ESREA holds a triennial European Research Conference. The conferences

ESREA

have been held in Strobl (1995), Bruxelles (1998), Lisbon (2001), Wroclaw (2004), Seville (2007), Linköping (2010), Berlin (2013) and Maynooth (2016).

ESREA JOURNAL

ESREA publishes a scientific open access journal entitled *The European Journal for Research on the Education and Learning of Adults* (RELA). All issues of the journal can be read at www.rela.ep.liu.se. You can also find more information about call for papers and submission procedures on this website.

ESREA BOOKS

ESREA's research networks and conferences have led to the publication of over forty books. A full list, giving details of the various publishers, and the books' availability, is on the ESREA website. ESREA's current book series is published in co-operation with Brill | Sense.

Further information on ESREA is available at www.esrea.org

Emilio Lucio-Villegas
Barbara Merrill
Marcella Milana
Henning Salling Olesen

BARBARA MERRILL, ADRIANNA NIZINSKA,
ANDREA GALIMBERTI AND JOSÉ GONZÁLEZ-MONTEAGUDO

INTRODUCTION

In recent years the economic crisis in Europe and beyond has had, and continues to have, social, economic and political consequences. New challenges, as well as threats are posed to adult education which both offer a potential way out of the crisis and an alternative to the dominant stories played out by the neoliberal economic discourse. Within this framework and context this book explores the role of adult education in relation to continuity and discontinuity of the learning careers of adults, and particularly non-traditional students, in a range of adult education learning contexts in Europe and also outside Europe. By non-traditional student we mean groups who, in some way, are under-represented in adult education. This includes quite a diverse range of groups such as mature students, working class students, women, students from ethnic minorities and students with disabilities who, in relation to higher education, are often the first generation in their family to go to university. Focusing on non-traditional students also raises issues of inequalities such as class, gender, race and age, (Finnegan & Merrill, 2017; Reay, 2005) and marginality which may impact upon their learning experiences and careers which for some may lead to discontinuous learning careers or even leading to dropping out of education. However, there are also other adults who use their agency and resilience to complete their studies in a continuous learning journey. The chapters in this book illustrate a similarity of experiences across countries and continents.

THE HISTORY OF THE BOOK

The chapters in this book arise from a conference and work of the ESREA Access Learning Careers and Identities Network, held in Seville in November 2015 where researchers from across Europe and Canada met to discuss, share and exchange ideas about continuities and discontinuities in the learning careers of adult students. This network was established in 1996 and a first network conference was held at the University of Leeds in the UK. At that time the network was called the Access research network reflecting the focus of adult education research at that time. The conference book publication entitled *Participation and Organisational Change* (Hill & Merrill, 1997) illuminates the narrow theme of the network as it only addressed access and participation in higher education. The network convenors were Chris Duke, Etienne Bourgeois and Barbara Merrill. This focus of the network continued to dominate the following two network conferences in Barcelona and Edinburgh. Subsequent network conferences (held every two years) were located at University of Barcelona (2000) for a second time, Louvain University, Belgium (2006), University of Seville, Spain (2008), University of Aveiro, Portugal (2011), Linköping, Sweden (2013) and again at the University of Seville (2015).

Ten years later responding to the changing nature of European adult education research and literature which was moving beyond research just on access and participation to other wider concerns and concepts the network name was changed to Access, Learning Careers and Identity. The narrow focus was thus widened away from just accessing and getting into an institution to experiences of learning in a wide range of educational contexts such as further and higher education, community education and vocational education. Importantly the network also explores the impact of biography and lifelong learning in shaping learning careers and how this process may result in a changing self and identity. This raises issues of agency and structure and their interaction by taking into account the socio-economic position in which adult learners are located and the actions that they take to develop their learner identity and career within a particular educational setting. In doing so the network examines the different conceptual approaches to understanding learning careers and learning identities. The network provides a forum for adult educators from a range of disciplines to discuss and debate these issues in relation to theory, policy, practice and methodology. The network is now convened by three co-ordinators: Barbara Merrill University of Warwick, UK), Andrea Galimberti (University Milano Bicocca, Italy) and Adrianna Nizinska (Gothenburg University, Sweden).

THE CHAPTERS IN THIS BOOK

The book assumes the same title as the 2015 conference held in Seville: *Continuity and Discontinuity in Learning Careers: Potentials for a Learning Space in a Changing World.* As stated above the network and this book in particular covers a wide range of adult groups, (prisoners, disabled students, working class students, women, ethnic minorities, those with mental health issues, and literacy students) concepts and adult education contexts and this is reflected in the division of the book into four distinct but also connecting parts. These are:

1. Continuity and discontinuity in formal education
2. Continuity and discontinuity in social institutions
3. Continuity and discontinuity around the job market
4. Continuity and discontinuity in professional contexts

The co-ordinators of the network invited Ted Fleming from Ireland, as a non-participant of the conference, to write an opening chapter. This chapter entitled *Learning Careers and Transformative Learning: Challenges of learning and work in neoliberal spaces* 'sets the scene' for the reader as he skilfully brings together the different threads of the chapters and book parts drawing out the key over-lapping

INTRODUCTION

and inter-locking themes. Fleming discusses the links and coherence of the chapters through an appropriate metaphor: 'lock and key' inferring that non-traditional students are both being kept out and excluded from education for a range of reasons but at the same time education also offers the potential for change and transformation of the self. Many non-traditional adult students find themselves being 'locked out' of education as a result of initial schooling experiences and life experiences more generally as well as because of issues of finance and inequalities such as class, gender, and ethnicity. In reference to other chapters in the book Fleming also identifies other categories of adults as being 'locked out' such as those with a disability, literacy difficulties, mental health issues and those who are unemployed. Still playing on the concept of lock he refers to the adult students in prison as discussed by Pillera as being 'locked up'. Thus, the metaphor of lock and key helps us to understand how the learning opportunities and identity of adults is shaped by both continuities and discontinuities in people's lives.

This chapter focuses on two aspects: work and education. Fleming explores the notion of work in the context of the global political context or neoliberalism and its relationship to lifelong learning and austerity. Drawing on the work of David Harvey he discusses current understandings of neoliberalism to illuminate how policy forces the educational agenda and practice to meet the needs of the market for workers. He criticises the way in which lifelong learning has been endorsed as a solution to society's social and economic needs with the emphasis on creating a more flexible workforce for a changing labour market. Lifelong learning discourse has become entrenched in meeting economic demands and this needs to be challenged by re-establishing the discourse of radical adult education which has the potential to 'unlock' and promote a critical pedagogy (Freire) and transformative learning (Mezirow). Non-traditional adult students are resilient and in a critical pedagogical learning context education will be experienced as emancipatory. Underpinning this is the need for adult educators to embrace critical theory and Honneth's concept of 'recognition' is one which Fleming argues for in his chapter.

We now take an overview of the rest of the chapters in this book.

Part 1

Moving on to Part 1 of the book, this part focuses on 'Continuity and discontinuity in formal education'.

Chapter 2 takes us to an interesting but under-researched area in relation to mature students and higher education: adults studying for an art and design degree in the UK. Sam Broadhead in her chapter titled *Friendship, discourse and belonging in the studio: The experiences of 'non-traditional students' in design higher education* explores the continuous and discontinuous narratives of two adult students who find themselves in a minority with younger students on textile design degrees. Both entered higher education through an Access programme (a programme aimed at adults for entrance to higher education) and the narratives were taken from a longitudinal study exploring the experiences of Access students in higher education. Broadhead draws on narrative inquiry to explore how the students managed, or not, their learning careers. In doing so she uses an unusual concept: phronesis (prudence or practical knowledge) as well as the work of Aristotle. The focus of learning takes place in a studio alongside other younger students and as Broadhead argues this can both be a friendly and alienating place. For these students friendship enabled them to overcome the challenges of studying in such an environment and continue with their studies.

Chapter 3 looks at another under-researched area in adult education: learning through an English language book club in a further education (FE) college (postcompulsory institution) in the UK and in a township in South Africa. Using a qualitative action research approach Ida Leal explores the potential for emancipatory and transformative learning through participation in a Book Club. She also examines to what extent involvement as a learner in a Book Club results in the development of a critical consciousness. Leal argues that empowerment can occur from being able to 'unmask and decipher' ideologies which underpin the texts enabling learners to perceive how they see themselves and the world. Theoretically she draws on the work of Freire and his concept of conscientization which importantly enables people to question and challenge the world and also thus to be human. She concludes that dialogue enables learners to critically reflect upon the world and challenge their existing beliefs.

In Chapter 4 we move to research from Canada by Alyson King, Allyson Eamer and Nawal Ammar. This chapter titled *Participation and persistence: An analysis of underserved students at UOIT* offers a case study of persistence and participation of underserved students at a Canadian university during the academic year of 2014–2015. This research was a pilot study which looked at the strategies used by successful students to complete their degree studies within the context of a multicultural Canadian society. The study focused on students from a diverse background and who are viewed as 'at risk students' in higher education coming from different ethnic backgrounds but despite this they were yet able to succeed with their studies.

Part 2

Part 2 of the book focuses on 'Continuity and discontinuity in social institutions' which are not formal educational institutions.

The first chapter in this part (Chapter 5) is by Shanti Irene Fernando and Alyson King focusing on an under-researched area of mental illness and adult students – *Education interrupted: Learning careers of adults living with mental illness.* Within the field of adult education this is yet another under-researched area. This chapter highlights how adult students living with mental illness can experience interruptions and discontinuities in their learning. Drawing on the work of Freire and his notion of hope in education the authors explore how a Canadian hospital based education programme

INTRODUCTION

provides hope, persistence, self-knowledge and confidence to adult learners. Through interviews with the adults they argue that such supported programmes enable adults with mental illness to make the transition from patient to student. Importantly these programmes have the potential to facilitate transformative learning frameworks enabling such adults to re-integrate into the community and workplace.

Chapter 6 focuses on a different institutional setting – that of prisons and higher education study in a comparative study of Italy and Spain by Giuseppe Pillera entitled *Inmates and university in Italy and Spain: Two models to grant higher education for non-traditional students on the margins*. In adult education research there are very few studies focusing on prisoners as a marginalised group of learners. Inmates studying for a university degree are in a minority in terms of numbers and this is sometimes because, as Pillera argues, many prisons do not offer this opportunity and as this study illustrates countries vary in their provision of university level prison education despite international agreements. Like the previous chapter the author argues that the availability of educational programmes in institutions such as prisons promotes transformative learning and in this particular situation also helps to reduce recidivism, encouraging a re-integration into society and work.

Part 3

The third part of the book looks at workplace learning and the job market as another important dimension of adult education under the heading of 'Continuity and discontinuity around the job market'.

Andrea Galimberti and Eva Ratti from Italy begin this part with a chapter entitled *Continuity and discontinuity around academia: The 'Find Your Doctor' project as a space for intervention and research in learning careers*. This chapter focuses on the increasing uncertainty of being a PhD student and the precariousness of transitioning out of academia and into the labour market. Galimberti and Ratti outline the findings of a research project – 'Find Your Doctor' which raises issues about competences, transversal skills and learning on the border of the academic world as PhD students and the implications this has for a professional career and lifelong learning. At the same time the authors take a critical stance in recognising that the labour market is embedded with power and political dimensions.

Chapter 8 continues with a European dimension (Austria) but this time looking at adults who have low qualifications. Monika Kastner's chapter is titled *Stimulating empowerment and supporting access to learning for formerly low qualified adults: Potentials of work-related competency assessment in social enterprises*. The chapter discusses the findings of a research and development project 'Competency Amelioration through Competency Assessment' (KOMKOM). The project focused on unemployed adults with low qualifications undertaking temporary employment in social enterprises with the aim of recognising and validating their learning outcomes acquired outside of formal learning. Theoretically the study draws on Honneth's theory of recognition and the development of a positive learning career.

Moving further north to Sweden Camilla Thunborg and Agnieszka Bron turn to higher education and employability in Chapter 9 *Policies for equality and employability: Consequences for non-traditional students in Sweden.* This chapter is set within the context of a European policy concern with the employability of graduate students from higher education into the labour market and a Swedish higher education system which has traditionally included widening access students. Thunborg and Bron highlight issues of inequality relating to employability particularly in relation to working class and minority ethnic students. Their study indicates that in relation to employability non-traditional students experience greater challenges than traditional students in the labour market resulting in a segregated labour market between traditional younger students and non-traditional students.

On the same theme of employability and higher education as the previous chapter Maria A. Tenorio-Rodriguez, Teresa Padilla-Carmona and José González-Monteagudo from Spain present a chapter entitled *Learning careers of non-traditional students and employability skills.* This chapter (Chapter 10) is based on research from a European project – EMPLOY – which looks at issues of inequalities and employability in relation to non-traditional graduate students. Using biographical methods the authors explore the experiences of the non-traditional adult students in their transition into the labour market and the challenges they face because of issues of social class, ethnicity and age.

The final chapter in Part 3 (Chapter 11) is by Ana Silva, Maria De Lourdes Dionisio and Juliana Cunha from Portugal and is entitled *Literacy practices in adult learning biographies: Possibilities and constraints.* This chapter discusses the process of Recognition, Validation and Certification of Prior Learning (PVCC) as a process of enabling adults to develop their literacy skills and their learning biography and as well as facilitate their learning career.

Part 4

The final part of the book (Part 4) 'Continuity and discontinuity in professional contexts' consists of four chapters.

The first chapter in this part before the conclusion is by Pascal Roquet from France who looks at *Adults' learning and career temporalities in the analysis of professionalization and professional identity construction.* This chapter draws on theories of temporalities and argues that the professionalisation of adults is embedded in temporal dynamics so that individuals engage in processes of professional identity construction at macro, meso and micro levels. The research focuses on French physiotherapists and junior community workers. The research illustrates how continuity and discontinuity produce differentiated forms of identity construction.

Chapter 13 *Learning ways of the adult educator in uncertain professional contexts* written by Catarina Paulos from Portugal discusses the changes in adult education and teaching in Portugal and the introduction of Recognition of Prior Learning for adult educators who lack teaching qualifications. As a result of recent policy changes the careers of adult educators have become uncertain and unsecure. This chapter is based on biographical interviews with adult educators who have undertaken Recognition of Prior Learning as part of their learning career and as an aim to have continuity in their career.

The final chapter in this part is by Carol Thompson and Peter Wolstencroft from the UK. Their chapter has an interesting title – *No more superheroes ... only avatars? Survival role play in English post compulsory education.* This chapter explores the professional identities of teachers and managers within the further education (post compulsory) sector and how they cope and survive in an era of austerity and neo-liberalism. These changes have placed middle managers in a situation where they have to compliant but research also indicates that the Avatar role is now being adapted in order to balance the demands of the organisation and their values as both a teacher and manager.

REFERENCES

Finnegan, F., & Merrill, B. (2017). 'We're as good as anybody else': A comparative study of working-class university students' experiences in England and Ireland. *British Journal of Sociology of Education, 38*(3), 307–324.

Reay, D., David, M. E., & Ball, S. (2005). *Degrees of choice: Class, race, gender and higher education.* Stoke on Trent: Trentham.

TED FLEMING

1. LEARNING CAREERS AND TRANSFORMATIVE LEARNING

Challenges of Learning and Work in Neoliberal Spaces

INTRODUCTION

Many adults have been 'locked out' of opportunities by their previous schooling, life experiences and continuing financial barriers. Disability and literacy difficulties also exclude many from the twin desires of education and work. Education and training are widely seen as providing keys to work and jobs. A number of the chapters in this book present broader understandings of how students experience the world that is unlocked by training and work that in turn lead to new identities and careers.

This chapter outlines a vision of education that 'unlocks' its emancipatory potential as articulated by Paulo Freire (critical pedagogy) and Jack Mezirow (transformative learning) and a vision of education that is an antidote to neoliberal policies. This chapter explores work in the global political and economic project known as neoliberalism and outlines current understandings of neoliberalism in a way that illustrates how public policy drives educational agendas towards addressing the needs of the market for workers rather than for the broader needs of individuals, communities and society. Mezirow and Freire are allies in this, as is Axel Honneth. The following chapters in this book are studies of continuities and discontinuities and of persistence and these issues are explored in the world of education and work.

Adults are resilient and if barriers such as finance are minimised and learning supports enhanced they will persist in education (Fleming, Loxley, & Finnegan, 2017). Real learning can be achieved and learning needs met by education, especially as it is an important source of recognition for learners. Recognition is a psychological and political spark that ignites and sustains learning that is deeply satisfying, critical, developmental and capable of delivering the educational promise of freedom and emancipation. It is the key that unlocks individual and social potential.

NEOLIBERALISM

As a recent iteration of capitalism, neoliberalism emphasises privatisation, downsizing the state as arbiter of the public good; encourages markets to supply everything; curtails organised labour often with legislation and dismantles the welfare state. The state is restructured to reflect the interests of business. According to Harvey (2005, p. 2) neoliberalism is;

> A theory of political economic practices that proposes that human well-being can best be advanced by liberating individual entrepreneurial freedoms and skills within an institutional framework characterized by strong private property rights, free markets and free trade.

Neoliberalism subjects the social functions of the state to economic calculation as if public services were private companies that regulated education, health, social security and employment (Bauman, 2014, p. 17). The state is compelled to cede functions they once considered their domain into the care of already deregulated market forces. Citizens lose faith in the ability of governments to deliver on their promises. The certainties of employment are demolished (or at least called into question) by part-time or zero-hours contracts thus adding to the insecurity of temporary employment.

Everything is subject to review so as to constantly reset priorities based on perceived shortages of public funding. Everything has become debatable, questionable, shaky, destined to remain standing or be wiped out with a stroke of the pen in response to more urgent needs, budget problems and compliance with European regulations (Bauman & Bordoni, 2014, p. 67). Everyone is expected to provide for themselves without burdening others (Bauman & Bordoni, 2014, p. 57). Consumerism 'may lubricate the wheels of the *economy* but sprinkles sand into the bearings of *morality*' (Bauman & Bardoni, 2014, p. 153). Discontinuities are embedded in the system.

We are required to do more with less and manage with scarce resources and adjustments – a euphemism for deep cuts in public expenditure, including education. Governments are preoccupied with austerity even though there is evidence that austerity makes the problem worse (Blyth, 2013). Austerity is first and foremost a transfer of wealth from the lower and middle classes to the classes above them. It furthers the neoliberal project of increasing inequality under the guise of freeing lower socio-economic groups from their social welfare supported unwillingness to work. These ideas are worked out in greater detail by Giroux (2014), Piketty (2014), and Sen (2015).

Neoliberalism does not aim to increase well-being but drives for a more competitive society and economy. Education is required to meet the needs of the economy for skilled workers and to re-focus its curriculum to become business friendly and produce graduates who are more 'work-ready'. State investment is expected to increase productivity and innovation, while investments in education are adjusted downward. The potential of lifelong learning to respond to the learning needs of active citizens is neglected (Fleming, 2011) and instead is implicated in the push to have everyone upskill and contribute to the economy (CEC, 2000). This context is important for this chapter and the following chapters in this book where the impacts of how work and education are reconfigured to fit the neoliberal agenda are addressed.

ROLE OF ADULT EDUCATION

Education has always been associated with progress, with freedom, democracy, justice and care. In its *Manifesto for Adult Learning for the 21st Century* the European Association for the Education of Adults (EAEA, 2016) asserts that adult education has a role in changing lives and transforming society. It sees adult education as a human right and a common good. But it needs investment. The *Manifesto* (p. 3) supports the traditional aims of adult education including citizenship, democracy, emancipation as well as life skills, health benefits, social cohesion and equality. Reskilling for work, second chance education and entrepreneurship are not neglected (pp. 4–5). By the conclusion of the document there is little that adult education cannot achieve about sustainability and other social, political, economic targets and aspirations.

How then is the rhetoric at odds with reality and public policy? Governments seem to be suspicious of learning that does not have an economic focus. The EU average participation rate for adult education is 10 per cent – though some countries have achieved rates between 25 and 30 per cent, e.g. Denmark, Sweden, Finland (European Commission, 2016, p. 80). Romania, Bulgaria, Croatia and Slovakia have participation rates in the range 1 to 3 per cent. Adult learners might be excused for thinking that their second chance opportunities are few and far between.

A number of current policy debates ask how the situation can be justified where the system is producing more graduates than the job market requires (Murphy, 2017; Sweeney, 2016). This conversation sees no point in taxi-drivers having PhDs! This concern about the excess supply of graduates, the resulting impact on the economy and the declining economic returns on education disconnect education from its value as a means of social mobility and advancement (Murphy, 2017).

Sweeney, a senior policy analyst at the National Economic and Social Forum (NESC) agrees that there are unresolved policy issues (state funding of education) concerning the learning needs and projects that adults undertake including how to create lives of fulfilment in families and society. Without learning and education it is difficult to achieve democracy, and participation in society and freedom. The implication is that the state abandons higher education for the masses and instead provide lower level skills for workers mostly through its further and adult education provision.

In contrast, in an interview in *The Nation*, Chantel Mouffe asserts that the gulf between the popular classes and the wealthy is growing and that there has been an oligarchization of politics (Shahid, 2016). Workers have been 'abandoned by neoliberalism' and suffer losses resulting from globalization (Shahid, 2016, p. 4). Politics has failed to respond and has no discourse about peoples' genuine problems. Mouffe is one of the preeminent theorists on democracy and social movements and she proposes a concerted reaction to this trend by 'creating a bond between those struggles in a way that recognises the specificities of different struggles' but also by fiercely recognising the commonalities and solidarities among the various struggles (Shahid, 2016, p. 7). This would involve recognising workers and other rights that have been taken away over recent years and engaging in a 'war of position' where 'progressive forces could build real influence in civil society, the dominant institutions, main stream culture and the media' (Shahid, 2016, p. 12). Education would have a social intent and not be just be preoccupied with training for jobs.

In recent times the field of education has been enriched by significant contributions to the understanding of adult education by Freire and Mezirow. They have defined the meaning and possibilities of adult learning in their respective theories of critical pedagogy and of transformative learning.

Mezirow (1978) defines one kind of learning that involves skills and techniques that for many lead to jobs. It is essential learning. Plumbers, accountants, farmers all kinds of scientists and engineers engage in technical learning that is about how best to do things. How to build a bridge in all its complexity is a good example of this kind of learning. These skills are taught mainly by demonstration. Technical learning offers freedom as it involves mastery and the ability to overcome the restrictions imposed on humans by nature.

Another kind of learning involves the humanities and social sciences, e.g. history, psychology, literature, etc. It involves understanding communications between people and understanding one self. Understanding is not a skill to be demonstrated but an ability to see things from the perspectives of others. Empathy and perspective taking are central and are taught through role play, case study and the kinds of discussions that one associates with adult education classes and seminars.

We each think and behave and make meaning within a paradigm constructed through the experiences we have in individual lives and through the impact of culture and society. This gives each a unique meaning making paradigm or frame of reference as Mezirow calls it. It is the educational process involved in changing these frames of reference that is known as Mezirow's Transformative Learning (Mezirow, 1978, 2000). For example, my frame of reference just happens to be white, male, middle class, Christian etc. and changing this is what Mezirow means by transformative learning.

Mezirow researched the learning experiences of adults returning to education and found that the learning process followed a path that normally began with a disorienting dilemma. This was followed by critical reflection on the genesis of the psycho-cultural assumptions that formed their frames of reference. The transformative process concluded with the adoption of new frames of reference and acting on the basis of these new ones. To become a feminist is a good example of such a transformation. Transformative learning is, according to Mezirow (2000, pp. 7–8):

> the process by which we transform our taken-for-granted frames of reference (meaning perspectives, habits of mind, mind-sets) to make them more inclusive, discriminating, open, emotionally capable of change, and reflective so that they may generate beliefs and opinions that will prove more true or justified to guide action.

Mezirow's theory of transformative learning clearly indicates the possibilities that can be realised through adult education.

Mezirow relied heavily on Jürgen Habermas for two elements of his theory that gave his theory academic rigor. First, the understanding of the kinds of learning outlined above – technical-skills, understanding and emancipatory or transformative learning (Fleming, 2002). Second, an understanding of the nature of the discourses or conversations that would lead to transformative learning, involving critical reflection. These Socratic conversations are linked to freedom and democratic will formation and follow rules that create open free debates in which all participants have the right to participate, ask questions and clarify their position on the understanding that the only force exercised is the force of the better argument. When these rules are followed the discussions approximate to an ideal speech situation (Habermas) in which people's real needs may emerge.

By relying on Habermas, Mezirow gave transformative learning theory an emancipatory intent that was further enhanced by his reliance on Paulo Freire. Both support knowledge and learning that go beyond the skills and mutual understandings of communications and propose an emancipatory process akin to ideology critique (Morrow & Torres, 2001).

In a less radical but interesting contribution Kreber (2015) identifies traditions in adult education that forge connections between skills learning on the one hand and democracy and social action on the other. The education of workers as not only members of an economy but as members of a democratic society was part of the mission of the Workers Education Association (WEA). Kreber highlights the historical link between work and the building of a life around that work that is a useful and productive life for individuals, families and society (Kreber, 2015, p. 102).

Relying on John Dewey and Hannah Arendt, Kreber shows how workers are motivated not just by pay but by the wish to do a good job (2015, p. 104). This involves not only being effective and efficient, not just following Health and Safety or Quality Assurance requirements but involves recognising the ethical and social dimensions of work. She takes hairdressers as an example. They are not only skilful operators but provide social cohesion in communities. As they produce well-groomed customers this has important social and personal consequences at work and elsewhere. At a minimum self-image is at stake. Appearance matters. This contributes to identity formation and enhancement.

Using hairdressing as her example may overstate the case slightly but she does provide an interesting understanding of the importance of what is usually seen as low paid, low skilled and unregulated work. She sees workers as civic agents, facilitating social interactions and community discussion. This is a public good and workers become enablers of democracy. 'Education might foster among future professionals a sense as civic agents capable of facilitating and participating in public deliberations' (Kreber, 2015, p. 111). Building on Biesta (2012), she goes on to explore the possibility that professionals may participate in activities that involve a concern for the 'public qualities of human togetherness' (Biesta, 2012, p. 683).

These issues are visible in many of the following chapters where learning has consequences for the individuals and for society.

HONNETH

Both Mezirow and Freire maintain a link with the emancipatory intent of critical theory. However, critical theory has moved on from the first generation (Marcuse and Fromm) and the second generation (Habermas) to the third generation that includes Honneth. Honneth moves beyond Habermas by expanding the theory of communicative action on which Mezirow relied. He shows how critical reflection, that in Mezirow's usage is often critiqued as overly rational, (Cranton & Taylor, 2012) requires and presupposes recognition. Without mutual recognition there can be no critical reflection. At the level of the family, recognition is given and received, for example, in the attachment experience between the infant and the adult carer. In this the parent recognises the fear or anxiety of the child and under the impact of a caring and empathetic response the child grows and develops (Fleming, 2016a).

Recognition is given and received in the intimate relations of the family, in communities, in society and at work (echoes of Hegel in this). The task of critical theory, according to Honneth, is to identify experiences in society that contain 'system-exploding energies and motivations' in pursuit of freedom and justice (Fraser & Honneth, 2003, p. 242). He offers 'a link between the social causes of widespread feelings of injustice and the normative objectives of emancipatory movements' (Fraser & Honneth, 2003, p. 113). Honneth re-writes critical theory so that damaged recognition is the pathology to be overcome, rather than distorted communication. Social change is driven by inadequate forms of recognition and internal (psychic) conflict leads to social change. The social and personal are connected. The individual search for identity is not isolated from political and social contexts and events. Distortions in identity are the motivation for struggle and social conflict and this moves the debate about emancipation away from the perceived highly cognitive and rational interest of Habermas (and indeed Mezirow) toward an alternative theory of intersubjectivity. It implies that not only is the personal political but the political is personal. Transformative learning is both personal and social (Fleming, 2014). In the following chapters of this book so many varied interventions are seen as transformative and based on this understanding the learning can be both personal and political.

Transformative learning and communicative action involve more than following linguistic rules of discourse (Habermas, 1987, p. 121). They involve mutuality and intersubjectivity (Honneth, 1995, pp. 92–95). The struggle for recognition, based on experiences of disrespect and the need for self-esteem, explains *social* development according to Honneth (1995, p. 92);

> It is by the way of the morally motivated struggles of social groups – their collective attempt to establish institutionally and culturally, expanded forms of recognition – that the normatively directional change of societies proceeds.

When citizens with a disability are recognised by the economy or the community or society (in its practices and laws) this moment is developmental at both personal and social levels. When Travellers are given status as an ethnic minority or gay rights are legislated for (the right to marry) these systemic policy and legislative moments are not only political but are profoundly developmental at an individual level. We have become accustomed to saying the personal is political. The political is personal. Work also provides moments of recognition and unfortunately (like school) too many moments of misrecognition. In a later chapter Fernando and King identify how hope is reclaimed through education. An enhanced learner identity is achieved according to Kastner in a later chapter.

THE FREEDOM TURN OF HONNETH

These ideas are of particular interest to educators looking for new ways of expressing a counter possibility for adult education – counter that is to dominant neoliberal imperatives. But Honneth goes beyond Habermas by seeking a broader vision of democracy involving not only the political sphere but emancipated families and a socialized market (Honneth, 2014, p. 345). The realisations of freedom in any one of these areas depends on its realisation in the others as democratic citizens, emancipated families and ethical markets 'mutually influence each other, because the properties of one cannot be realized without the other two' (Honneth, 2014, pp. 330–331). For Honneth (2014, p. 15) freedom is the key value of modern life;

> Of all the ethical values prevailing and competing for dominance in modern society, only one has been capable of leaving a truly lasting impression on our institutional order: freedom, i.e. the autonomy of the individual ... all modern ethical ideals have been placed under the spell of freedom ....

Freedom involves the ability to realise one's own desires, intentions and values in the social environment of roles and obligations. As one might anticipate, individual and social freedom are connected – and not in some vague or superficial way but essentially. In addition, he asserts that markets, interpersonal relationships and the spaces of public politics are best understood as places of potential social freedom. Places such as work, friendships, family, work, laws, are all justified only if they promote, support and bring about a free society for all. These institutions can be evaluated as successful to the extent that they encourage and bring about social freedom and a better life. Education and the right to education (though not referred to by Honneth) are part of that emancipatory project. Later chapters in this book highlight the development of autonomy, identity and social freedom experienced by students in Spain and Portugal on a literacy programme.

Social freedom is connected to the sphere of markets that offer co-operative activities that are in the interest of all participants and these involve offering goods for sale and jobs. In markets there are of course consumer rights; regulations as to what can be sold and how; regulations about pricing, wages, imports, illegal commodities and so on. There are also regulations about fairness in business transactions (Honneth, 2014, p. 202). These areas of economic activity are structured by the values they serve by meeting peoples' needs for goods (Honneth, 2014, p. 199) and recognising their achievements at work. Honneth outlines changes in society that contribute to disconnecting the markets from social freedom. Neoliberalism does not increase or support social freedom (2014, pp. 176–177) and is a social misdevelopment that makes individual identity development more difficult to achieve. Later chapters refer to and emphasise the potential negative impact for students. Any explicit critique of neoliberalism should not be interpreted as a negation of the important role that markets play in social, community and political life as of right.

The most important sphere of social freedom is what he calls the 'We' of democratic will formation (2014, p. 253). This leads Honneth to his theory of democracy where democratic interactions enable citizens to make their lives and conditions better through a process of discourse or democratic will formation (2014, p. 254). Again, with reference to Habermas and his radical discursive democracy, the democratic state acts as an agent of the democratic public sphere (2014, pp. 305–307). This suggests that learning (and teaching) for the development of the 'we' of democratic discourse may be a vital task of education and a necessary one for transformative learning. One's identity development is not merely an individual task but necessarily involves a social dimension. Educators may be at risk of not perceiving how social and political many outcomes are for students studying what are on first appearance quite individual learning projects.

Social movements have been important in enhancing democratic moments of the public sphere and current indignations and insurgent social movements in places such as Barcelona, Athens and Wall Street are typical of the expanded 'we' that are, in Honneth's view, spheres of social freedom. Only through agreed and mutually supportive cooperations with others can there be political freedom. Freedom of this kind is inherently social as it cannot be realised if one is not involved in the 'we' of democratic will formation where the same weight is afforded to all contributions of citizens (p. 261). This is reminiscent of Dewey's affirmation that 'democracy is a name for a way of life of free and enriching communication' (Dewey, 1954, p. 148). A new vision of adult education would involve supporting through tuition, seminars and its entire pedagogy and indeed its management systems a collaborative environment that supports and teaches how to be democratic.

IMPLICATIONS AND DISCUSSION

These ideas of Honneth have had little impact on education apart from a few (Brown & Murphy, 2012; Huttunen, 2008; Murphy & Brown, 2012). Some work has been done on the connection with transformative learning (Fleming, 2014). Transformative learning requires critical reflection and recognition becomes central to the learning process. In order to engage in the critical discourse associated with transformative learning and critical pedagogy we now paraphrase Honneth who asserts that the formation of democratic discussions requires three forms of self-relating or identity. We need caring and loving individuals (teachers). It requires recognition of the reciprocal nature of legal rights. And thirdly, a democratic discursive society requires the reciprocal recognition provided by work and solidarity. Freire's culture circles are good examples of how these processes might operate in practice (Souto-Manning, 2010). Everything is connected.

This 'recognition turn' suggests that the high rationality of the critique required by transformative learning is 'softened' by this understanding of the interpersonal recognition that underpins the democratic discourse of a learning environment. Teaching might usefully address the struggles of students for recognition as motivations for their learning. Without altering the importance of critical reflection for transformative learning and critical pedagogy there is now the possibility of reframing these learning theories so that rational discourse is seen as based on an interpersonal process of support and recognition that builds self-confidence, self-respect and self-esteem. Mezirow (and Dewey and Freire and Habermas) see democratic participation as an important means of self-development that produces individuals who are more tolerant of difference, sensitive to reciprocity and better able to engage in discourse (Mezirow, 2003, p. 60). It is important not to sink into a sentimental subjectivity here but build on this understanding; this is a precondition for rational discourse and this does not involve a loss of rigor or the ambition to remain within the emancipatory agenda of critical theory.

The emphasis on whether learning is individual or social (Fleming, 2016b, p. 78) can be re-configured in a similar way to how Freire reconfigured the dualisms of subject/object, teacher/learner and reflection/action best expressed in his concept of *praxis* (1972, p. 75). The perceived individualism of Mezirow's theory can now be reframed as built on a fundamentally intersubjective process of mutual recognition. These relations of mutuality are preconditions for self-realisation, critical reflection, identity development and transformative learning. Recognition and emancipation are connected; recognition becomes the foundation on which emancipatory learning and social change are based. This implies that learning, whether in transformative learning or in adult education in general, is best supported by interactions that are not only respectful but that explicitly recognise the individual worth of each individual along with the aspirations and dreams that prompt their struggle for recognition. The pursuit of identity is both an individual learning and developmental project as well as a social, political and economic task. Freire reconfigured the relationship between the traditional dualism of thinking and action by relying on the concept of *praxis* (Freire, 1972, p. 60). He also connected teaching and learning in a similar way (Freire, 1998, p. 29) so that these apparent opposites were defined as connected dialectically: 'there is no teaching without learning' (Freire, 1998, pp. 29–48).

The process of transformative learning commences with a 'disorienting dilemma' and includes a stage where one's individual 'problem' becomes identified with a major/significant social issue (Mezirow, 2000, p. 22). In Mezirow's work this perplexity normally involves a disconnect and discomfort between old inadequate frames of reference and the possibility offered by new ones. The dilemma for the learner is whether to stay with old ways of making meaning that have lost their ability to usefully guide understanding and action or search for new ones. The struggle for recognition acts as a disorienting dilemma. It motivates the search for new meaning schemes and identities. The struggle for recognition is a form of perplexity (Dewey, 1997, p. 11). It has within it the possibility that this may be the paradigmatic form of disorienting dilemma. The dilemma involves whether to stay in a world circumscribed by old experiences of misrecognition or respond to the struggle to be recognised and acknowledged through learning. This search for new meanings is found in social struggles, new social movements and in adult education. Of necessity, there are continuities and discontinuities in these explorations.

One of the stages in the transformative process involves making connections between one's own individual problem (that may have prompted learning) and broader social issues. From this study of Honneth it is proposed that personal problems are intimately connected to broader social issues. Many of the following chapters outline such issues and can be seen in this way. The connection is not just an empirically grounded finding in research on transformation theory but is a philosophically essential step in properly interpreting the world. Now the political is personal and the learning process necessarily involves making this connection. At an obvious level, adult education requires the ability to perceive the world in this way – the personal and political and social are connected.

Adult education now becomes a learning project with the practical intent of increasing freedom, justice, care and equality in the spheres of family, law and work and involves transformation not just of the individual but of society also.

It is important to attend to teaching as a process of mutual recognition between teacher and learner. Teaching that is informed in this way has the potential to strengthen identity development. With the current emphasis on functional learning, competency and behavioural outcomes that are supported by neoliberal states it is important to take seriously the contribution of intersubjectivity in teaching and learning. The motivation to engage in learning becomes less economic, functional and instrumental and more social and potentially transformative, critical and emancipatory. This is achieved not just by an emphasis on critical reflection but on the always presupposed imperative of recognition. This assists in reclaiming the emancipatory potential of adult education that has the long standing intention of bringing about a better society in which to live, grow and create environments in which families can take care of children – and not just a society as a place in which to work. This is evocative of the thoroughly human and humanizing task of education as outlined by Freire in *Pedagogy of the Oppressed* (1972, p. 21) where he frames critical reflection, dialogue and changing the world as an exercise in love (1972, p. 62).

The critical role of education is to work in solidarity with workers and citizens to insert democratic imperatives into the system world. The foundations of democracy are under threat from the monopoly of technical and instrumental reason in society. The forces of technical control must be made subject to the consensus of acting citizens who in dialogue redeem the power of reflection and intersubjectivity. The preoccupation shifts from prioritising how to get things done to realising genuine democracy. By adding insights from the third generation of critical theorists the vision that recognises the struggle of people to exercise their right to learn is developmental and a necessary condition for emancipation. The reliance on Honneth is mostly about securing a theoretical base for concepts that are intersubjective, political and social and connected with each other.

CONCLUSION

Many adult education programmes are quite individual in their focus. These include many of those described in later chapters, on literacy (Silva, DeLourdes Dionísio & Cunha), on book clubs (Leal), on textile design (Broadhead) and taking on board prior learning (Paulos). Even in the various groups the focus is individual whether disadvantaged, non-traditional, underserved, low qualified, at risk students (King, Eamer & Ammar), students with mental health issues (Fernando & King), or prisoners (Pillera). Others (Thunborg & Bron; Tenirio-Rodriguez, Padilla-Carmona & González-Monteagudo) pay attention to the links between education and labour market transitions and to the ways that higher education contributes to the stratification of the academic labour market. Issues concerning teacher education is the topic in other chapters (Thompson & Wolstencroft; Galimberti & Ratti). And all appear to focus on individuals.

But it is deceptive because when the experiences are analysed it becomes clear that the transformative learning or increased critical awareness is not just an individual experience but has (whether the programmes perceive this or not) a clear political and/or social dimension. The connection is the experience of recognition. Recognising the students' intelligence and ability as well as providing experiences of friendship, connection and support in open free democratic conversations open at least the possibility that something quite profound is happening. Identities are being forged and equally important the impetus and momentum may be given to realise more democratic moments in classrooms, in families, in communities and at work. This is the opposite to and the antidote to the experiences of being 'locked out' of their desires for education and work.

REFERENCES

Bauman, Z. (2014). *What use is sociology?* Cambridge: Polity Press.
Bauman, Z., & Bordoni, C. (2014). *State of crisis*. Cambridge: Polity Press.
Biesta, G. J. (2012). Becoming public: Public pedagogy, citizenship and the public sphere. *Social and Cultural Geography, 13*, 683–697.
Blyth, M. (2013). *Austerity: The history of a dangerous idea*. Oxford: Oxford University Press.
Bourdieu, P. (1984). *Distinction: A social critique of the judgement of taste*. London: Routledge.
Brown, T., & Murphy, M. (2012). The dynamics of student identity: The threats from a neoliberal model and the benefits for a relational pedagogy. In L. West & A. Bainbridge (Eds.), *Psychoanalysis and education: Minding the gap* (pp. 217–242). London: Karnak.

CEC (Commission of the European Community). (2000). *A memorandum on lifelong learning: Commission staff working paper.* Brussels: European Commission.

Cranton, P., & Taylor, E. W. (2012). Transforming learning theory: Seeking a more unified theory. In E. W. Taylor, P. Cranton, & Associates (Eds.), *The handbook of transformative learning* (pp. 3–20). San Francisco, CA: Jossey-Bass.

Dewey, J. (1954). *The public and its problems.* Chicago, IL: Swallow Press.

Dewey, J. (1997). *How we think.* New York, NY: Dover.

European Association for the Education of Adults (EAEA). (2016). *Manifesto for adult learning in the 21st century.* Brussels: EAEA. Retrieved March 21, 2017, from http://www.eaea.org/media/policy-advocacy/manifesto/manifesto.pdf

European Commission. (2016). *Education and training monitor 2016.* Retrieved March 25, from https://ec.europa.eu/education/sites/education/files/monitor2016_en.pdf

Fleming, T. (2002). Habermas on civil society, lifeworld and system: Unearthing the social in transformation theory. *Teachers College Record On-line, 2002,* 1–17. Retrieved June 25, 2015, from http://www.tcrecord.org/content.asp?ContentID=10877

Fleming, T. (2011). Models of lifelong learning: An overview. In M. London (Ed.), *Oxford handbook of lifelong learning* (pp. 29–39). New York, NY: Oxford University Press.

Fleming, T. (2014). Axel Honneth and the struggle for recognition: Implications for transformative learning. In A. Nicolaides & D. Holt (Eds.), *Spaces of transformation and transformation of space. Proceedings of the 11th international transformative learning conference* (pp. 318–324). New York, NY: Teachers College.

Fleming, T. (2016a). Reclaiming the emancipatory potential of adult education: Honneth's critical theory and the struggle for recognition. *European Journal for Research on the Education and Learning of Adults, 7*(1), 13–24.

Fleming, T. (2016b). The critical theory of Axel Honneth: Implications for transformative learning and higher education. In V. Wang & P. Cranton (Eds.), *Theory and practice of adult and higher education* (pp. 63–85). Little Rock: Information Age Publishing.

Fleming, T., Finnegan, F., & Loxley, A. (2017). Retention in Ireland's higher education institutions. In T. Fleming, A. Loxley, & F. Finnegan (Eds.), *Access and participation in Irish higher education.* London: Palgrave Macmillan.

Fraser, N., & Honneth, A. (2003). *Redistribution or recognition? A political-philosophical exchange.* London: Verso Books.

Freire, P. (1972). *Pedagogy of the oppressed.* New York, NY: Seabury.

Freire, P. (1998). *Pedagogy of freedom: Ethics, democracy and civic courage.* New York, NY: Rowman and Littlefield.

Giroux, H. (2014). *Neoliberalism's war on higher education.* Chicago, IL: Haymarket.

Habermas, J. (1987). *The theory of communicative action: The critique of functionalist reason* (Vol. 2). Boston, MA: Beacon.

Harvey, D. (2005). *A brief history of neoliberalism.* Oxford: Oxford University Press.

Honneth, A. (1995). *The struggle for recognition: The moral grammar of social conflicts.* Cambridge, MA: MIT Press.

Honneth, A. (2014). *Freedom's right: The social foundations of democratic life.* Cambridge: Polity Press.

Huttunen, R. (2008). *Habermas, Honneth and education.* Köln: Lambert.

Kreber, C. (2015). Transforming employment-oriented education to foster Arendtian action: Rebuilding bridges between community and vocational education. *Adult Education Quarterly, 65*(2), 100–115.

Mezirow, J. (1978). Perspective transformation. *Adult Education, 28,* 100–110.

Mezirow, J. (1991). *Transformative dimensions of adult learning.* San Francisco, CA: Jossey-Bass.

Mezirow, J. (2000). Learning to think like an adult: Core concepts of transformation theory. In J. Mezirow & Associates (Eds.), *Learning as transformation: Critical perspectives on a theory in process* (pp. 3–34). San Francisco, CA: Jossey-Bass.

Morrow, R. A., & Torres, C. A. (2002). *Reading Freire and Habermas: Critical pedagogy and transformative social change.* New York, NY: Teachers College Press.

Murphy, M. (2017). *Who is to blame for overeducation: Graduates, employers or policy makers?* Glasgow: Robert Owen Centre for Educational Change, University of Glasgow. Retrieved on March 24, 2017, from http://robertowencentre.academicblogs.co.uk/who-is-to-blame-for-overeducation-graduates-employers-or-policy-makers/

Murphy, M., & Brown, T. (2012). Learning as relational: Intersubjectivity and pedagogy in higher education. *International Journal of Lifelong Education, 31*(5), 643–654.

Piketty, T. (2014). *Capital in the twenty-first century.* Cambridge, MA: Harvard University Press.

Shahid, W. (2016). *America in populist times: An interview with Chantal Mouffe.* Retrieved March 24, 2017, from https://www.thenation.com/article/america-in-populist-times-an-interview-with-chantal-mouffe/

Sweeney, J. (2016, March 14). *Raising the status and quality of further education and training: The labour market as an ally.* Paper presented at the Further Education and Training Forum, The National College of Ireland, Dublin.

Sen, A. (2015, June 4). The economic consequences of austerity. *New Statesman.* Retrieved March 26, 2017, from http://www.newstatesman.com/politics/2015/06/amartya-sen-economic-consequences-austerity

Souto-Manning, M. (2010). *Freire, teaching and learning: Culture circles across contexts.* New York, NY: Peter Lang.

Ted Fleming
Columbia University
New York, USA

PART 1

CONTINUITY AND DISCONTINUITY IN FORMAL EDUCATION

SAMANTHA BROADHEAD

2. FRIENDSHIP, DISCOURSE AND BELONGING IN THE STUDIO

The Experiences of 'Non-Traditional' Students in Design Higher Education

INTRODUCTION

This chapter draws upon the narratives of continuity and discontinuity from two design students collected during three years of their degrees in textiles which they studied in the north of England. This was part of a longitudinal study (2011–2014) that sought to investigate the experiences of post-Access to HE students in art and design higher education. The Access to HE Diploma route gives students a broad introduction to art and design skills at level three, which is the required standard for entry to higher education in the UK and it enables them to develop a portfolio of work for their submission through the Universities and Colleges Admissions Service (UCAS). Narrative inquiry was used to show the ways in which students reflected on and took stock of their learning careers (Clandinin & Connelly, 2004; Butler-Kisber, 2010). 'Chad' and 'Eliza' were participants who had gained places on textile degrees with an Access to HE Diploma, rather than with the more conventional A levels (school leaving qualifications). They were representative of those mature students (both were over 40 years old) who have diverse social backgrounds and non-traditional educational histories (Hudson, 2009, p. 25; Penketh & Goddard, 2008, p. 316; Burke, 2002, p. 81). The students were both studying textile design but at different Higher Education Institutions (HEIs). Chad was in full-time education and Eliza was part-time due to working and family commitments. Textile designers are concerned with designing for surfaces and embellishments which could include wallpapers, fabrics for fashion or interiors, flooring, and packaging.

The concept of phronesis/practical wisdom or prudence was used as a theoretical lens. Aristotle aligned phronesis with gaining life experience that, alongside other capacities, could be used to guide good judgements about acting well for the self and others. Aristotle claimed that only a person of experience could practice practical wisdom, and a young person was unlikely to have extensive life experience (Aristotle, Nicomachean Ethics, Book VI, Chapter 8). By referring to the work of Paul Ricoeur (1994) it was possible to argue that generous or virtuous acts of friendship were an important aspect of phronesis.

The narratives were considered in relation to the ideas of phronesis and in particular the role friendship between post-Access students and others in their cohort played in supporting their learning. Both students revealed how they decided to continue or discontinue with their studies, because it seemed at that point in time the most prudent course of action. However, it was the virtuous actions by their friends that ultimately enabled Chad and Eliza to continue with their studies. It is of note that it was the generous interventions of younger students that helped the post-Access students overcome self-doubt and exclusion.

The discussion recounts some of the critical incidents within Chad's and Eliza's stories where I have noticed evidence of phronesis or at some points the absence of wise judgement. It is suggested that within the context of higher education mature students sometimes made poor decisions leading them to act in ways that continued their sufferings. This was because they did not always exercise their potential to act with prudence (Aristotle, Nicomachean Ethics, Book VI, Chapter 5). In some instances the younger students did have the capacity to act well for others.

It was due to the day-to-day discourse within the design studio space that enabled friendships between students from different backgrounds to develop. Inhabiting and working in the physical space with others were recognised to be important aspects of developing a student's sense of belonging and eventually their capacities for resilience and motivation. Edstrom (2008) has carried out similar research into the studio conversations of postgraduate fine art students in Sweden. However, the focus was on interactions between staff and students and these conversations related to the actual art work the students had made.

The study, discussed in this chapter, captured the more informal, everyday talk occurring between students that promoted connection and friendship. At the same time this interaction between students in the design studio was a means of sharing information about projects and assignments. Those part-time students who could not spend as much time in the studio relied on the institutions' virtual learning environments (VLE) for information about their course. Unfortunately, in Eliza's case the VLE seemed only to invite frustration and confusion. She commented on the difficulties she had accessing information from Moodle which was her institution's VLE.

PHRONESIS AND FRIENDSHIP

Book six of Aristotle's Nicomachean Ethics offers a model of deliberation known as phronesis, practical wisdom or prudence where the person who practises this was known as the phronimos (Ricoeur, 1994, p. 174):

> A sagacious man is supposed be to characterised by his ability to reach sound conclusions in his deliberations about what is good for himself and advantage to him, and this not in one department of life – in what concerns his health, for example, or his physical strength – but what conduces to the good life as a whole. (Aristotle, Nicomachean Ethics, Book VI, Chapter 5, p. 176)

The phronimos firstly recognised the singularity of a particular situation and was able to determine a best course of action. They understood what it meant to act well, justly and with courage (Wall, 2005, p. 315). Phronesis was about being able make good decisions that allowed people to act well for themselves and others in order to live a good life together. It was an intellectual virtue where acting well was not through habit or conditioning, but through thought and deliberation. It sat with the other forms of intellect; sophia (purely theoretical intelligence) and techne (technical expertise) (Skilleas, 2006, p. 267).

Practical wisdom was closely interconnected with cardinal virtues such as temperance, fortitude and justice. The phronimos was guided by these virtues in determining the correct course of action (Nussbaum, 2001, p. 306). Thus the person of practical wisdom could identify a situation where courage was needed or perhaps another one where moderation was required.

Being able to judge and act well was seen as intrinsic to being a human and living a good life. How someone lived well was in some ways dependant on context and the particularities of the situations thrown up by life. For Ricoeur (1994, p. 177) the word 'life' designated the person as a whole rather than a series of practices. Ricoeur said that to live a life well was the standard of excellence which he called the life plan. The 'good life' was a nebulous collection of ideals and dreams of achievements in regard to a life to be fulfilled or unfulfilled (Ricoeur, 1994, p. 179). The good life was where all actions (even though they may have ends in themselves) were directed by these ideals and dreams. It seemed that this was very pertinent to those mature students who chose to make difficult decisions in order to pursue the good life, by achieving a degree so they could ultimately become designers.

Aristotle (Nicomachean Ethics, Book VI, Chapter 11, p. 186) talked about how acting with practical wisdom was based on a good or fellow-feeling towards others; this could also be seen as an important aspect of inclusion. Within an educational context for example, students and teachers could have empathy for others whether or not they were similar or different to themselves. Ricoeur (1994) extended this idea of 'good feeling towards others' to a mutual responsibility, where an individual – to be an individual – must be part of a social relation. For Aristotle too, living a good life entailed acting well for and with others; friendship could be seen as an important aspect of this. Including others in education, for example, and being responsible for people who were not always like us entailed thinking with practical wisdom, whether one was a student, a teacher or a manager. Imagination also played a role in that subjects needed to imagine the impact of their actions on the lives of other people. The risks associated with being open to newness and difference might be experienced as fearful but at the same time as an opportunity for creativity and innovation in everyone's conduct. To paraphrase Ricoeur (1994, p. 189) the 'other' could count on him and it was this that made him accountable, as he was 'summoned to responsibility'. He identified an asymmetrical power relationship between the self and other (doctor/patient; teacher/student; lawyer/client). Ricoeur acknowledged that this needed to be considered during the practices of phronesis. Although he also explored the possibility of mutual friendship between self and other, he saw the relationship as being fragile (Ricoeur, 1994, pp. 184–189). Acting with phronesis meant that other people were included when deliberations, decisions and judgments were made. Being included in this way could improve a subject's confidence just as being excluded could erode a person's self-belief.

Duckworth (2014, p. 184) has also argued that friendship not only facilitated practical support it could be a way to counter any exclusion or symbolic violence a person might experience within a group or institution. Within the context of higher education the significance of friendships has been identified as a means of giving students a sense of belonging which in turn promotes increased student retention (Thomas, 2012). Similar to the work of Thomas (2012), Kane et al. (2014) carried out a cross-institutional, collaborative project that investigated students' sense of belonging in higher education within three neighbouring universities. The work was carried out during the first semester of the first year. They used a questionnaire approach that drew upon the responses from 1346 students. The researchers used Goodenow's (1993) Psychological Sense of School Membership Measurement. The results showed that ten to fifteen percent of students were unable to feel accepted at university. They suggested that mature students found it more difficult to fit into higher education. Through the narratives of Chad and Eliza it was possible to show how they deliberated about whether or not they should continue with their studies in higher education and the role different friendships made in their decisions.

TWO STORIES OF DISCONTINUITY/CONTINUITY

Chad and Eliza were two post-Access to HE students whose narratives referred to them carefully deliberating about whether to continue their degrees in textile design. Both appeared to use practical wisdom in order to come to a decision, and both had support from their friends. However, Chad who studied full-time was able to build friendships very quickly within the first year. Eliza who was part-time and could not spend as much time in the studio space did not seem to have such strong friendships nor did she seem to find her relationship with the staff very conducive to learning.

Chad did not socialise with the younger students; her friendships were created through the day-to-day participation in the studio. This was a space where people could move around, chat to each other whilst working and sharing ideas. It enabled discourse and creativity. My second meeting with Chad was in the design studio. We talked in her work space where there were sketches pinned to the wall which were inspired by the 1950s. She appeared to be very tired and was a little wider around her middle:

C: At the start of the year I was full of energy and really, really looking forward to starting and actually it didn't disappoint. This first term was excellent – I enjoyed it in fact, I enjoyed the whole year – but obviously I'm expecting! I'm six months pregnant now so at my age I'm feeling it – really feeling it – but the whole year has been ... I've really enjoyed it – absolutely enjoyed it. It's been fantastic. (Chad, June 2012)

It remained unclear as to whether the decision to become pregnant was planned or unexpected. Nussbaum (2001, p. 305) has said that the phronimos should be open to life's surprises and be flexible in order to change a course of action; to act well in response to an unexpected situation. The question was now how would Chad deal with motherhood, pregnancy and a demanding course. Would she be motivated enough to remain at the HEI or would this be an extra burden that meant her dream to be a textile designer was untenable? She told me she intended to take a year out, but was already planning how to turn this unexpected break in her studies into an opportunity to improve her own skills and abilities:

S: You don't have to start again at Year one?

C: You do in a way with new people, I'll start the second year with a completely new group and they'll have established themselves as a group. So it'll be more difficult for me to fit into that year. But my classmates in this particular year will be in third year and be next door. It won't be so bad, my friends will be around so ... (Sam & Chad, June 2012)

Chad demonstrated foresight (Providentia) in how she imagined her return to education after a year at home; showing a concern for possibly feeling isolated. She recognised the importance of the social aspects of the studio culture. Indeed, this first year had been about establishing that she belonged on the course both academically and socially. She now felt she was part of the cohort; Vallerand (1997, p. 300) has defined a sense of belonging as being connected to the institution and feeling that one is accepted as part of the social milieu. As the only mature or 'non-traditional' student in this cohort there had been a danger of Chad not feeling a subjective sense of belonging (Thomas, 2012), but actually she had been successful not just academically but in establishing a body of friends.

She tried to moderate her fear of future isolation by seeing that she could position herself next to her old friends in the studio. Chad had been able to make friends during her first year and has recognised their importance in contributing to her future success. However, she did not seem to have confidence that, as she had already made friends with younger students this year, she would be able to bond with a new body of students again in a year's time.

Chad did take a year out but continued as a participant in the research project. She came into the HEI's library bringing her new born with her so she could talk to me. It became apparent that the bonds of friendship still continued:

C: They text me all the time. I was really busy at one point and I didn't ... I wasn't in touch with them for a couple of weeks and they were worried. They kept sending me a succession of text messages – all of them – Lorraine, Vicky, Ryan, Sophie, Eleanor – all of them. "What's the matter, are you alright?"

So I missed them more than anything. I missed the class more than anything and I'm kind of apprehensive about going back because again I'm starting from scratch. (Chad, December 2012)

S: Good, so last time I saw you, you said you were going to spend time sorting out files and everything, did you do that?

C: No, I have got them – they are continuous – they are not something that I've put on the side-line. The files are there but he has to go to nursery, as soon as we get Christmas over and done with I'm doing them on an evening as soon as he's going to nursery. He goes in June for the odd day, till he gets to full-time in September – then I'll get back on to PPP [Personal Professional Planning] and all the rest but I've got loads of stuff in the pipeline especially with my friends. Still I got lots of friends off this course that have just left and they're keeping me up to date with what's going on and what's needed for the next year, which is lovely and it gives me … I won't feel so bad about going back – I won't feel as rusty because I've already got a couple of projects in mind. (Chad, December 2012)

It was interesting that Chad drew upon the experience of others in order to plan for her future projects. It was the stories her friends told her about their own experiences on the second year that allowed Chad to imagine what would be expected from her when she began her education again. By staying connected with her friends Chad continued her sense of belonging and they provided her with a vicarious learning experience. Her work in the short term involved continued planning with her friends who had kept her in the loop about what was going on at college. The person of practical wisdom could draw upon the stories of others based on their actual experiences because they could empathise with people and could gain an insight into their motivations (Skilleas, 2006, p. 268). It was an indication of how well she had established herself on the degree during the first year that her friends were so supportive.

In Chad's previous career (in the Merchant Navy) she had been part of a team, working closely together in highly regulated situations; these past experiences may have given her the good social skills needed to cultivate friends. Inherent in her narrative was the importance of being well-prepared when she returned as she was not sure how she would manage her course and two young children. The next meeting was in July 2013 and Chad would be beginning the second year in two months' time. Chad continued to acknowledge how important her friends had been:

C: I haven't done any work sketch-wise. Research – have been writing notes down and thinking about what to get into when I go back. Friends have helped me a lot, the guys that have just left and they're going back to third year they've been fantastic. They've been so encouraging and I see them all the time so they come to the house. It's nice to have that contact I know they're in the third year now because I've had to take a year out it's almost like starting from scratch yet again. So this is about the third break I've had. So it's been like from what a normal person would take to do a degree in three years, it's taken me seven or eight years to finally get to the end of it. (Chad, July, 2013)

For Ricoeur (1994, p. 180) phronesis aimed at the ethical intention of, 'the good life with and for others in just institutions', where people of practical wisdom were of good character and were concerned with friendship, justice, courage moderation and generosity. It could be seen that the practices of Chad's friends had been driven by these virtues in determining the correct course of action, which was to support her through her year out (Nussbaum, 2001, p. 306). Ricoeur (1994, pp. 184–189) explored the possibility of mutual friendship between self and other; the relationship was seen as fragile. However, at this point, in time even though Chad thought of herself as different to the 'younger students' they had a bond that had stood the test of separation. Her friends had taken time out of a busy course and had shared their experiences with her which was a generous and moral thing to do. It also could be seen as a democratic act where those on the margins were included (Bernstein, 2000, p. xx). The studio space enabled people through day-to-day contact and discourse to get to know each other facilitating virtuous actions. Although Chad temporarily discontinued her course, she was in a good position to return to her studies again.

Eliza was studying a similar subject of textile design but at a different institution. She studied part-time as she needed to keep working during her education, but this meant she did not have the same day-to-day contact with students in the studio space. So, her sense of belonging was not as quickly established. Unlike Chad, Eliza had begun to seriously consider leaving her course at the end of level four (or at the end of the second year as she was studying part-time). The reasons she considered leaving were to do with not understanding how she would be assessed, what she needed to do to improve her work and how to manage her practice alongside her sketchbook work:

> E: I am thinking about leaving this ridiculous course. I was looking forward to the third year (moving up to the level five now as it is a part-time course). I was so looking forward to doing a new brief as I had done quite well on the previous one. But it was not a positive brief. Our six designs were to be given to an American firm – six designs – so I knew I had to produce the work. But my sketch book wasn't progressing or up-to-date as I was working hard in the print room. I knew it was supposed to follow your working process. The tutor told me to leave it to the end – but I wasn't sure about that. The last project I did really well, but I didn't really understand visual research – every time I was stuck I asked for help. (Eliza, February 2014)

Eliza did act with wisdom to some extent as she was not averse to asking for help when she required it. For example, she was struggling with computer aided design (CAD) and she told me that, 'One of the younger students was so sweet they put together *a how to do CAD* guide for me'. This was an example of virtuous and unselfish action by another student designed to help another person. However, common themes within Eliza's story were about her frustrations with the systems of communication used to tell students about their assessment. Briefs (the assignments by which art and design work by students is assessed) were not written specifically for part-time students so they had difficulty in understanding the volume and quality of work they should produce. But also communication with staff had proved to be difficult, especially as a part-time student Eliza was not in the studio as often as she would have liked and so was not freely available to talk to staff. A year later Eliza was still questioning whether or not she belonged on the course.

> E: I got my last lot of work back which was not too bad you know. I did talk to the tutor and basically said, "You know I'm not sure if this is for me and you know really I'm not enjoying it and if I'm spending two days of my life for the next three years, it's not a good use of my time really". And she was a bit shocked and bit surprised and basically said to me, if I could get through the next year (which is this coming year), things will be a lot easier in the final two years because it's much more bio-self-direct stuff. (Eliza, February 2015)

Eliza had thought about her time-commitment and was making a rational decision about whether to stay or leave. She was asking the tutor about it so she seemed to be taking into account the opinions of others. The tutor was surprised that Eliza had considered dropping out, so it could be assumed that she had not noticed how frustrated Eliza had been and this supported the notion that communication had been very difficult. Eliza had been encouraged to stay, to 'get through' the second year as if it would be a trial with the promise that the final two years at level six would be easier because they were more self-directed. There was no suggestion that the course would change in order to address some of the problems Eliza had been having. Why would level six be easier than level five? Eliza had felt frustrated when working at levels four and five so there was a danger that this would continue at level six. Although the tutor had been encouraging, the underlying problems were not really thought about in depth or addressed. The tutor had not listened to what Eliza was unhappy about and assumed it was do with finding the course difficult when actually the issues had been to do with communication, misunderstanding and exclusion. Eliza decided to stay for another year and was attempting to accept that she would have to keep being pro-active in getting the support she needed as a part-time student. Liz was another part-time mature student who was studying on a fine art undergraduate course; she was also the department's student representative. Her role was to communicate with the staff about any issues the students were having with their studies. Eliza asked for Liz's help in requesting that staff populate the VLE with relevant and current information.

> E: So now we've started this new brief and again it starts. I need to start now; sit down and go through everything. So again I emailed last week and said, Can you let me know if I need to bring anything this Friday nothing is on the

Moodle? Do we have our own [part-time] brief on the internet?" Liz is now the course rep. so she's actually sent an email to say, "You know nothing is on the Moodle. Just read the brief today and it says very clearly that a lot of information will be put on the Moodle. We're expecting you to do that". I went on Moodle again today – nothing there. I kind of know what I need to do. I know that I've got to start doing surface design trend forecasting. I just need to have designs ready to go by Friday. Also I'm working at night so I'm thinking, "Right I need to get this done and it's quite an interesting brief or not as the case may be, about being innovative; innovative through fabrics and I don't understand what that means. (Eliza, February 2015)

The Moodle or VLE was very important for students who were part-time as this could be a means of including people who were not able to attend certain sessions. However, as had happened previously, Eliza and Liz did not get what had been promised and continued to work in the dark. In effect the request had not been heard. The student representative system would only instigate innovation and change if students were listened to and their concerns acted upon (Biesta, 2010, p. 122). Eliza said she 'kind of knows' what she needed to do, but then went on to say that she did not understand what the phrase 'innovative through fabrics' meant. More information on Moodle could have helped her respond to the brief well. The scenario that Eliza described was very similar to the problems she had had in the first year: there was no brief designed for part-time students; no understanding that last minute time changes made it hard for students to plan their time and, finally, information was not made explicit on Moodle. The VLE had not been used to create a virtual community of friends and did not seem as effective a way of sharing experiences as the physical engagement and immersion in the learning space had been for Chad.

CONCLUSION

The method of narrative inquiry, carried out over three years, successfully revealed how Chad and Eliza thought about and responded to various issues over time. The consequences or impact of their actions and those of other people were also suggested from their narratives, for example how making friends helped them decide to continue or discontinue studying on their courses. Unfortunately, only the students' points of views were captured; staff could have provided additional perspectives which could have been illuminating.

Both Chad and Eliza used their ability to act with practical wisdom to deliberate about whether they should continue or discontinue their courses; they did this for different reasons. Chad recognised that she needed to take a year away from her degree based upon her finding the later part of her first year tiring. She knew it would be a physically demanding time in her life. However, she was able to plan how to use her time when she was away from her degree. She was also able to temper her fears about returning to education by imagining the support she would get from her friends. She anticipated being close to them in the studio and this comforted her. Her younger friends also showed their capacity for practical wisdom when they took time out to see Chad when she had had her baby. They shared with her strategies for future success, by telling her about their experiences on the course in the second year. The bonds of friendship meant that Chad was more motivated to return to education after she had taken a year out.

Eliza also deliberated about leaving her degree. She was uncertain about her ability to improve her work. Often she felt the channels of communication were difficult, so she could not find out how she would be assessed. Because she could not spend as much time in the studio due to her other commitments Eliza had not developed a range of friendships with other students and a rapport with her tutors. She also struggled to learn the more practical skills such as CAD However, even in her story there were examples of virtuous actions from others, such as the young student who took the time to make a CAD guide for her to use. The relationship with Liz the student representative demonstrated how Eliza was recruiting supporters to help in her quest to get the information she needed. Eliza had listened to her tutor and had decided to stay on her course even though she recognised it would be challenging. From Eliza's previous experiences it is possible that she may continue to 'suffer' in that she may continue to find studying textile design on a part-time basis very difficult; perhaps it is an unrealistic dream? This could be an instance where it would have been prudent to give the course up and continue when she had more time to give to her study.

From these accounts it was possible to speculate that younger students in higher education as well as the mature ones had a capacity to act well with and for others and were capable of acts of generosity and friendship with people who may be very different from themselves. As Ricoeur (1994) argued, recognising that someone else had a particular need and acting for that person was an important aspect of phronesis. This qualified Aristotle's claim that it was most likely that older people had the experience to act with practical wisdom.

The design studio space (both in its physical and virtual form) was revealed to be a place where horizontal discourse took place between students from different backgrounds, enabling friendships to grow (Broadhead, 2015). Through friendship and a sense of belonging students were able to continue with their studies even though they met with unexpected and difficult challenges. The help given by others was practical but also supportive emotionally. It entailed the sharing of knowledge and learning experiences. At the same time, the studio in its wider sense could also be an alienating space that potentially confused and frustrated some students, making them consider discontinuing their course. When relying mostly on a virtual learning space rather than being physically present in the studio it seemed more difficult to cultivate those relationships with others which could enhance a person's chance of achievement in art and design.

This study suggests that design educators should facilitate and celebrate friendship and virtuous action within and outside the studio by feeding back how well students interact with others. They should also listen to students who are under-represented on their courses who may have a valuable perspective that has not been considered before. This perspective may introduce innovation and change into the staff's own teaching practices. If VLEs are promoted to students as spaces where they can glean information and advice then these should be kept up-to-date. However it seems that VLEs are an addition to rather than a replacement of the physical and social interactions of the design studio which are necessary for creative development (Candy, 1991).

Further work is still needed on identifying the ways educators could encourage and celebrate phronesis or wise judgments so that students feel they have agency over their own learning. It seems that the confidence needed to be a self-directed learner, one of the aims of higher education, can be diminished, if a student feels under pressure to succeed whilst studying part-time. Strategies need to be devised to enable students to share their anxieties with staff and peers without being made to feel they are failing. Accepting a mix of students with different educational histories and ages onto a design degree can facilitate intergenerational friendships; the impact of this on their creativity and innovation needs to be investigated further.

REFERENCES

Aristotle. (1953). *Ethics of Aristotle.* Middlesex: Penguin Putnam Trade.
Bernstein, B. (2000). *Pedagogy, symbolic control, and identity: Theory, research, critique.* Lanham, MD: Rowman and Littlefield Publishers.
Biesta, G. (2010). *Good education in an age of measurement: Ethics, politics, democracy.* Boulder, CO: Paradigm Publishers.
Broadhead, S. (2015). Inclusion in the art and design curriculum: Revisiting Bernstein and 'class' issues. In K. Hatton (Ed.), *Towards an inclusive arts education.* London: Trentham Books.
Burke, P. J. (2002). *Accessing education: Effectively widening participation.* Stoke on Trent: Trentham.
Butler-Kisber, L. (2010). *Qualitative inquiry: Thematic, narrative and arts-informed perspectives.* London: Sage Publications.
Candy, P. C. (1991). *Self-direction for lifelong learning: A comprehensive guide to theory and practice.* San Francisco, CA: Jossey-Bass.
Clandinin, D. J., & Connelly, F. M. (2004). *Narrative inquiry: Experience and story in qualitative research.* San Francisco, CA: Jossey-Bass.
Duckworth, V. (2014). *Learning trajectories, violence and empowerment amongst adult basic skills learners.* New York, NY: Routledge.
Edström, A. (2008). Art students making use of studio conversations. *Art, Design & Communication in Higher Education. 7*(1), 31–44
Goodenow, C. (1993). The psychological sense of school membership among adolescents: Scale development and educational correlates. *Psychology in the Schools, 30*(1), 70–90.
Hudson, C. (2009). *Art from the heart. The perceptions of students from widening participation backgrounds of progression to and through HE art and design.* London: National Arts Learning Network.
Kane, S., Chalcraft, D., & Volpe, G. (2014). Notions of belonging: First year, first semester higher education students enrolled on business or economics degree programmes. *The International Journal of Management Education, 12*, 193–201.
Nussbaum, M. C. (2001). *The fragility of goodness.* Cambridge: Cambridge University Press.
Penketh, C., & Goddard, G. (2008). Students in transition: Mature women students moving from foundation degree to honours level 6. *Research in Post-Compulsory Education, 13*(3), 315–327.
Ricœur, P. (1994). *Oneself as another.* Chicago, IL: University of Chicago Press.

Skilleås, O. M. (2006). Knowledge and imagination in fiction and autobiography. *Metaphilosophy, 37*(2), 259–276.
Thomas, P. L. (2012). *Building student engagement and belonging in higher education at a time of change: Final report from the what works? Student retention and success programme* [Online]. Retrieved July 10, 2014, from http://www.heacademy.ac.uk/resources/detail/retention/What_works_final_report
Vallerand, R. (1997). Toward a hierarchical model of intrinsic and extrinsic motivation. In M. Zanna (Ed.), *Advances in experimental social psychology.* New York, NY: Academic Press.
Wall, J. (2005). Phronesis as poetic: Moral creativity in contemporary Aristotelianism. *The Review of Metaphysics, 59*, 313–331.

Samantha Broadhead
Leeds College of Art
England

IDA LEAL

3. ENGLISH LANGUAGE BOOK CLUB AND TRANSFORMATIVE LEARNING

Developing Critical Consciousness in the English Language Classroom in a UK Further Education (FE) College and in a South African Township

INTRODUCTION

Education does not make us educable. It is our awareness of being unfinished that makes us educable. (Freire, 2001, p. 58)

Do not conform to the patterns of this world, instead be transformed by the renewing of your mind. (Romans 12, 2)

This chapter aims to discuss the results of a qualitative action research study which sets out to capture the extent to which a 'Book Club' strategy can lead to transformative learning. The research was in two phases and in two distinct contexts. The first, with English language learners at London's South Thames College and the second, Delft, a township in Cape Town, South Africa, to explore whether transformative learning and a greater sense of critical consciousness would also occur.

BOOK CLUB STRATEGY

'Book Club' is an extensive reading programme where the books read are self-selected graded readers. The rationale behind using graded readers was to facilitate comprehension and to enable the readers to immerse themselves in the story (Lantolf, 2000; Laberge & Samuels, 1974), whilst also encouraging word recognition and subsequently reducing the affective filter (Krashen, 2003). Graded readers enable English language learners to engage fully with the text, which means interpreting the text through the lens of their self-narrative (Duncan, 2012). This is key if learners are to use their cultural imagination, which is the process of re-examining our cultural histories and adapting these as we engage in discussions with other cultural perspectives which may differ from our own (Florio-Ruane & DeTar, 2001).

The learners were given two weeks to read their graded readers outside of class and told to be prepared to discuss these different books on book club day where they would share food and drinks in the school café as they discussed the themes in the book and the themes that would naturally arise throughout the discussion. Conversational learning and dialogue are attributed great value by hooks (2010) and to this end, the teacher takes a Socratic role to encourage deeper discussion by asking questions, whilst being careful not to tell learners what to think or lead them to a 'right' answer and providing vocabulary to bridge gaps in communication. Instead, learners are encouraged to challenge each other and themselves. The teacher is meant to take a passive role and enable learners to lead discussion, 'thus sharing conversational leadership by combining viewpoints rather than arguing for a single interpretation' (Florio-Ruane & DeTar, 2001, p. 69.) and for the discourse to invite contribution of personal narratives. 'Instead, the conversations unfolded as hybrid literary events in which voices and styles of reading and responding mingled' (Florio-Ruane & DeTar, 2001, p. 67).

BACKGROUND

'Book Club' was piloted 3 years ago at London's South Thames College with a group of adult international English language learners from a range of countries including: Thailand, Turkey, South Korea, Colombia and Cameroon, who were studying English with a view to getting a British degree and for some in order to teach English in their country.

'Book Club' came about initially as a strategy to encourage learners to read in English. Most had expressed the opinion that reading was purely instrumental and all expressed their negative experience of reading in English as demoralising, tedious and labour-intensive due to the enormous load of unknown vocabulary. The idea was to foster the love of reading and in so doing also change the learner's reading identity as a reader in English with a view to incorporating reading in English as a social practice (Duncan, 2012). It was hoped this would subsequently have a positive effect on their English language acquisition and experience of learning English.

During this time, I had also started a BA in Lifelong Learning at Canterbury Christchurch in southern England as a mature student. The course led me to conduct a small-scale pilot study of these learners to explore the impact that their involvement with Book Club was having and to determine whether further investigation was warranted for an action research study.

The hegemony of globalisation, neoliberal policies and English as an international language as vehicles to prosperity and forces for good, calls for educators to empower their learners by providing opportunities in the classroom which foster and develop critical consciousness. The speed of change and degree of uncertainty we live in today, along with changing markets coupled with unprecedented levels of unemployment forcing people to migrate for work, demand that we know who we are as individuals and that we possess a strong sense of self that is confident enough to choose a course of life that we can be content with (Illeris, 2014).

I contend that the role of the educator is to provide opportunities for learners which facilitate, require and encourage questioning, validating and justifying. Lange (2012, p. 205) posits that 'although we cannot direct meaningful change, we can disturb a system by introducing a meaning-rich idea, question, or practice that responds to a shared need' (Lange, 2012, p. 205). These changes, I argue, can occur within a formal or informal context. Orr (2004) disagrees with the emphasis on the mastery of content and acquiring qualifications. This mirrors what Freire (1972) refers to as the 'Banking Mode' of education, where learners are not more than passive receptacles. This passivity leads to what C. Wright Mills (1959) refers to as 'cheerful robots' in the 'Sociological Imagination'.

Being critically aware enables the learner to engage with the world with greater discernment (Freire, 1987) and leads to the premise underlying this chapter which seeks to explore the following research question: To what extent does 'Book Club' lead to transformative learning and the development of critical consciousness?

The author maintains that taking an approach to English language teaching which fosters transformative learning, helps to enable adult English language learners to think more democratically and more critically, which in turn fosters a greater sense of agency in the construction and re-construction of beliefs or frames of reference. It is argued that this skill is necessary to negotiate meaning and to navigate in the multi-cultural world they live in as *Subjects* rather than objects. For Freire (1993, p. 18) a Subject can be described as, someone who 'knows and acts whereas objects are acted upon'.

> They perceive that through their consciousness, even when they are not makers of their social reality, they transcend the constituting reality and question it ... students assume a critical posture to the extent that they comprehend how and what constitutes the consciousness of the world. (Freire & Macedo, 1987, p. 49)

The epistemological stance underpinning transformative learning is constructivist and as such, views meaning as being socially constructed (Cranton & Taylor, 2012, p. 5). This is manifest in the conceptual assumptions upon which Book Club is based: the principle that language use is inextricably linked to what is learned by any individual and begins in the social interactions in which he or she engages (Vygotsky, 1997). This chapter claims that a 'Book Club' strategy can spark a rebuilding and reconstructing process, which is the result of being exposed to other realities and world views. These frames of reference undergo scrutiny, which leads to a dialogue with the self and with others. Tisdell and Tolliver (2009) assert that engaging and working with the cultural imagination can lead to transformative learning by stimulating critical discussion.

Comparably, Freire (1972) refers to "conscientization" or critical consciousness and the empowerment which comes from being able to 'unmask and decipher' the ideologies underpinning texts, institutions as well as social and cultural practices. He argues that we '... first read the world and then the text'. Emphasising the importance of being critically conscious so as to challenge and question, which both he and Mezirow believe is a condition of being human (Mezirow, 2009; Freire, 1972).

RATIONALE FOR RESEARCH

This research project is informed by the findings of an earlier small-scale study which was designed mainly to alter beliefs and preconceptions regarding reading in English as a second language and to foster a love for reading. Upon further observation of these same learners and my reflection-in-action (Schön, 1983), I noticed a change in their behaviour. They seemed much more critical and open to dialogue at a much deeper level, whilst also displaying a marked willingness and openness to other points of view and a desire to explore possibilities in class discussion that they had not considered in the past. In addition, and of great importance, was a sense of empowerment that was observable in the way they spoke and in the way that they carried themselves. It was this 'awakening' that spurred me to conduct a fresh literature review.

Furthermore, I contend that the reason I was able to recognise this 'awakening' in my learners is due to the fact that I myself was also undergoing transformative learning. Mezirow (2009, p. 22) defines this learning as a 'learning that transforms problematic frames of reference to make them more inclusive, discriminating, reflective, open and emotionally able to change'. Among the ten stages outlined, the first is what is referred to as a 'disorientating dilemma' (Mezirow, 2009, p. 19). Early on in the BA in Lifelong Learning, as a mature learner returning to higher education, I was experiencing an internal struggle which was highly emotive, as I faced the fear of failure and not measuring up coupled with a different learning culture. Despite a strong desire to learn and open my mind, there was also enormous anger and frustration as I was faced with ideas and concepts which not only challenged my established ways of thinking, but also compelled me to reflect critically coupled with a profound need to voice these reflections.

Although I did not understand what was happening, I was acutely aware that I was in the process of extreme change. There was no doubt that it was profound and that I was changing the way I viewed the world and this directly affected my role as a teacher, which in turn affected my perception of my learners.

The findings of the focus group, which had been taped but were informal, revealed surprising evidence which would suggest that the participants involved in Book Club had experienced transformative learning in terms of re-framing their negative frame of reference regarding reading in English (Mezirow, 2009). Furthermore, participants expressed increased levels of confidence, which had led to most feeling confident enough to read newspapers independently.

LITERATURE REVIEW

The fresh literature review included Mezirow and Associates' (2000) 'Learning as Transformation', Mezirow, Edward W. Taylor & Associates' Transformative Learning in Practice: Insights from Community, Workplace, and Higher Education (2009), Freire (1993, 1972) 'Pedagogy of the Oppressed' and C. Wright Mills (2000)

'The Sociological Imagination'. These have introduced me to critical theory, transformative learning theory, 'conscientization' and the 'Banking Model' of Education and the creation of the 'sociological imagination'. Overall, this is the bedrock for this research project.

METHODOLOGY

The methodology is qualitative Action Research (AR) within a transformative learning framework. AR is designed to improve professional practice, and is an approach which aims to improve education by changing it and learning from those changes, which resonates with transformative learning. My understanding of action research is encapsulated by Carr and Kemmis (1985) who describe action research as:

> Simply a form of self-reflective enquiry undertaken by participants (teachers, students or principals for example) in social (including educational) situations in order to improve the rationality and justice of (a) their own social or educational practices, (b) their understanding of these practices, and (c) the situations (and institutions) in which these practices are carried out. (Carr & Kemmis, 1985, p. 162)

It is a cyclical process which leads to critical reflection. The democratic participation emphasised in AR respects the contributions of the participants and recognises the practitioner as 'expert' and a significant contributor in his/her professional development' (McNiff, 1988).

Qualitative methods were used to collect data, which was in two phases. In phase one individual semi-structured interviews were used to obtain a more-detailed description of their experiences. Participants were given a copy of the questions to refer to, so as to support listening comprehension. These participants are also English language learners from London's South Thames College. 'Jane', a 42-year old woman from South Korea is married and has taken a year's sabbatical from work in the Cyber Crime division to come to London with her husband. She clearly identifies Confucianism as the foundation of her beliefs, values and frames of reference. 'Patricia' is a 24-year-old woman from Cameroon, who aims to gain a British degree. She has expressed that her culture places great value on marriage and qualifications. Both have received a banking model of education (Freire, 1996), especially in Jane's case, which she highlights as extremely negative. 'We just memorise ... never discuss'.

Significantly, both candidates were profoundly impacted by this process, with Patricia experiencing a moment of epiphany as she realised at the end of the interview that she loved reading (Mezirow, 2009). Jane felt compelled to critically reflect and expressed this at the second interview, explaining that she went on to research Confucianism to get a clearer understanding of her long-held beliefs to understand her own behaviour and perceptions. She seemed disoriented by the fact that she had never questioned them before.

33

I. LEAL

Selection of participants was based on the researcher's observation of them in class and observable perceived changes. However, both participants are generally guarded and have had negative experiences of authority figures. There was a meeting before the interview to explain the process thoroughly and to allow for any questions. They were reminded that they could leave the process at any time and were under no obligation to participate. Both seemed excited, but also apprehensive. Furthermore, participants were given a copy of the transcript (verbatim) before the second interview for member checking (Kvale, 2010). Interestingly, both checked for grammatical mistakes.

With a view to making the process democratic and to maintaining authenticity and fidelity (Kvale, 2010) interviewees were given the option to bring visual aids, such as photographs, art and examples of narratives which expressed their feelings. The researcher was aware of Jane's keen interest in art and felt it would help Jane to express how she experiences and makes sense of the world. Interestingly, Jane chose Bacon's *Three Sides of Freud* and brought the print with her and used it to explain her experience of speaking in English.

Another strategy was to use concept questions, or questions to check understanding and paraphrasing to deal with unknown vocabulary (British Council, 2006). For instance, 'Is powerful the right word? Is that what you want to say?' Interestingly, Jane chose Bacon's *Three Sides of Freud* to help her express herself.

Interviews were recorded and subsequently transcribed to aid the analytical process and highlight salient themes. This was time-consuming but thematic analysis was found to be appropriate. Participants were given copies before the second interview for member checking (Kvale, 2010).

Phase 2 involved a change in context in terms of learning culture and background of participants. These learners are from Delft, a township in Cape Town, South Africa, who were attending an English Club I was running as a volunteer, at Bettaway Community Church. This was my second visit to Delft. Delft is a township in Cape Town and has one of the highest crime rates and substandard education. The method chosen was a focus group, conducted via Skype consisting of two females. The reasons for this were distance, and to obtain as much data as possible via their interaction with each other. This was later transcribed verbatim and used in the text.

Rochelle is what is referred to as 'coloured' and her first language is Africaans. She is married and has two sons. Zodwa is referred to as 'black', and her first language is Xhosa. She is a single mother of two sons. She lives with no clean running water or indoor toilet and lives in one of the most dangerous areas in Delft. Both have an elementary level education. By means of triangulation data collection methods and findings were compared, as were context and background.

DISCUSSION OF FINDINGS

The results of the semi-structured interviews revealed three salient themes where there is persuasive evidence which demonstrates that the participants exhibit signs of having undergone 'perspective transformation' (Mezirow, 2009) in the areas of: attitudes to learning English, the freedom to be fully who you are and heightened cultural awareness. Furthermore, there are examples of what Freire (1972) refers to as 'conscientization' or critical consciousness, and how Book Club, through the books that are read and what Iser (1972) refers to as the 'work', fosters conditions for critical reflection. He explains that first, there is the 'text', and that it is through the interplay between the reader and the reader's interpretation of the 'text', informed by the reader's self-narrative, that meaning is given. There is a constant reconstructing and constructing of meaning, which mirrors transformative learning.

Zodwa seems to be engaging with her cultural imagination (Florio-Ruane & De Tar, 2001) and bringing her personal narrative as she interprets the book which mirrors what life is like for her and Rochelle. She is re-examining her frames of reference and identifying other ways of being.

Zodwa: Look, like when I read the book 'Street Life' it tells about our life, no? And you think "How did the writer think of this book, these characters? If you are reading this book and you find that a person is in a certain situation and what is the solution, we can really think It's not so bad. Sometimes when you read a book maybe you upset, and you find yourself thinking Wow!
Researcher: So it changes your way of thinking?
Zodwa: Yeah, it's a good thing!

This process triggered critical reflection as she engaged with topics and issues not only from her reading, but also through dialogue, which in some cases compelled the participants to reassess and reconstruct their 'frames of reference' with a greater sense of agency and critical consciousness. hooks (2010, p. 46) reminds us that conversational learning is powerful and exposes us to 'different ways of seeing and knowing'. Significantly, she emphasises that the act of conversation can create a safe space which generates compassion. According to hooks (2010, p. 46) compassion is essential as it stimulates a desire to communicate and understand.

These are learners who are no longer happy to blindly or passively accept ways of thinking without challenge. There has been an 'awakening' in their consciousness. Taylor and Jarecke (2009, p. 277) refer to a kind of learning which is profound and goes beyond instrumental learning, which seeks only to improve performance (Taylor, 2009, p. 20), whereas communicative learning is concerned with understanding what people mean when they communicate (Taylor, 2009, p. 20). Long-held beliefs and values are called into question through dialogue, requiring critical reflection. This is learning where learners 'experience personal social empowerment' (Taylor & Jarecke, 2009, p. 277).

Significantly, the participants from the townships in Delft have become more autonomous and are taking ownership of their learning by making it their own. The agency demonstrated suggests an increase in confidence to take initiative and in their own ability. It is important to remember that these women have not been educated past elementary school and have never demonstrated this level of autonomy before. In addition, it is interesting to note their interest in individual words. When I was there teaching and setting up Book Club in August 2015, they learnt the word 'enthusiastic', and 'unwind' was learnt in August 2011, during my first visit there. Both Rochelle and Zodwa make a point of showing me they know these words and can use them in the correct context.

> Rochelle: Yes! We decided that if there are words that we don't understand that we make copies for each one. At the back of the book is the words and the meanings of the words. So, everyone get a copy and we go over it. We try to pronounce it and so on.
> Zodwa: Yes, we very *enthusiastic*!
> Rochelle: We don't want just to read it. We want to understand so we make copies for each one to go over it at home and so on.
> Researcher: What happens in your mind when you're reading?
> Rochelle: Like you *unwind*.

One major theme of transformational learning was language learning, which further corroborates the experience voiced by participants in the earlier pilot study. In a study conducted by King (1999) into which found that language learning is conducive to fostering transformative learning in English language learners. For example, Patricia described her experience of reading as purely instrumental.

> We just read to pass an exam … reading is just losing your time … reading is just for when you have to … Before, I was angry when I was reading and I don't understand. I would just give up … How am I going to do it … I was afraid to read and to explain in English … Now I sometimes find newspapers and I just pick it.

This is significant because it demonstrates a desire in Patricia to engage with reading as a social practice (Duncan, 2012). This is a dramatic paradigm shift for Patricia, which supports Duncan's view (2012, p. 2) that there is persuasive evidence which strongly supports the notion that reading circles develop not only reading and discussion skills, but also 'independent study skills, confidence as both readers and members of the community, the exploration of personal identity and the development of personal reading practices'.

Jane from South Korea and Patricia from Cameroon expressed an increased desire to read more and increased confidence levels due to Book Club. Significantly, the same was true for Rochelle and Zodwa, from Delft, despite the vast differences in their backgrounds in terms of education, cultural background and standard of living. Both contexts seem to be examples of what Duncan (2010) describes as a shift in 'reading identity' and illustrates an example of 'internal' change due to participation in Book Club. This change in perspective was incremental, occurring over a period of time, and as a result of feeling a sense of achievement at being able to finish an entire book and discuss it fluently and confidently.

In addition, Rochelle also seems to be reflecting critically and there is persuasive evidence to suggest that Book Club is enabling them to pass on the love and habit of reading to their children. Bourdieu (1986) refers to these dispositions as *habitus*.

> Rochelle: I am reading more now. In the evening Keon asks "Are we not gonna read Mommy?" He want to read in the evening and now I must read again. So, it's more now. It's our duty to read for them. We must also read the books. We do it and then they do it also.

This is significant because it will enable not only Rochelle but her children to move within a wider range of 'fields' as they gain social and linguistic capital (Bourdieu, 1986).

> Rochelle: That book that I read about scientists. There is stuff that I didn't know so through that book I did learn about stuff that I didn't know. It's good because there's a lot of stuff that you don't know. Then you read and I think then your thinking and your mind set I think it changes. Like let's say your child might have a project about scientists, you can help him.

Both Rochelle and Zodwa feel more empowered to help their children and themselves despite the apparently insurmountable challenges they face on a daily basis. A second major theme of transformational learning is the freedom to be fully who you are.

> When I choose new book it was interesting because for example South Africa president ... I choose Mandela's book. He was famous in the world and I choose when he was not died. So ... he is black president ... so I heard his story but when I read the book I understand his life and why people choose ... after I read book when I listened to the news about South Africa I interested in that news. It's connected.

Jane was intentional and discriminating in her book selection. Furthermore, her choice of book reveals a desire to explore and broaden her cultural awareness so as to open her mind (Cranton & Taylor, 2013, p. 37) to other ways of thinking and other ways of knowing, which are far-removed from her own (Belenky et al., 1997). It also demonstrates a willingness to change, which is one of the democratic ideals in communicative learning as stipulated by Mezirow (2009) and is also an example of what Florio-Roune and DeTar (2001) describe as 'cultural imagination. There is reasonable evidence to suggest that Jane is experiencing the beginnings of conscientization or critical consciousness as she demonstrates signs of 'reading the world' (Freire & Macedo, 1987).

I. LEAL

> So … when I came here I saw another country classmates and they are very free!! I was surprised and I wanted to be like them!

Comparably, the feeling of disorientation in Mezirow's (2009) stages of transformative learning can also be seen in stage 2 of culture shock as experienced when there is a meeting between different cultures (McClinton, 2005). When faced with her Colombian and Italian classmates Jane was stunned by their expressiveness and perceived lack of inhibitions, causing her to experience culture shock, which acted as a catalyst for her to challenge her established way of thinking and behaviour. Jane explains that because of her Confucian principles she had always obeyed teachers and parents. And now realises she had been conditioned to conform and follow convention unquestioningly. There is also convincing evidence to suggest that this is also an example of what Freire (1993) means by "conscientization" and Habermas (no date, cited in Mezirow, 1981, p. 7) regards as emancipatory action, which is when taken-for-granted social roles and expectations and habitual ways of behaving are challenged by the process, Freire (1972) calls these 'problem-posing'.

> My background culture is Confucianism. I checked this. Children respect parent and teachers. So when I was growing up I didn't have questions for anything because children respect adults because Confucianism, so I ALWAYS obeyed people in authority. So when I had Book Club it's very useful for me to read the book and then explain to another classmate … I have chance to explain my book and I give my opinion to another classmate. I share my opinion. It's very good.

Jane comes from a Banking Model of education, which is designed to destroy any desire to question and renders individuals passive and unable to think critically. Added to this, her society is underpinned by the Confucian saying 'Silence is Gold' and expressing one's opinion is frowned upon. This is maintained through the threat of alienation. Despite these seemingly insurmountable obstacles, Jane is engaging in what Brookfield (1995) describes as ideology critique.

Jane selected Bacon's painting *Three sides of Freud*, as a metaphor to represent how not being able to speak fluently in English constrains her and also to represent the freedom she longs for. Initially, she feels trapped, but there is now more space, which she explains represents an increase in self-confidence. The affective factor, which Mezirow has been criticised for not addressing in depth, would seem to be a significant factor in her transformative learning. Her feelings and emotions are powerful and have played a major role, compelling her to critically reflect and challenge the values and beliefs that had been assimilated unquestioningly (Mezirow, 2009).

> Jane: My speaking is not good. So when I speaking during the Book Club I'm like him, sitting on the chair and I want to go out of the swing.
> Researcher: So … does that mean that in this painting he's trapped?
> Jane: Yes, so this colour (the golden yellow) … it's very beautiful … so if I stand outside, I can enjoy this space.

Researcher: And that space represents?
Jane: Free!

Vygotsky (2012) explains that the 'flow of thought is not accompanied by a simultaneous unfolding of speech' and he stresses that the cognitive process has its own framework and reminds us that the transition from thought to the speech act is not an easy one. He adds, 'Every sentence that we say … has some kind of subtext, a thought behind it' (Vygotsky, 2012, pp. 264–265). Jane is illustrating the internal struggle, which can be involved in perspective transformation, and which Meizirow (2009, p. 19) describes as Phase 2, where there is a 'recognition of a connection between one's discontent and the process of transformation'.

It could also be argued that Jane is struggling with not being able to be her 'true' self in English. She seems to be struggling with 'losing her genuineness' (Foster, p. 35) due to the restrictions imposed by her limited range of competence in English, which she does not experience in Korean. This sense of loss can contribute to transformative learning as the language learner's self-perception is made vulnerable or re-examined, and is often a painful and disturbing process (Mezirow, 1991; McClinton, 2005).

Belenky et al. (1997) posit that there is a correlation between women whose sense of self is embedded in external definitions, institutions and roles and women who gain fulfilment from pleasing others or measuring up to external standards such as 'the good woman', 'the good student' or the 'successful woman'. Jane explains that one of the reasons why she feels torn about embracing the freedom she claims to desire or aspire to, is that she enjoys the approval, validation and praise she receives when she complies with the stereotypical roles and principles of Confucianism.

> Because my parents say 'You are very good child … my friends say You are very good person … my colleagues Oh! You are the best partner! I want to be that kind of person. I always give something to everyone so that they will tell me Oh! You are a very kind person!

This seems to be an example of what Mills (2000) refers to as the problem of 'the cheerful robot' and asserts that apparent desire for freedom is not inherent in Man. Jane refers to the fear that came with that desire for freedom. Her fears of alienation and losing the comfort and security of the life and reality she has known.

Rochelle now realises that others saw her as one-dimensional, funny and someone who didn't take anything seriously. She is no longer content to be seen this way and now enjoys the fact that she is more highly-regarded. She has found her voice and enjoys using it.

Zodwa: I was feeling excited because I was sharing that story with them and they were like asking even more questions 'What happened …?'
Researcher: How did you feel doing that?
Zodwa: I feel great man!

I. LEAL

Rochelle: They are LISTENING to you!
Researcher: And that's important?
Rochelle: Some people say "You don't even take notice of this and that and now you talking about this book that you have read and explaining everything.
Researcher: So it's changing the way other people see you?
Rochelle: Yes, it's a good thing. You know, people think Rochelle is JUST funny. But there's a serious part of me also. If they see that side they think 'What's up with Rochelle?' Maybe they ask me Sister Rochelle, are you OK? You're so quiet. But I think to myself, No I'm not quiet, I'm just THINKING. They say "I never saw you like that before".
Researcher: How did that make you feel?
Rochelle: It's nice to let people see another side of me. Not only that side that they know. It's not always jokes, jokes! It's just that stuff changes. Sometimes they catch me in the middle of thinking mood and they think something's wrong, but nothing's wrong.

Conversational learning is powerful in transformative learning because it not only provides the place to be heard, but also its democratic nature assumes every voice is worthy, generating compassion and a 'book club' discourse where participants combine 'book talk' with 'self-talk' (Florio-Ruane & de Tar, 2001).

The third theme highlighted was heightened cultural awareness and critical consciousness.

Jane: So ... another for example ... I read Barack Obama book ... yeah ... before I liked Barack Obama ... who is president ... yeah ... he's a good person ... I just know information about him ... and I read Barack Obama story book ... yeah ... Why in America big issue Barack Obama's religion? ... and then ... Why Barack Obama wanted to change the politics in the USA? ... and in the world ... in Afghanistan ... Why USA fight Afghanistan? Before I don't ... didn't interested in that kind of book. It's not my life.
Researcher: So you weren't interested ... it was completely ... J
Jane: Different.
Researcher: From you ... separate from you?
Jane: Yeah, I didn't even think about it.

There is evidence to show that she is beginning to 'read the world and then the text' (Freire & Macedo, 1987, p. 49) by unmasking and deciphering the ideologies, underpinning texts, institutions, social and cultural practices. She is showing signs of critical consciousness and engagement with the world as a Subject and no longer an object.

Both Patricia, from Cameroon and Zodwa, from Delft highlight the importance of being more tolerant and not judging. When asked how 'Book Club' had changed her life Zodwa replied:

Zodwa: Now as we come together to explain our books, I will explain it my way and she will explain it her way. It came into to my mind that you expect another explanation and you don't have to judge that explanation of that person.

Patricia: Now I am more tolerant. The first Book Club when she said she didn't like children I was very angry and I wanted to punish her. Now, I don't need to judge. I am more tolerant.

CONCLUSION

Fostering an environment which leads to transformative learning, where individuals cultivate a greater sense of agency and are empowered to make sense of the world through consciousness-raising, is in my view significant and crucial in adult learning.

As English language learners, these learners not only have the formidable task of learning the language, but also the culture, whilst being immersed in the second language culture. This research has highlighted areas such as acculturation and the importance of identity and being authentic in a second language, which had not previously been considered as elements which could foster transformative learning.

There is strong support for incorporating strategies such as Book Club, where these learners can have a voice. This was evident in all the participants. Furthermore, there is persuasive evidence to suggest that a 'Book Club' strategy does seem to foster transformative learning. I believe that the 'book club' discourse, which is a mixing of 'book talk' with 'life talk', not normally welcome in the classroom, promotes engagement with their cultural imagination, triggering critical reflection and a re-shaping of these cultural histories as they encounter different cultural perspectives (Florio-Ruane & DeTar, 2001).

Practically, Action Research has had a profound impact on my practice, not only instrumentally, but in terms of my identity as an English language teacher. It has served as a catalyst to a re-examining of my own frames of reference, as I have become convinced that this role comes laden with my ideologies, my beliefs and my self-narrative, and as such there is the responsibility not to preach or to manipulate learners into taking on what teachers regard as true, fair or the right way of thinking or living. Freire (1993) reminds us to be careful not to become the new oppressor, however well-meaning.

To conclude, there was evidence which strongly supports the ideas of Freire (1972) and C. Wright Mills (2000), who highlight the detrimental effects of a Banking Model of education, which is characteristically 'necrophilic' as the relentless process of narration eradicates critical consciousness and the desire to question, producing "cheerful robots", who cannot make the effort to question the existing power system.

Not only have these learners incorporated reading as a social practice and improved language acquisition, there is evidence of consciousness-raising and greater agency and ownership of their re-constructed frames of reference.

Therefore, the findings support an adult curriculum which incorporates strategies in English language teaching and learning, that are designed intentionally to help foster transformative learning.

REFERENCES

Belenky, M. F., Clinchy, M. B., Goldberger, R. N., & Tarule, M. J. (1997). *Women's ways of knowing: The development of self, voice, and mind*. New York, NY: Basic Books.

Bourdieu, P. (1986). *The forms of capital* [Online]. Retrieved from August 12, 2015, from https://www.marxists.org/reference/subject/philosophy/works/fr/bourdieu-forms-capital.htm

Brookfield, S. (1995). *The power of critical theory for adult learning and teaching*. Maidenhead: Open University Press.

Cranton, P., & Taylor, E. (2012). *The handbook of transformative learning: Theory, research, and practice*. San Francisco, CA: Jossey-Bass.

Duncan, S. (2012). *Reading circles, novels and adult reading development*. London: Continuum.

Florio-Ruane, S., & DeTar, J. (2001). *Teacher education and the cultural imagination: Autobiography, conversation and narrative*. Mahwah, NJ: Lawrence Erlbaum Associates.

Foster, E. (1997). *'Transformative learning in adult second language learning' new directions for adult and continuing education, no. 74, Summer, Jossey-Bass Publishers* [Online]. Retrieved from http://onlinelibrary.wiley.com/doi/10.1002/ace.7404/epdf?r3_referer=wol&tracking_action=preview_click&show_checkout=1&purchase_referrer=onlinelibrary.wiley.com&purchase_site_license=LICENSE_DENIED

Freire, P. (1972). *The pedagogy of the oppressed*. London: Penguin Group.

Freire, P. (1993). *The pedagogy of the oppressed*. London: Penguin Group.

Freire, P. (2001). *Pedagogy of freedom: Ethics, democracy, and civic courage*. Lanham, MD: Rowman and Littlefield, Publishers.

Freire, P., & Macedo, D. (1987). *Literacy: Reading the word and the world*. London: Routledge and Kegan Paul Ltd.

hooks, b. (2010). *Teaching critical thinking: Practical wisdom*. New York, NY: Routledge.

Ileris, K. (2014). *Transformative learning and identity*. Oxon: Routledge, Taylor and Francis Group.

Iser, W. (1972). *The reading process: 'A phenomenological approach': A new literary history, on interpretation* (Vol. 3, no. 2, pp. 279–299). Baltimore, MD: The Johns Hopkins University Press. Retrieved April 12, 2015, from http://www.jstor.org/stable/468316

King, K. P. (1999). *Changing languages, cultures and self: The adult ESL experience of perspective transformation*. Retrieved from http://www.adulterc.org/applications/ClassifiedListingsManager/inc_classifiedlistingsmanager.asp?ItemID=458&CategoryID=134

Krashen, S. (1988). *Steven Krashen's theory of second language acquisition* [Online]. Retrieved April 14, 2014, from http://www.sk.com.br/sk-krash.html

LaBerge, D., & Samuels, S. J. (1974). Toward a theory of automatic information processing in reading. *Cognitive Psychology, 6*, 293–323.

Lange, E. A. (2012). Transforming transformative learning through sustainability and the new science. In E. W. Taylor, P. Cranton, & Associates (Eds.), *The handbook of transformative learning: Theory, research, and practice* (Chapter 12). San Francisco, CA: Jossey-Bass.

Lantolf, J. P. (2000). *Sociocultural theory and second language learning*. Oxford: Oxford University Press.

Mertens, D. (2009). *Transformative research and evaluation*. London: The Guilford Press.

Mezirow, J. (1991). *Transformative dimensions of higher and adult education* [Online]. San Francisco, CA: Jossey-Bass. Retrieved from https://www.amazon.co.uk/Transformative-Dimensions-Jossey-Bass-Education-Hardcover/dp/1555423396

Mezirow, J., & Associates. (2000). *Learning as transformation*. San Francisco, CA: Jossey-Bass.

Mezirow, J., & Taylor, E. W. (2009). Transformative learning theory. In J. Mezirow, E. W. Taylor, & Associates (Eds.), *Transformative learning in practice: Insights from community, workplace, and higher education*. San Francisco, CA: Jossey-Bass.

McClinton, J. (2005). Transformative learning: The English as a second language teacher's experience. *The CATESOL Journal, 17*, 1. Retrieved from http://www.catesoljournal.org/wp-content/uploads/2014/07/CJ17_mcclinton.pdf

McNiff, J. (1988). *Action research principles and practice*. London: MacMillan Education Ltd.

Mills, C. W. (2000). *The sociological imagination.* Oxford: Oxford University Press.

Orr, D. (2004). *Earth in mind*. Washington, DC: Island Press.

Power, J. (2012). *Does Confucianism have a role in Korea today?* [Online]. Retrieved July 3, 2014, from http://www.koreaherald.com/view.php?ud=20120213001231

Raphael, T. E., Florio-Ruane, S., & George, M. (2001). Book club plus: A conceptual framework to organize literacy instruction. *Language Arts, 79*(1), 159–168. Retrieved July 5, 2014, from https://www.learner.org/libraries/engagingliterature/support/book-club-plus.pdf

Romans 12, v2, New International Version of the Bible.

Schon, D. (1983). *The reflective practitioner: How professionals think in action*. New York, NY: Basic Books.

Taylor, E. W. (2009). Fostering transformative learning. In J. Mezirow, E. W. Taylor, & Associates (Eds.), *Transformative learning in practice: Insights from community, workplace, and higher education*. San Francisco, CA: Jossey-Bass.

Taylor, E. W., & Cranton, P. (2013). A theory in progress? Issues in transformative learning theory. *European Journal for Research on the Education and Learning of Adults, 4*(1), 33–47. Retrieved July 19, 2014, from http://www.pedocs.de/volltexte/2013/7705/pdf/RELA_2013_1_Taylor_Cranton_A_theory_in_progress.pdf

Taylor, E. W., & Jarecke, J. (2009). Transformative learning theory. In J. Mezirow, E. W. Taylor, & Associates (Eds.), *Transformative learning in practice: Insights from community, workplace, and higher education*. San Francisco, CA: Jossey-Bass.

Vygotsky, L. (1997). *Mind and society Interaction between learning* (pp. 77–91) [Online]. Retrieved form http://www.psy.cmu.edu/~siegler/vygotsky78.pdf

Vygotsky, L. (2012). *thought and Language*. Cambridge, MA: MIT Press.

Ida Leal
South Thames College
England

ALYSON E. KING, ALLYSON EAMER AND NAWAL AMMAR

4. PARTICIPATION AND PERSISTENCE

An Analysis of Underserved Students at UOIT

INTRODUCTION

In Canada's multicultural society, identifying and understanding how students from diverse backgrounds are able to persist at university until graduation is important, especially given the impact of postsecondary degrees on employment opportunities, individual income and long term earnings, as well as the education requirements for newly created jobs (e.g., Zeman, McMullen, & de Broucker, 2010). Since research has identified the importance of higher education for future earnings (Ostrovsky & Frenette, 2014), quality of life and life chances (Banerjee & Verma, 2012), we must understand how to enable "at-risk" students to succeed in higher education (instead of studying only barriers).

According to Statistics Canada (2010), about fifty percent of the population over the age of 15 will be foreign-born or have one foreign-born parent by 2030. The University of Ontario Institute of Technology (UOIT), where this study took place, is located on the rural-urban fringe at the edge of the Greater Toronto Area and provides a good snapshot of this demographic trend, with 44% of the students self-identifying as visible minorities and a large number receiving loans or working more than 15 hours per week to pay their university tuition fees (NSSE, 2012). Broad trends show that there are differences between ethnic groups and the educational success of young adult immigrants (Reitz, Zhang, & Hawkins, 2011; Vaccaro, 2012), but most of that research is American and focuses on the barriers that create such differentials in educational success among ethnic or national groups (Armstrong & McMahon, 2013; Boyd, 2009; Davies & Maldonado, 2008), explores the stage of transition from high school to the university (Roxas & Roy, 2012; Sweetman & Dicks, 1999), examines labour market success after degree completion (Anisef, Sweet, & Frempong, 2003; Ferrer & Riddell, 2008; Mata & Krauth, 2008) and uses quantitative methodologies that provide little detail about the nuances of students' experiences (Ferede, 2010). This pilot study complements these by beginning to develop a more nuanced examination of the reasons why some students successfully persist to graduation.

LITERATURE REVIEW

Research on the barriers to and the levels of participation in higher education for students of different ethnic, racial and class backgrounds is extensive (e.g., Kilpi-Jakonen,

2011; Ashton & Esses, 1999). In Canada, much of the research has relied on the rich longitudinal data collected in the Youth in Transition survey (e.g., Finnie et al., 2015) and provides information on financial barriers, family income, parental education background, and the like. Others have delved into these quantitative data to analyse their impact on student aspirations for, barriers to, and influence on attending and persisting in post-secondary education (e.g., Childs et al., 2012).

In addition, researchers in Canada and the United States have examined the role that family background plays in the participation of immigrant youth in post-secondary education and the transition process and integration of immigrant youth into schools and communities (e.g., Teranishi et al., 2011; Matthews & Mahoney, 2005; Sinacore & Lerner, 2013). Much of that research refers to quantitative data collected in the 1980s and 1990s (e.g., Glick & White, 2004; Keller & Tillman, 2008; Tseng, 2004). Some researchers utilising traditional assimilation theory have found that immigrant youth and children of recent immigrants face barriers to accessing post-secondary education (Keller & Tillman, 2008), but others have found that some groups of immigrants have higher levels of aspiration for and participation in higher education (e.g., Baum & Flores, 2011) and point to generational differences between categories of children from immigrant families (Glick & White, 2004; Keller & Tillman, 2008; Baum & Flores, 2011), even when researchers controlled for socio-economic background (SES). Related research has identified an "immigrant paradox" where 2nd and 3rd generation immigrant students experience lower academic achievement than their 1st generation counterparts (Suarez-Orozco et al., 2009). There is also considerable research about retention and student participation in higher education in Ontario (e.g., Finnie, Childs, & Wismer, 2011; Norrie & Zhao, 2010; Sweet et al., 2010). These reports are valuable in providing information related to individual institutions, specific programmes targeted at the retention of 1st generation university students, overviews of factors impacting access and persistence, and the like. Few studies focus on what students themselves say about how and why they are successful at persisting to graduation.

Recent programmes that targeted First Generation students (i.e., those whose parents have never attended university) and overall first-year retention have been important in improving first-year persistence rates (e.g., Torenbeek et al., 2010; Bailey & Alfonso, 2005). These include mentoring and early integration experience programmes (e.g., Collier & Fellows, 2008; Soria & Stebleton, 2012), first-year seminar courses (Miller et al., 2007), participation in learning communities to improve engagement and persistence (e.g., Engstrom & Tinto, 2008), institutional policies and practices (e.g., Calcagno et al., 2008; Lee et al., 2009), institutional structures (e.g., Scott et al., 2008; Parkin & Baldwin, 2009), and the influence of faculty interactions with students (Sax et al., 2005). Other researchers have focussed on students who are English language learners to determine how they acculturate to the academic environment (e.g., Cheng & Fox, 2008; Schwartz et al., 2013), the ways in which immigrant students socialize on university campuses and maintain their cultural values and identities in a diverse environment (Grasmuck & Kim, 2010;

Rosenblum et al., 2009), and how resilience and self-esteem impacts student experiences and success (Jaret & Reitzes, 2009; Seror et al., 2005). In spite of the success of targeted first-year retention programmes, most universities in Ontario have much lower degree completion rates. According to CUDO (Common University Data Ontario, 2014), for instance, Laurentian University's year 1 to 2 retention rate in 2012 was 83.1% and its graduation rate was 70.9%. Few studies examine what happens between years two and four to cause this attrition or which students are most affected. Our research takes up these questions to make a holistic and comparative analysis of the success strategies used by different demographic segments of student groups at varying levels of risk. This comparative approach reduces the "othering" that often emerges when examining only "at risk" populations (Seigel, 2005; Viveiros de Castro, 2004). This case study is the result of a pilot project to begin considering the potential for such a comparative analysis.

METHODOLOGY

We used a concurrent mixed methods approach and drew on a variety of theoretical frameworks: critical race theory, resilience theory, post-colonialism and Indigenous paradigms. Understanding how underrepresented students successfully persist in university in spite of barriers to access requires methodologies that challenge the notion that "the social system is open and individual mobility can be attained through hard work" (Sleeter, 1993, p. 160). Resilience theory, like Indigenous research paradigms, holds that oppressive methods dislocate trust and unfairly position the researcher as the one with the 'power to define' (Liebenberg & Ungar, 2009). Volunteers for the project were solicited and were chosen through purposeful selection to ensure an even split between first and fourth year students, between visible minority immigrant students and those who did not identify as visible minority immigrant, and for a balance in gender.

This pilot study of a total of 29 individuals including surveys of 24 students (13 first-year students and 11 fourth-year students) and interviews with eight students (4 first-year and 4 fourth-year), three of whom did both the interview and the survey. Seven participants were male students and 17 were female, ranging in age from 17 (1) to 25 (1), with most aged 18 (10) and 21 (8). Only one student surveyed was living common law; the remaining 23 were single and never married. Fifteen of the students were Canadian citizens by birth, four were Canadian citizens by naturalisation, and five were permanent residents. Of the 15 Canadian citizens by birth, all were born in Ontario. Students identified with a wide range of ethnicities, including Canadian, and several identified with multiple ethnicities, such as Italian, German and Scottish or South Asian and West Indian or Jamaican and Indian. In terms of the importance of their ethnic identity, four stated that their identity was not at all important, while eleven felt their identity was very important; the remaining nine students fell in between, with five rating their identity as neither important nor very important. For most students, English was the main language they spoke regularly and used for reading and writing, but there was a wide range of languages spoken at home and with friends.

Volunteers were sought from all Faculties within the university. Fourteen of the students were enrolled in a programme in the Faculty of Social Science and Humanities, three were in a Science programme, four were from the Faculty of Engineering and Applied Science and three (one in each Faculty) were in the Faculty of Business & Information Technology, Faculty of Energy Systems & Nuclear Engineering, and the Faculty of Health Science. Participants were enrolled in a total of twelve different programmes (4 in Criminology, 8 in Forensic Psychology, 2 in Legal Studies, 2 in Electrical Engineering, and one in each of the following programmes: Automotive Engineering, Commerce, Biology, Communication, Community Development & Policy Studies, Health Science, Mechanical Engineering, and Nuclear Engineering).

FINDINGS

The survey and interview questions were designed to solicit information about the influence of family and personal lives, as well as available academic resources and activities. In both the survey and interviews, open-ended questions were used to capture the voices of the students as they reflected on their experiences at university. Most respondents' parents (21 mothers and 19 fathers) had at least a high school education or higher (see Table 1). In addition, fifteen students had an older sibling who had pursued a higher education. Having family members who value education has been shown to be important for the successful completion of both high school and post-secondary education for young people (Glick & White, 2004; Picot & Hou, 2013).

Most of the respondents grew up knowing they would go to university (n=18), while four decided to go to university while in high school and two said they were still not sure why they were attending university. Twenty students came directly from secondary school, while four arrived at UOIT after attending another university

Table 1. Parents' education

Highest level of schooling	Mother	Father
Earned doctorate (Ph.D., D.Sc., Ed.D.)	0	1
Master's degree (M.A., M.Sc., M.Ed.)	2	0
Bachelor's or undergraduate university degree (including B.A., B.Sc.N., LL.B., B.Ed.)	4	6
Diploma or certificate (community college, CEGEP or apprenticeship)	9	4
Some trade, technical or vocational school, or business college	0	5
High school diploma	6	3
Some high school	2	4
Don't know	1	1

(n=3) or college (n=2). Three of the students who came from another university or college felt more successful in their new program. Twelve students had completed their secondary school diploma requirements in June 2014 and six in June 2011; the remaining six students had completed secondary school in 2008 (n=1), 2009 (n=2), and 2010 (n=2). Most participants identified their overall grade average in their final year of secondary school as 80% to 89%; however, eight said their secondary school grades were between 70%–79% and three said their grades were 90% or higher. When asked whether their secondary school adequately prepared them for university, opinions were split evenly: twelve felt their secondary school did prepare them well for university and twelve did not (see Table 2).

Students were also asked about their motivation levels. Thirteen stated that they were very motivated ("I attend all classes and regularly do homework, readings and study"), ten stated that they were somewhat motivated ("I attend most classes and do

Table 2. Secondary school preparation for university

Felt adequately or well-prepared for university	Number	Did not feel adequately prepared for university	Number
Course workload expectations	3	Lack of efficient grading system	1
Difficulty of courses, level of expectations	3	Lack of consequences for missing assignments	1
Time management	3	Lack of detailed explanations of concepts needed for university courses	1
Organization	2	Below standard high school courses	1
Learned to work hard	1	"babied" in high school & victory lap	1
Learned to study	1	Lack of note taking, managing exam schedules, life skills (for living on own)	3
Well-prepared for assignments;	1	Lack of practical assignments	1
Examinations	1	Pressure to study more	1
Course content	1	Grammar, writing skills	3
Writing & citing	1	Citation methods	1
Everything overall	2	Professionalism	1
		Technology	1
		Amount of work	1
		Irrelevant subject matter not related to field of interest	1
TOTAL [Some respondents provided multiple answers]	19		18

most of my homework or readings, and study only when necessary"), and one said s/he was unmotivated ("I often miss class, rarely do homework or readings, and minimally study".). The fact that we solicited volunteers for this project has the potential to skew the results regarding motivation level since unmotivated students are less likely to voluntarily do anything extra. We tried to mitigate this problem by offering a $10 incentive for completing the survey and a $20 incentive for taking part in the interview.

In terms of the importance of religion to individual students, seven stated that religion was not important at all and six stated religion was very important; the remaining eleven students ranked religion in between with six stating that religion was neither important nor unimportant (see Table 3). Interestingly, in the interviews, those who said they were religious also said that their religion really did not have an impact on their schooling or ability to be successful beyond providing a stable base for their life in general.

However, when students were asked about how they overcame any challenges in their education and what helped them to succeed at university, religion played a role for some students. Seven students stated that their religion or spirituality regularly helped them with challenges and stresses, five said religion or spirituality sometimes helped them, and twelve stated that religion or spirituality never plays that kind of role in their lives.

Other factors tended to play a more important role in overcoming challenges (see Table 4). Eighteen respondents stated that one or more professors had encouraged and helped them when they had questions, while six said that professors had not helped them. Only six students said that the Student Learning Centre had helped them. Eleven students said that they used online tools (such as NOOL.uoit.ca, OWL@Purdue), but thirteen had not used online tools. Overall, surprisingly few students made use of the free resources available on and off campus. This may be the result of who volunteered for the study. Most of the students felt that they were able to cope well with a difficult course, assignments or other challenges: Sixteen said that they cope well ("Yes, I can usually cope with any problems"), six said that they sometimes cope well ("Sometimes I cope well, but there are times when I give up or do not complete a difficult task"), and one said that s/he does not cope well with problems. Students were also asked about what factors would help them to cope with challenges (see Table 5).

Financial problems cause stress for many students. Using a feeling thermometer scale out of 100, students were asked to identify how much the cost of university worries them (the lower the number, the less worried; the higher the number, the more worried) (see Table 6). Most of the students pay for university tuition through

Table 3. Importance of religion in student lives

Very Important	Neither Important nor Unimportant	Not at all Important
6	17	7

Table 4. Factors to help succeed in university

Factors	Yes, I use	No, I did not use
Professors	18	6
Student Learning Centre (i.e., peer tutoring, subject area support)	6	18
Online tools (i.e., NOOL.uoit.ca, OWL@Purdue)	11	13
Academic Advisors	9	15
Services for Students with Disabilities	2	22
Student Association	1	23
University association or centre (i.e., Aboriginal Resource Centre)	1	23
Study groups with peers	9	15
Other	3	21

Table 5. Factors that help (or would help) in coping with problems

Factors	Yes, it helps	No, it doesn't help
A quiet place to think or study	20	4
An opportunity to talk with my peers in the course	21	3
Encouragement from my family or friends	17	7
Fewer hours of paid employment	2	22
Being enrolled in fewer courses	7	17
Fewer personal problems	18	6
Fewer financial problems	11	13
Other	1	23

government loans (n=17), only three students have parents who pay for all of their tuition, one student received scholarships and bursaries for tuition, two students share the cost with their parents, and one did not respond to this question. Living expenses were similarly a cause for concern with seven paying for living expenses mainly through government loans, three mainly by working part-time, seven whose parents paid for all living expenses, one who lived at home, and five who shared the cost with their parents. In terms of how finances impacted their studies, just over half of the students (n=13) either found that finances were not a problem or that they had found a way to balance work and school, but just less than half either worried about finances (n=8) or had been negatively impacted by financial concerns (see Table 7). Given that we know from other internally collected data that most UOIT students are from lower income families and work while attending university, these findings

Table 6. Worry about finances

Range	46/100 Not worried	60–69/100 Worried	70–79/100 Moderately worried	80–89/100 Very worried	90–99/100 Extremely worried	100 Extremely worried
Number	1	4	5	6	3	3

Table 7. Impact of finances

How have finances impacted ability to pursue your studies?	Number
Finances are not a problem	8
I work hard, but work and school are manageable	5
I constantly worry about paying tuition and other bills	8
My long working hours have a negative impact on my ability to do well in school	1
I delayed my university education to earn money for school	1

suggest that there is some skewing happening – those with the most challenges have the least amount of time to participate in voluntary research. A larger sample size in the future may mitigate this problem.

Because involvement with family, friends and non-academic activities can impact student success, we asked about social supports. Nineteen students said that their family encouraged them to go to university and to attend classes regularly and four students said that some of their family encouraged them. Most of the students had friends either at UOIT or at another university or college; only two said all their friends only worked at jobs and did not attend university or college. Eleven students said they had friends at UOIT with whom they studied, while thirteen stated that they preferred to study alone. Seventeen students participated in the activities of a group or organisation (such as, a sports team, a hobby club, community organisation, or an ethnic organisation) in the past 12 months, but six had not. They were also asked about the type of organisation (see Table 8).

Most of the students who took part in an organisation of some sort, did so at least once a week (n=11) or once a month (n=4); two said they did so once or twice a year, two not at all, one did not know, and four did not answer. Fifteen students had volunteered their time with their organisation. Eight students voted in the last federal, provincial, and/or municipal election, ten did not vote, and five were not yet eligible to do so. Students were also asked if they ever felt uncomfortable or out of place due to their ethnicity, culture, race, skin colour, language, accent, and/or religion (see Table 9). One student reported feeling uncomfortable or out of place all of the time, one did so most of the time, twelve felt uncomfortable some of the time, five did so rarely, three never felt uncomfortable, one did not know and one did not answer. In order to try to get a more complete picture of student experiences of discrimination, we asked them where they had felt discriminated against or treated unfairly in the

Table 8. Participation in non-academic activities

Type of organisation	Yes	No
Sports club/team	5	18
Religious-affiliated group	3	20
Community organisation (i.e., YMCA/YWCA, community centre)	4	19
Service club (i.e., Kiwanis, Rotary, hospital auxiliary)	3	20
Charitable organisation (i.e., Cancer Society)	3	20
Hobby club (i.e., garden club, book club)	3	20
Political or citizen's group	0	23
Youth organisation (i.e., Scouts, Guides, Boys & Girls Club)	1	22
Children's school group (i.e., Parent/Teacher Assn, school volunteer)	4	19
Job related association (i.e., union, professional association)	6	17
Ethnic or immigrant association	0	23
Other	2	21

Table 9. Feelings of belongingness

Reason for feeling uncomfortable or out of place	Yes	No
Ethnicity/culture	12	11
Race or skin colour	13	10
Language or accent	6	17
Religion	5	18
Don't know	5	18
Never felt uncomfortable	3	20

past five years (see Table 10). Students were also asked if they felt uncomfortable or out of place at UOIT in particular (see Table 11). Three felt they did so most of the time, one did so some of the time, ten rarely felt out of place or uncomfortable, eight never felt out of place or uncomfortable, one did not know and one did not answer. We explored this question further by asking for the reasons for feeling out of place while on the UOIT campus. These questions about volunteerism and feelings of comfort in different locations speaks to the sense of community and inclusion students feel. We suggest that without a sense of community and belongingness, students are less likely to be successful.

The survey concluded with questions to help determine students' overall sense of life satisfaction and their advice for other students. Using a feeling thermometer, students were asked to identify: "All things considered, how satisfied are you with your personal life as a whole these days?" (see Table 12). Responses were spread almost evenly from not at all satisfied to extremely satisfied. To help gain a sense

Table 10. Location of discrimination/lack of belongingness

Where did you experience discrimination or been treated unfairly in the past 5 years?	Yes	No
On the street	11	12
In a store, bank or restaurant	7	16
At work or applying for a job or promotion	7	16
When dealing with police or courts	1	22
When on the UOIT north campus	2	21
When on the UOIT south campus	2	21
In class at UOIT	2	21
When working with other students for class projects	2	21
When speaking with a lecturer, professor or TA	1	22
Other	6	17
Don't know	1	22
Never experienced discrimination	6	17

Table 11. Reasons for lack of belongingness at UOIT

Reason for feeling uncomfortable or out of place while at UOIT	Yes	No
Ethnicity/culture	7	16
Race or skin colour	10	13
Language or accent	3	20
Religion	1	22
Don't know	0	0

Table 12. Life satisfaction

Range	2 Not at all satisfied	25	30–39	40–49	52	60–69	70–79	80–89	90–99 Extremely satisfied
Number	1	1	2	4	2	3	2	5	3

of what students did to succeed at school, they were asked what advice they would give to incoming students in order to be successful. A common comment by several students who faced academic struggles was that they "should have tried harder". Another regular comment was that they needed better time management and to make sure to do the readings regularly. One non-immigrant student commented that after doing badly in her first term, she began typing out her notes after class and reviewing them daily. She made sure to review regularly and keep up with assignments. These comments reflect a sense of personal responsibility for students' success or lack of success, rather than any attribution to external influences.

DISCUSSION AND CONCLUSIONS

The most interesting findings came from fourth-year students, since first-year students had not yet had enough experience in their university studies to really understand and be able to articulate how they were successful and how they overcame any obstacles. When asked what advice they would give to a new student, the comments were remarkably similar and were connected to their analysis of their own perceived failings. Students indicated that knowing someone who had been to university prior to starting was helpful in understanding what to expect. At the same time, making new friends early in their programme of study was just as helpful. Having at least one person to share experiences, complaints and studying helped with motivation, problem-solving and the like. In many ways, these findings are not surprising. Success in education is regularly attributed to personal factors rather than external ones. Discrimination off-campus was seen as occurring more frequently than on campus and as causing feelings of discomfort. A lack of a sense of community may be one of the key factors inhibiting success. Many students indicate that having like-minded friends who study together and support each other is important to their success. Yet, our findings indicate that students do not access on-campus resources (such as the writing centre or peer tutoring) largely because the hours to access them are limited. Additionally, few students are involved in extra-curricular or volunteer groups in spite of the fact that they know such activities are important for building skills and networking with potential employers. For students at small commuter campuses who have to work to pay for tuition, there is little time or money to become involved or to access resources on or off campus. Indeed, after speaking with a professor when help is needed, the most frequently used resources are online tools.

The number of our participants was quite small, so we do not have a strong sense of differences between different groups of students. However, one of the last questions students were asked on the survey was: "If there is something you wanted to say about how your background impacts you (either at school, University, society in general), but we did not address in the questions above, please tell us in the space below". Only one of the non-visible minority/immigrant students made a comment ("Sometimes I feel I am treated differently in society because of the colour of my skin"), but four of the immigrant/visible minority students did. They commented on feeling uncomfortable in a larger city with more diversity after growing up in a small pre-dominantly white town without experiencing any racism and on being yourself even when you are feeling judged. One student specifically commented on the loneliness of not fitting into any groups on campus, even an 'African' student group, because her accent was wrong: 'It's hard to open up when you feel alone. I've never been able to identify with the African society (sic) because the majority of the group acts as though I don't belong simply because my accent is different which upsets me'. Not surprisingly, these comments suggest that there are influences beyond personal actions (such as studying more) that impact on students' successfulness. In future research, the goal will be to involve more students who are close to graduation or recently graduated and to include students from across Canada to allow for comparative analysis based on location of study as well as immigrant status, ethnicity, class, and gender.

REFERENCES

Anisef, P., Sweet, R., & Frempong, G. (2003). Labour market outcomes of immigrant and racial minority university graduates in Canada. *Journal of International Migration and Integration, 4*, 499–502.

Armstrong, D. E., & McMahon, B. J. (2013). Developing socially just leaders: Integrative antiracist approaches in a transformational paradigm. In A. H. Normore & N. Erbe (Eds.), *Collective efficacy: Interdisciplinary perspectives on international leadership* (pp. 23–39). Bingley: Emerald Group Publishing Limited.

Ashton, M., & Esses, V. M. (1999). Stereotype accuracy: Estimating the academic performance of ethnic groups. *Personality and Social Psychology Bulletin, 25*(2), 225–236.

Bailey, T. R., & Alfonso, M. (2005). *Paths to persistence: An analysis of research on program effectiveness at community colleges*. Indianapolis, IN: Lumina Foundation for Education, New Agenda Series. Retrieved from http://ccrc.tc.columbia.edu/media/k2/attachments/paths-persistence-program-effectiveness.pdf

Banerjee, R., & Verma, A. (2012). Post-migration education among recent adult immigrants to Canada. *Journal of International Migration & Integration, 13*(1), 59–82.

Baum, S., & Flores, S. M. (2011). Higher education and children in immigrant families. *The Future of Children, 21*(1), 171–193.

Boyd, M. (2009). Social origins and the educational and occupational achievements of the 1.5 and second generations. *Canadian Review of Sociology/Revue canadienne de sociologie, 46*(4), 339–369.

Calcagno, J. C., Bailey, T., Jenkins, D., Kienzl, G., & Leinbach, T. (2008). Community college student success: What institutional characteristics make a difference? *Economics of Education Review, 27*(6), 632–645.

Cheng, L., & Fox, J. (2008). Towards a better understanding of academic acculturation: Second language students in Canadian universities. *The Canadian Modern Language, 65*(2), 307–333.

Childs, S., Finnie, R., & Mueller, R. (2012). *University attendance and the children of immigrants: Patterns of participation and the role of background factors*. Ottawa: Education Policy Research Initiative, University of Ottawa. Retrieved from http://socialsciences.uottawa.ca/education-policy-research-initiative/sites/socialsciences.uottawa.ca.education-policy-research-initiative/files/mesa_carmichael_finnie/childs.finnie.mueller.immigrant.EPRI.july.2012.pdf

Collier, P. J., & Fellows, C. (2008). *Expertise-development mentoring: An intervention to improve first-generation college freshmen's academic performance and retention*. Washington, DC: American Sociological Association.

Common University Data Ontario (CUDO). (2014). *Laurentian University*. Retrieved from http://cou.on.ca/numbers/cudo/

Davies, S., & Maldonado, V. (2008). Socioeconomic inequalities in Canadian education. In E. Grabb & N. Guppy (Eds.), *Social inequality in Canada: Patterns, problems, and policies* (5th ed.). Toronto: Prentice Hall.

Engstrom, C., & Tinto, V. (2008). Access without support is not opportunity. *Change: The Magazine of Higher Learning, 40*, 46–50.

Ferede, M. K. (2010). Structural factors associated with higher education access for first-generation refugees in Canada: An Agenda for Research. *Refuge, 27*(2), 79–88.

Ferrer, A., & Riddell, C. (2008). Education, credentials and immigrant earnings. *Canadian Journal of Economics, 41*(1), 186–216.

Finnie, R., Childs, S., & Wismer, A. (2011). *Access to postsecondary education: How Ontario compares*. Toronto: Higher Education Quality Council of Ontario.

Finnie, R., Wismer, A., & Mueller, R. (2015). Access and barriers to postsecondary education: Evidence from the youth in transition survey. *Canadian Journal of Higher Education, 45*(2), 229–262.

Glick, J. E., & White, M. J. (2004). Post-secondary school participation of immigrant and native youth: The role of familial resources and educational expectations. *Social Science Research, 33*(2), 272–299.

Grasmuck, S., & Kim, J. (2010). Embracing and resisting ethno-racial boundaries: Second-generation immigrant and African-American students in a multicultural university. *Sociological Forum, 25*(2), 221–247.

Jaret, C., & Reitzes, D. C. (2009). Currents in a stream: College student identities and ethnic identities and their relationship with self-esteem, efficacy, and grade point average in an urban university. *Social Science Quarterly, 90*(2), 345–367.

Keller, U., & Tillman, K. H. (2008). Post-secondary educational attainment of immigrant and native youth. *Social Forces, 87*(1), 121–152.

Kilpi-Jakonen, E. (2011). Continuation to upper secondary education in Finland: Children of immigrants and the majority compared. *Acta Sociological, 54*(1), 77–106. doi:10.1177/0001699310392604

Lee, D., Olson, E. A., Locke, B., Michelson, S. T., & Odes, E. (2009). The effects of college counselling services on academic performance and retention. *Journal of College Student Development, 50*(3), 305–319.

Liebenberg, L., & Ungar, M. (Eds.). (2009). *Researching resilience*. Toronto: University of Toronto Press.

Mata, F., & Krauth, B. (2008). *Exploring linkages between the country of post-secondary education completion and labour market activity of immigrants in Canada*. Vancouver: Metropolis British Columbia, Centre of Excellence for Research on Immigration and Diversity.

Matthews, L., & Mahoney, A. (2005). Facilitating a smooth transitional process for immigrant Caribbean children: The role of teachers, social workers, and related professional staff. *Journal of Ethnic & Cultural Diversity in Social Work, 14*(1–2), 69–92. doi:10.1300/J051v14n01_04

Miller, J. W., Janz, J. C., & Chen, C. (2007). The retention impact of a first-year seminar on students with varying pre-college academic performance. *Journal of the First-Year Experience & Students in Transition, 19*(1), 47–62.

National Survey of Student Engagement (NSSE). (2012). *2011 Results Summary*. Office of institutional research & analysis, UOIT.

Norrie, K., & Zhao, H. (2010). *An overview of PSE accessibility in Ontario*. Toronto: Higher Education Quality Council of Ontario.

Ostrovsky, Y., & Frenette, M. (2014, October). *The cumulative earnings of postsecondary graduates over 20 years: Results by field of study* (Economic Insights No. 040, Catalogue No. 11-626-X). Ottawa: Statistics Canada.

Parkin, A., & Baldwin, N. (2009). *Persistence in post-secondary education in Canada: The latest research*. Montreal: Canadian Millennium Scholarship Foundation. Retrieved from http://www.yorku.ca/pathways/literature/Aspirations/090212_Persistence_EN.pdf

Picot, G., & Hou, F. (2013). Why immigrant background matters for university participation: A comparison of Switzerland and Canada. *International Migration Review, 47*(3), 612–642.

Reitz, J. G., Zhang, H., & Hawkins, N. (2011). Comparisons of the success of racial minority immigrant offspring in the United States, Canada and Australia. *Social Science Research, 40*(4), 1051–1066.

Rosenblum, K., Zhou, Y., & Gentemann, K. (2009). Ambivalence: Exploring the American university experience of the children of immigrant. *Race Ethnicity and Education, 12*(3), 337–348.

Roxas, K., & Roy, L. (2012). "Where to start": Learning from Somali Bantu Refugee students and families. *Teacher Education and Practice, 25*(1), 100–118.

Sax, L. J., Bryant, A. N., & Harper, C. E. (2005). The differential effects of student-faculty interaction on college outcomes for women and men. *Journal of College Student Development, 46*(6), 642–657.

Schwartz, S. J., Waterman, A. S., Umaña-Taylor, A. J., Lee, R. M., Kim, S. Y., Vazsonyi, A. T., Huynh, Q. L., Whitbourne, S. K., Park, I. J., Hudson, M., Zamboanga, B. L., Bersamin, M. M., & Williams, M. K. (2013). Acculturation and well-being among college students from immigrant families. *Journal of Clinical Psychology, 69*(4), 298–318. doi:10.1002/jclp21847

Scott, G., Shah, M., Grebennikov, L., & Singh, H. (2008). Improving student retention: A University of Western Sydney case study. *Journal of Institutional Research, 14*(1), 9–23.
Seigel, M. (2005). Beyond compare: Comparative method after the transnational turn. *Radical History Review, 91*(1), 62–90.
Seror, J., Chen, L., & Gunderson, L. (2005). Multiple perspectives on educationally resilient immigrant students. *TESL Canadian Journal, 22*(2), 55–74.
Sinacore, A. L., & Lerner, S. (2013). The cultural and educational transitioning of first generation immigrant undergraduate students in Quebec, Canada. *International Journal for Educational and Vocational Guidance, 13*(1), 67–85. doi:10.1007/s10775-013-9238-y
Sleeter, C. (1993). How white teachers construct race. In C. McCarthy & W. Crichlow (Eds.), *Race, identity and representation in education* (pp. 157–171). New York, NY: Routledge.
Soria, K. M., & Stebleton, M. J. (2012). First generation students' academic engagement and retention. *Teaching in Higher Education, 17*(6), 673–685.
Statistics Canada. (2010). *Projections of the diversity of the Canadian population, 2006 to 2031* (Catalogue No. 91-551-X). Ottawa: Statistics Canada.
Suarez-Orozco, C., Rhodes, J., & Milburn, M. (2009). Unraveling the immigration paradox: Academic engagement and disengagement among recently arrived immigrant youth. *Youth & Society, 41*(2), 151–185.
Sweet, R., Anisef, P., Brown, R., Walters, D., & Phythian, K. (2010). *Post-high school pathways of immigrant youth*. Toronto: Higher Education Quality Council of Ontario.
Sweetman, A., & Dicks, G. (1999). Education and ethnicity in Canada: An intergenerational perspective. *The Journal of Human Resources, 34*(4), 668–696.
Teranishi, R. T., Suarez-Orozco, C., & Suarez-Orozco, M. (2011). Immigrants in community colleges. *The Future of Children, 21*(1), 153–169. doi:10.1353/foc.2011.0009
Torenbeek, M., Jansen, E., & Hofman, A. (2010). The effect of the fit between secondary schools and university education on first-year achievement. *Studies in Higher Education, 35*(6), 659–675.
Tseng, V. (2004). Family interdependence and academic adjustment in college: Youth from immigrant and U.S.-born families. *Child Development, 75*(3), 996–983.
Vaccaro, A. (2012). An analysis of access barriers to post-secondary education. *College Quarterly, 15*(4).
Viveiros de Castro, E. (2004). Perspectival anthropology and the method of controlled equivocation. *Tipití: Journal of the Society for the Anthropology of Lowland South America, 2*(1), Article 1.
Zeman, K., McMullen, K., & de Broucker, P. (2010). *The high education/low income paradox: College and university graduates with low earnings, Ontario, 2006*. Ottawa: Statistics Canada.

Alyson E. King
University of Ontario Institute of Technology
Canada

Allyson Eamer
University of Ontario Institute of Technology
Canada

Nawal H. Ammar
Rowan University
New Jersey, USA

PART 2

CONTINUITY AND DISCONTINUITY IN SOCIAL INSTITUTIONS

SHANTI IRENE FERNANDO AND ALYSON E. KING

5. EDUCATION INTERRUPTED

Learning Careers of Adults Living with Mental Illness

INTRODUCTION

This chapter identifies mental illness as one of the reasons for the interruption of the learning careers of adults and as a continuing barrier to learning. It examines themes that relate to how learning careers are interrupted and how they can be resumed through supported education programmes which accommodate the individual needs and goals of adult students living with mental illness. Supported education (SEd) has evolved as a best practice that assists individuals with psychiatric disabilities in exploring their educational options and provides ongoing support during their study period (Collins, Mowbray, & Bybee, 1999; Mowbray et al., 2003; Mowbray, 2004). Students attend programmes in the community, on college and university campuses, or in hospitals, supported by a combination of mental health services and academic accommodations. Success in such programmes serves not only to advance their education, but also to improve students' self-esteem and quality of life. According to the Mental Health Commission of Canada (2012), in any given year, one in five people in Canada experiences a mental health problem or illness. Therefore all service providers including adult educators need to be cognisant of the significant effects of mental illness on learning careers and lifelong learning experiences.

Funded by an Insight Development grant from the Social Sciences and Humanities Research Council of Canada, we conducted interviews with learners and staff in a Canadian hospital-based supported education programme. We use the findings from these interviews to discuss themes related to how discontinuity of learning careers played themselves out in students' lives in the past and how access to supported education programmes has afforded continuity in both formal and informal education paths. These learning careers reveal the centrality of mental illness as an on-going determining factor in educational discontinuity. These are careers shaped by barriers related to mental illness, the full extent of which the learners themselves are not always fully aware. Therefore, a key part of supported education is about gaining self-knowledge and beginning to fully understand one's own learning biography in order to change its trajectory. Our study revealed hope, persistence and improved self-knowledge and confidence among its students. The interviews also revealed that all students had varying levels of negative educational experiences in the past, some of which they blamed on others and some of which they blamed on themselves or their illness. We argue that there is hope for continuity of learning through supported education programmes that can help shift students' learning careers to reflect a new self-awareness and control of knowledge through new learning spaces (Fernando, King, & Loney, 2014). Doing so affords these students access to improved community connections and can help create labour market and community integration transitions (Wong, Metzendorf, & Young, 2006; McIntyre, 2012). We argue, therefore, that greater policy and funding support of such programmes is needed to foster and capitalise upon supported education's positive impact on the social and economic welfare of adults living with mental illness.

We interviewed 47 students in a hospital-based supported education programme in Ontario, Canada; five of these students were English Language Learners (ELL) taking part in English as a Second Language classes. These were semi-structured interviews in which we simultaneously collected quantitative (demographic details and self-reported improvements during the programme) and qualitative information (regarding attitudes towards education, their lives and their experiences in the programme). The interviews served a dual purpose: they were intended to allow for a better understanding of the impact of SEd programmes generally and to provide an opportunity for an outside assessment of the programme. In order to understand student needs and experiences, student voices must be heard. The themes which characterised their learning were helpful in understanding the strengths and weaknesses of the programme. In addition, the analysis of the interviews revealed a number of themes and collective issues that illustrated common educational experiences.

The students we interviewed wanted to be known and understood; most were eager to tell their stories. We had prepared ourselves for negative reactions to our interview questions but encountered very little substantial resistance to the interview process. Of the 42 English-speaking students in the SEd programme, 65% were male and 89.1% were single. Most of the participants (81%) had some high school education, with about 21% having attained a Grade 9 and 27.3% a Grade 10 education. While a few students refused to take part in the interviews, this number was quite small compared with the students who wanted to be interviewed. Since people living with mental illness often experience anxiety, this might account for the refusals. Anxiety did not seem to be an issue with those who consented to the interviews. Instead, the fact of being asked for their stories and opinions seemed to be an anxiety release. The vulnerable nature of our interviewees meant that we were limited conducting one interview with each person and immediately anonymising all of the data; so, unlike Barabasch and Merrill (2014) or Sagan (2007), we were unable to create in-depth learning biographies through repeated interviewing and relationship building. Because we had to identify participants only by number, rather than name, we were unable to build the rapport necessary for a more extensive and personal biography. Nonetheless, the analysis of the interviews revealed several themes related to the continuity and discontinuity of education: educational struggles; experience of stigma; gains in self-awareness, independence and confidence; and, increased social skills. These themes came out in the interviews with students, staff and volunteers (see Table 1).

Table 1. Themes arising from interviews

Themes from student interviews	Themes from staff & volunteer interviews
Past educational struggles	Limited gains in literacy
Experiences of social stigma	Need for less stigma around mental illness
Gains in self-awareness, independence and confidence	Student gains in independence and confidence
Increased social skills decreasing feelings of isolation	The value of socialization for student learning career
The value of continuing their education for quality of life	The value of literacy instruction for nurturing hope

The interviews with the five staff members and nine of the volunteers working in the supported education programme revealed a number of themes that complemented those of the students. These interviews were much more open-ended than the student interviews, in part because we were interested in gaining feedback about the programme overall, but also to allow the instructors and volunteers the opportunity to reflect upon their interactions with the students. The interviews with the staff and volunteers were qualitatively different for several reasons; in particular, they were a less vulnerable population and they were not being questioned about their personal lives. The main themes related to discontinuity of education that emerged from the interviews with staff and volunteers were the problems of the stigma of mental illness and the impact of students' illness on their formal education. The main themes related to continuity of education included improvements in social skills, confidence and independence among the students. In general, all the staff and volunteers felt positively about the programme; however, they acknowledged there were limitations to the programme and there was resistance from some students because of their past educational experiences even when they recognised that literacy instruction provided an opportunity to gain the skills and education that would help them move forward with their lives.

DISCONTINUITY IN LEARNING CAREERS: DEALING WITH MENTAL ILLNESS AND ITS STIGMA

While it is sometimes hard to trace the genesis of educational problems and eventual disruption (see Table 2), the onset of mental illness is often identified as one determining factor. For example, the onset of schizophrenia often occurs among males between the ages of 17 to 24 (CAMH) which are the years during which young people often attain the specialised education needed for the workplace and for careers. Other forms of mental illness, such as anxiety and depression, also make for learning difficulties that are not always supported or understood (see for example, Ennals et al., 2014). Among our student interviewees, some described themselves as initially good students who encountered difficulties in high school

Table 2. Barriers to education*

Mental health issues	52.2%
Learning disabilities	34.8%
Social isolation	30.4%
Medication(s)	23.9%
Lack of access to an education programme	19.6%

* Some participants indicated more than one barrier

because of their illness. Other students blamed themselves for not understanding the importance of education, while others blamed their problems in school on a lack of accommodation or on the drugs and alcohol to which they turned to as coping mechanisms. In addition, finding the right medication for treating their illness may also present a barrier because some drugs can interfere with their ability to function and concentrate. Once the right type and dosage was found, however, interviewees found that the drugs helped them with anxiety and other symptoms that impeded learning. Participants commented, for example, that:

> I didn't really have any education … I went to high school, but differently than other people.

> [Anxiety]'s been a part of my life as long as I can remember [so] probably why I wasn't able to finish high school.

> I started grade 11… I liked it, but there was things getting in my way. Like I was addicted to drugs at the time, and I thought drugs were more important than school.

> I think I was doing stuff because it was an excuse to not have to go to school … Nope, I was doing awesome at school when I tried, I was above average, straight A's.

> I have always been a good student. I got sick and I neglected my school work. I was in school when I got sick but I was an A student and an A plus student before I got sick.

Study participants tended to be accepting of their past experiences with education and recognised both the importance and challenges of seeking to further their education.

Not surprisingly, the stigma of mental illness was identified as having a negative impact on students' past and present life. Students reported struggling to overcome social stigma and negative stereotypes from those around them. Most participants did not have paid work, except on an occasional basis, and were supported financially by family or some form of social or employment assistance. When mental illness and its impacts are not fully understood by family and friends, there is a resulting lack of understanding about and compassion for their struggle to integrate into society and the labour market. Students commented:

> I have a roommate that is working at Tim Horton's and we got into a fight and she said at least I have a job and you don't she says to me, so it kind of makes me feel different.

> My brother's worked for 20 years at *The Star* and he's like 'what happened to you?'

Most of the participants aimed to attain employment of some sort and felt limited by their lack of education. For instance, one student commented:

> I already have five years hands on experience with a landscaping construction company and I just want the credentials so I can say that I have the schooling and the experience and I have actually started my own portfolio and all those things look good in terms of starting my own business.

Others told us:

> I used to do dry walling and painting, I am really good at painting and I am pretty good at dry walling and I think that if maybe I could take a business course to help manage money, because I am horrible with money, HORRIBLE! ... my dad owns his own company and one day I want to take it over down the road.

> I think if I just stay focused and stay off the drugs and stay off the booze, I think in 6–8 months I could achieve my grade twelve and get my grade twelve math and two compulsory courses, I'll probably take like a business class, a couple of business classes ... Well, I'm thinking about going back to school, I'm just too lazy to get off my butt and go.

Similarly, among the ELL participants, even those with experience working in English found it difficult to find and hold a job. For instance, one had previously worked as a sushi chef in the United States, but had been unable to find similar employment in Ontario. Another aimed to become a personal support worker (or similar), but that required a college diploma. Only one stated that employment in Canada was not a goal; he hoped to return to his home country to work on a family farm. For most participants, employment is clearly important for more than simply financial reasons; work can help to provide a sense of stability and normality to one's life. It can also provide a more positive identity that allows for greater acceptance in their family and community.

Interviews with staff and volunteers similarly revealed that the discontinuity that many students experienced was the result of mental illness and its stigma. The staff and volunteers recognized the importance of working towards greater acceptance of individuals, no matter what illnesses they experience:

I think it's important for us to respect everyone's situation, everyone has a different life situation/circumstances, it's important to recognise that everyone is dealing with something different and that there's no shame connected with mental illness, which traditionally has been something in the past and we still struggle with that today. Some people view it as a sign of weakness. That it's some sort of character flaw which it's not of course.

There are people that can contribute to society but you need to work with them so I think that it is important to get them to that level and make them feel useful as well [in] society not be a burden on society.

I think there is a lot of stigma associated with mental illness and if you look at the people around here they might have some issues but they are also really nice everyday people and they did not choose to be mentally ill and it's like having diabetes or anything else like that, so yeah you definitely need education around that.

The ELL participants faced additional barriers to their education due to their lack of English. For these participants, their educational experiences began in schools outside of Canada and were interrupted by inability to pay school fees, migration, and other factors. Nonetheless, all had some education in at least their first language, with four having been introduced to English prior to arriving in Canada. In spite of their prior education, the fact that these participants had been in Canada between three and nineteen years, and that four of the five have been or were currently employed in Canada, which are usually facilitative factors for learning a second language, all of them were still struggling with learning English. Our research suggests that factors related to their mental illness had more impact in impeding their language learning than the factors that would normally be expected to facilitate language learning (Eamer, Fernando, & King, 2017). Although there is little research on the educational needs of English Language Learners living with mental illness, our findings suggest that SEd programmes for English Language Learners will be increasingly important with the rising number of refugees and immigrants to Canada to ensure their integration into the social and economic fabric of Canadian communities.

Staff and volunteers believe that the SEd programme affords students the opportunity to resume their educational path in a manner that is both safe but challenging. Students' past negative experiences with the education system make it difficult for them to resume their education in a traditional classroom setting. In addition, if they have not completed high school, alternative programmes are needed because they may be too old to return to their former school. The most fundamental positive change for adults living with mental illness is their transition from patient to student; supported education allows for the resumption of their student identity. The SEd programme is one that is accessible to both in- and out-patients of the mental health hospital, so it can help patients to return to their learning careers while still living at the hospital and continue to support them after discharge.

CONTINUITY THROUGH SUPPORTED EDUCATION: DEVELOPING CONFIDENCE AND INDEPENDENCE

Our study of the supported education programme revealed that there were some areas in which continuity was clearly visible in terms of connecting students to their own biographies and increasing their independence and confidence. Learning is often described as a process of identity development which can be gained through new opportunities and learning spaces (Brown & Bimrose, 2014). Supported education is one way to create learning spaces that are individually-focused rather than classroom-based. SEd programmes have more flexibility in curriculum and programming because it is less regulated than the school system; as a result, supported education has evolved as a best practice to support individuals with psychiatric disabilities in exploring their educational options and providing ongoing support during their study period. With SEd programmes located in hospitals as well as in communities, students living with mental illness can begin to re-engage in their education at their own pace before moving into programmes in the community or on college and university campuses. Supports can come in the form of educational counselling and academic skill building or accommodations such as modifying tests and test environments to suit people's individual needs (Gregg, 2012). Students can receive general upgrading and skill improvement or high school credits through the programme, which serves not only to advance their education, but also to improve their self-esteem and quality of life (Unger, Pfaltzgraf, & Nikkel, 2010; Mowbray, 1999; Leonard & Bruer, 2007; Mowbray et al., 2003; Mowbray, 2004). Education is an essential element of recovery for people with mental health conditions and can lead to better jobs and improved community and social integration (Prince & Gerber, 2005; Taylor, Trumpower, & Pavic, 2012; McIntyre, 2012).

Barabasch and Merrill's (2014) description of the determination and resilience of individuals to achieve their educational goals was reflected in the comments of our participant students despite their increased challenges. Our interviews revealed that while only 23.8% reported having reached their general goals of education, 73.8% believed that they would achieve them. This finding was also reflected in responses to questions about increases in confidence, with 85.7% stating that they now felt more confident. In addition, a related positive theme in the student interviews was an increase in self-awareness of their abilities and learning style. One student commented: "I am more defined in my situation of understanding my skills". Similarly, an important shift in students' sense of self was in their increased sense of independence; indeed, 81% of participants reported an increase in feelings of independence. This increased self-confidence and feelings of independence was directly connected (by the students) to their participation in the SEd programme.

> I didn't know what I could do until I came here. They continued to give me questions and see what I can do and everything they gave me I could do.

> I have even spoken at the lecture hall on graduation day … That would not have been possible 5 years ago, it wouldn't have happened.
>
> It makes you a better person at work because you have full confidence in the things that you say and you sound smarter if you use proper English.

These gains in a sense of self-awareness, independence and confidence can help in the process of building resilience within individuals. Even if that resilience is hidden (i.e., others cannot see their ability to cope), participants often feel better able to handle the challenges of day-to-day living because of their improved confidence and sense of independence. This can mean that SEd students experience their lives subjectively as successful (Liebenberg & Ungar, 2009), even if others do not.

Interviews with the staff and volunteers demonstrated that they recognised the value of the programme in promoting an improved sense of confidence and independence among some students, even when measurable educational gains were slow to manifest. A sense of independence and confidence is needed in order for the students to use the benefits of education. Staff and volunteers commented on these issues specifically:

> Independence, like fostering that will and independent learning, that's very important I think for them to go out and search for ways to learn themselves.
>
> Self-confidence, they feel that they are achieving something in life, they get important skills that will help them in jobs.
>
> […] you can see just sort of how people are becoming more confident and you know, more comfortable and confident in themselves. I mean in the beginning, like you said usually it can be very intimidating when you're starting a course or programme and so through the support that people are given it builds up their confidence and they are able to say okay you know I am able to do this. Because a lot of people may have been put down in the past and told that you know, you're not capable and this is a way for them to build up their confidence.

Alongside the development of independence and self-confidence, some students needed to strengthen the social skills and social capital that are a necessary part of community and labour market integration (McIntyre, 2012). The ability to interact in socially appropriate and acceptable ways is something that can develop when one is successful in learning and in building confidence and self-esteem. Mental illness, however, can disrupt one's ability to learn and use the social skills that are generally expected in schools and the workplace. Students commented on their efforts to improve these skills and their sense of improvement.

> When I first came here I was shy … and now I am outgoing and try to speak more.
>
> I just find it easy to talk to people now, I know it used to be a big problem before. I didn't know what to talk about and I have learned how to ask people questions about what they are interested in and keep [the] conversation going.

My social skills, I would say they were pretty poor. They have improved.

You get to meet friends, meet people, learn.

Participants in this SEd programme demonstrated a sense of pride in their learning which tended to lead to improved comfort in social interactions. The community atmosphere of the SEd programme itself also provided a space for learning to work with or alongside others with similar goals. Without these skills learners would be unable to fully integrate into society or be attractive to employers. Furthermore, the fact that students enjoy education in this programme in a way that they had not before bodes well for them continuing their education beyond the programme. It also demonstrates that supported education facilitates lifelong learning through a positive environment.

I like to learn, I never want to stop learning.

Day dreaming almost every day doesn't allow you to do a lot because you live in your head, everything you do is in your head. You don't actually do anything. And with education, you go back to thinking that writing and reading, and explaining, and understanding things, how they are done.

Staff and volunteers similarly point to the value of literacy instruction as a way for students to improve their life chances and quality of life. This continuity of their learning careers allows for greater continuity of their lives in general and provides hope for improved quality of life.

Well I think [the programme is] very important for people, for outpatients and inpatients to move forward with their lives.

I think that is so helpful for in trying to reintegrate back into society for all the inpatients for sure, and helps with getting a job [and] just functioning in society.

It gives them, like, a sense of a purpose and something to work towards, goals, and that's always important for recovery. It's having, like, a sense of where you want to end up, how you want to be when you … what kind of goals you achieve.

Adult learners who are living with mental illness inherently face more challenges in continuing their formal (and informal) education. These adult learners, and the staff and volunteers who support them, see Supported Education programmes as providing opportunities for moving forward and opening doors for improved integration into their communities and the workplace.

CREATING COMMUNITY AND LABOUR MARKET TRANSITIONS

Some of the barriers to community and labour market integration for individuals living with a mental illness that have been identified include lack of confidence, independence and relevant work skills, and these barriers are magnified for those who are also English Language Learners. Wong et al. (2006) identified a number of factors that were needed for the community integration of persons with psychiatric disabilities. She argues that addressing "social and independent living skills deficits is a requisite step toward building normalized social relationships" along with having a supportive "safety net" of a community for students when they are out in the community (p. 56). Such community offers a platform for consumers to learn and practice their social and independent living skills and to procure support and assurance in the face of social rejection (Wong et al., 2006). Additionally, for immigrants with mental illness, that community integration positively impacts their ability to learn English (Eamer, Fernando, & King, 2017). Our interviews indicate that these elements are present in the supported education programme we examined, as was discussed above, and would be elements of most such programmes. In today's economy, meaningful workforce participation is increasingly determined by education and literacy level (Murray & Shillington, 2011). Persons with disabilities, especially those with a mental health disability, are more likely to be in low paying work or to be unemployed. Brown and Bimrose (2014) argue that "the key processes to support learning for career and labour market transitions can be represented as occurring across four domains: relational development; cognitive development; practical development; and emotional development" (p. 278). They argue that learning is part of a process of identity development and is reflected in the idea of 'learning as becoming' which appears in many strategic career and learning biographies. This is particularly relevant to those living with mental illness because their literacy skills, as well as their self-knowledge and identity, is often at a low level and need effective supported education and recovery programmes to address these areas of development.

Arbesman and Logsdon (2011) describe supported education as creating a conduit to employment, providing meaningful activity and access to the role of student. They found that supported education increased enrollment in school or vocational education. They identify supported education in individual and group forms as one of the best programmes to keep people in paid and unpaid employment, since people with psychiatric disorders and serious mental illness have the lowest employment rates. Furthermore, education helps to empower students to become effective advocates for change and to avoid the social isolation that persons living with mental illnesses tend to experience. This is ultimately about understanding the oppression and discrimination that one has experienced and continues to experience. Oppression includes, as Freire (1999) argues, attitudes towards physical and mental disability along with class, race and gender. For those who have felt that oppression, the empowerment of education can lead to improved self-advocacy and ability to understand how to deal with that oppression.

CONCLUSION

Students who have experienced mental illness tend to experience discontinuity in their learning careers that often leaves them feeling isolated and which impedes their ability to integrate into the labour market and their communities. Our interview findings indicate that the new learning spaces created by supported education programmes can take student learning careers in new and positive directions. These findings illustrate that education is a continuous need rather than a finite time of preparation during youth. The impact of SEd programmes extends well beyond the personal. Supported education programmes help to create more equitable communities and labour markets. With the large number of refugees and immigrants being welcomed in Canada in recent years, it is inevitable that there will be an increased demand for not only mental healthcare, but also SEd programmes for English Language Learners. Supported education is one of the many lifelong learning policies that should be supported at the institutional, regional, provincial and federal levels. The Mental Health Commission of Canada was established in 2007 by the Government of Canada in order to consult with people living with mental health problems and illnesses, families, stakeholder organizations, governments, and experts and to make recommendations for a mental health strategy for Canada. There are six strategic directions including one which recommends the Government help increase accessibility to treatment services and supports including supported education (Mental Health Commission of Canada, 2012, p. 8). This accessibility is a necessity, especially for those who have experienced discontinuities in their education, career and life, in order to integrate all members of Canadian society into their communities and the labour market in an equitable way.

REFERENCES

Arbesman, M., & Logsdon, D. W. (2011). Occupational therapy interventions for employment and education for adults with serious mental illness: A systematic review. *The American Journal of Occupational Therapy, 65*(3), 238–246.

Barabasch, A., & Merrill, B. (2014). Cross-cultural approaches to biographical interviews: Looking at career transitions and lifelong learning. *Research in Comparative and International Education, 9*(3), 287–300. Retrieved from http://dx.doi.org/10.2304/rcie.2014.9.3.287

Brown, A., & Bimrose, J. (2014). Model of learning for career and labour market transitions. *Research in Comparative and International Education, 9*(3), 270–286.

Centre for Addiction and Mental Health. (2012). *Mental illness and addictions: Facts and statistics*. Retrieved from http://www.camh.ca/en/hospital/about_camh/newsroom/for_reporters/Pages/addictionmentalhealthstatistics.aspx

Collins, M., Mowbray, C., & Bybee, D. (1999). Establishing individualized goals in a supported education intervention: Program influences on goal-setting and attainment. *Research on Social Work Practice, 9*(4), 483–507.

Eamer, A., Fernando, S. I., & King, A. E. (2017, March 8). Still on the margins: Migration, English language learning and mental health in immigrant psychiatric patients. *Diaspora, Indigenous, and Minority Education* (Published online). Retrieved from http://dx.doi.org/10.1080/15595692.2017.1289918

Ennals, P., Fossey, E. M., Harvey, C. A., & Killackey, E. (2014). Postsecondary education: Kindling opportunities for people with mental illness. *Asia-Pacific Psychiatry, 6*, 115–119.

Fernando, S., King, A., & Loney, D. (2014). Helping them help themselves: Supported adult education for persons living with mental illness. *Canadian Journal for Studies in Adult Education, 27*(1), 15–28.

Freire, P. (1999). *Pedagogy of the oppressed* (30th Anniversary ed.). New York, NY: Continuum International Publishing Group.

Gregg, N. (2012). Increasing access to learning for the adult basic education learner with learning disabilities: Evidence-based accommodation research. *Journal of Learning Disabilities, 45*(1), 47–63.

Leonard, E., & Bruer, R. (2007). Supported education strategies for people with severe mental illness: A review of evidence based practice. *International Journal of Psychosocial Rehabilitation, 11*, 97–109.

Liebenberg, L., & Ungar, M. (2009). Introduction: The challenges in researching resilience. In L. Liebenberg & M. Ungar (Eds.), *Researching resilience*. Toronto: University of Toronto Press.

McIntyre, J. (2012). The development and recovery of social capital through community-based adult learning. *International Journal of Lifelong Education, 31*(5), 607–621.

Mental Health Commission of Canada. (2012). *Changing directions, changing lives: The mental health strategy for Canada*. Calgary: Author. Retrieved from http://www.cpa.ca/docs/File/Practice/strategy-text-en.pdf

Mowbray, C. T. (1999). The benefits and challenges of supported education: A personal perspective. *Psychiatric Rehabilitation Journal, 22*, 248–254.

Mowbray, C. T. (2004). Supported education: Diversity, essential ingredients, and future directions. *American Journal of Psychiatric Rehabilitation, 7*, 347–362.

Mowbray, C. T., Megivern, D., & Holter, M. (2003). Supported education programming for adults with psychiatric disabilities: Results from a national survey. *Psychiatric Rehabilitation Journal, 27*, 159–168.

Murray, T. S., & Shillington, R. (2011). *From poverty to prosperity: Literacy's impact on Canada's economic success*. Ottawa: Canadian Literacy and Learning Network.

Prince, P. N., & Gerber, G. J. (2005). Subjective well-being and community integration among clients of assertive community treatment. *Quality of Life Research, 14*(1), 161–169.

Sagan, O. (2007). An interplay of learning, creativity and narrative biography in a mental health setting: Bertie's story. *Journal of Social Work Practice, 21*(3), 311–321. doi:10.1080/02650530701553617

Taylor, M., Trumpower, D., & Pavic, I. (2012). A social capital inventory for adult literacy learners. *International Forum of Teaching and Studies, 8*(2), 12–24.

Unger, K., Pfaltzgraf, B., & Nikkel, R. (2010). A supported education program in a state psychiatric hospital. *Psychiatric Services, 61*, 632.

Wong, Y. I., Metzendorf, D., & Young, M. (2006). Neighbourhood experiences and community integration. *Social Work in Mental Health, 4*(3), 45–59. doi:10.1300/J200v04n03_03

Shanti Irene Fernando
University of Ontario Institute of Technology
Ontario, Canada

Alyson E. King
University of Ontario Institute of Technology
Ontario, Canada

GIUSEPPE PILLERA

6. INMATES IN HIGHER EDUCATION IN ITALY AND SPAIN

Legal, Cultural and Technological Issues in a Complex Network of Continuity and Discontinuity

INTRODUCTION

Inmates who attend university may be considered non-traditional students, presenting one or more of the features that are usually attributed to this definition: break between high school and university, full time job, part-time attendance at university, independent financial situation, presence of children or dependants other than their own partner, being a single parent, attaining only a GED (not a high school diploma).[1] Moreover, for all the students in prison, each stage of the training process (choice, enrolment, didactics, individual study) is strongly influenced and limited by the space in which they are incarcerated. The physical, socio-cultural and professional discontinuity induced by the environment and its rules (official, unofficial, explicit and implicit) determine for all the imprisoned people a marginal condition that, beyond the different orientations of the criminal law, was and continues to be a summary of the prison sentence, where *the wall* – the fundamental instrument of containment and control – is not only its symbol but also its deeper raison d'être.

Nevertheless, according to the correctional paradigm (endorsed by the international rules and adopted, at least on paper, by a wide range of nations), the penalty should not only punish (retributive function) but also rehabilitate the convicts. In this design the prison, still the main recourse for penalising offenders,[2] should operate as a *positive discontinuity* of life-style and opportunities (principally learning and working) to target changes in convicts' judgements, values and behaviours, providing them with the motivation to make a definitive switch from a criminal route to that of integration into a law-abiding society. However, too often prison still represents a place of *negative discontinuity*, where the physical isolation and the consequent social deprivation are accompanied by a lack of opportunities, resulting in further marginalisation and in attacks (sometimes systemic) on human dignity, unfortunately more frequent than the cases confirmed by the courts of national and international justice.

Confronted with this scenario, why focus specifically on detainees in higher education, who represent a small minority of students in prison and a very limited cross-section of inmates overall? Academic study behind bars deserves to be encouraged and supported because not only does it involve an increasing number of prisoners, but it also has a particular significance: as we will see for the two considered countries. University can offer the opportunity of transformation not only of the convict but of the prison itself, in terms of its human, cultural and physical environment.

Even if education, up to its higher levels, is often sanctioned as an inalienable human right, a series of obstacles (legislative, organisational, cultural, technical) *de facto* restrict full access of prisoners to the higher grades of education, especially with regard to university. These threaten both the *continuity* of the learning career for students that want to continue their academic pursuits after a custodial sentence or while in custody, as well as the choice, in positive *discontinuity*, of beginning a course during the period of incarceration.

As a result in this context, both the concepts of *continuity* and *discontinuity* can be meant in a positive or negative way according to whether they might produce empowerment or marginalisation, and consequently they appear interwoven in a complex relationship, complementary yet at the same time circular.[3]

This short comparative research focuses on Italy and Spain: these two major Euro-Mediterranean countries have common roots and a lot of cultural similarities; furthermore, they are comparable in the dimensions and the general structures of their penal systems but they present remarkable differences in the management and the outcomes of academic education in prison (Table 1, Figures 1–2).

Through a lecture in three dimensions – legislative, cultural and technological – the study aims, on the one hand, to identify and analyse the adopted models, checking if they comply with international agreements, especially at the continental level; while on the other hand, to compare the main outcomes, highlighting the best and most replicable practices.

Table 1. University students in prison during 2009 in Italy and Spain, by gender and nationality

Countries	Gender						Foreigners	
	F univ. students	M univ. students	Tot.	F inmates	M inmates	Tot.	Overall univ. students	Overall tot. inmates
Italy (31/12/09)	79 (26%)	224 (74%)	303	2751 (4%)	62040 (96%)	64791	13%	24067 (37%)
Spain (31/10/09)	128 (11%)	1065 (89%)	1193	6076 (8%)	70003 (92%)	76079	35%	27162 (35%)

Sources: www.giustizia.it, Viedma Rojas (2013 for students in Spain, Ministerio del Interior (2013) for total in Spain

INMATES IN HIGHER EDUCATION IN ITALY AND SPAIN

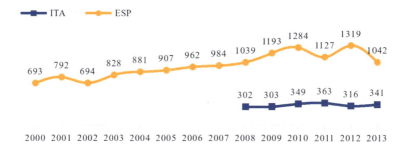

Figure 1. Yearly results of jailed university students in Italy (2013) and Spain (2000–2013). Sources: www.giustizia.it for Italy; Viedma Rojas, 2013 for Spain

Figure 2. Percentage of jailed university students in Italy and Spain (2013) overall the total prison population (respectively 62536 and 66765) and overall the total number of students in jail (respectively 16836 and 18385).
Sources: www.giustizia.it for Italy; SGIP (2014) for Spain. Note: the Italian data relates to December the 31st while the Spanish data relates to October 31st each year

PRISON EDUCATION AND UNIVERSITY: NOTES OF INTERNATIONAL LAW

In 1955 the United Nations (UN) adopted the *Standard Minimum Rules for the Treatment of Prisoners*, that sanctioned, for the first time on a global level, the contrarieties to penal treatment that are prejudicial to human rights and dignity. They were inspired by the principle of accountability of the condemned (free and conscious participation in treatment) in preparation for their return to the outside world as an active force. Furthermore, the UN Rules identified in education the principal vehicle for the development of the person as a whole, through a project that takes into account their social and cultural background (arts. 65, 77, 78).

The Council of Europe welcomed the UN resolution, integrating it in a text known under the title of *European Prison Rules* (EPR). Issued for the first time in 1973 (R [73] 5), then updated in 1987 (R [87] 3) and in 2006 (R [06] 2), they cover all aspects of everyday life of the inmates, as well as various questions concerning the prison staff. Their programmatic nature and the progressive reception of previous recommendations made the EPR the main source of Continental law in this field.

On the question of education in prison, the EPR (arts. 77–82 in the '73 and '87 editions, art. 28 in the 2006 edition) essentially echo the approach of the UN Rules.

Although the EPR, as well as the UN Rules, never mention explicitly the university, we will highlight a few points most involved with the academic study, referring to the last edition of the text (2006).

1. Par. 4 of art. 28 encourages full parity of education with work, even from the point of view of pay, so preventing the economic penalty arising from the choice of studying instead of working. This is particularly relevant with regards to higher education, which can absorb a considerable part of the day and proves difficult to reconcile with a job.
2. Par. 7 of art. 28 draws attention to the need to integrate prison education into the public system of education and vocational training, following two policies: on the one hand, making compatible the learning programmes both in and out of prison, so as to promote continuity after release; on the other hand, allowing prisoners to attend external courses, whenever possible.
3. Finally, pars. 5 and 6 of art. 28 recommend that each prison make available to all convicts a comprehensive library ('adequately stocked with a wide range of both recreational and education' "in co-operation with community library services'.

The specific theme of the university had not been addressed directly even in 1989, in the 17 points which made up the Recommendation on education in prison (R [89] 12), which, however, was issued together with an explanatory memorandum. This analytical report, compiled by a committee of experts, observes the prison education systems of the member countries according to two circuits: external and internal to prisons. This time the university is mentioned in both paths: in one case, briefly, to promote once again the integration with the public education system outside the prison; in the other case, more extensively, to analyse and recommend opportunities and best practices across European prisons, with a strong focus on distance learning (traditional and electronic), as well as on access to MOOCs (Massive Open Online Courses), which are offered by many universities at the present time, with even more institutions expected to adopt this method over the coming years.

UNIVERSITY STUDY IN PRISON: FRAMEWORKS IN ITALY AND SPAIN

Both the Italian (1948) and Spanish (1978) Constitutions affirm the right-duty to compulsory education (respectively arts. 33–34 and art. 27) and the former adds constitutional protection of access to higher education for the deserving underprivileged (art. 34 pars. 3–4). In addition, both provide new ethical foundations to penalty, prescribing non-afflictive methods and rehabilitative aims (respectively art. 27 par. 3 and art. 25 par. 2), even if, naturally, they are silent about the contents of the penalty, a field left open to the legislator, but still characterised – more so in Italy than in Spain – by prison sentences. Therefore, we will examine the laws in force in the two countries, trying to evaluate how, and to what extent, they have taken action to encourage academic study among detainees, focusing particularly on the three issues raised in the European context.

The Laws and the Actors in Italy

The Italian L. n. 354/1975 (henceforward OP: *Ordinamento Penitenziario*) embodies, and in some ways anticipates, the principles that were successful at the international level: humanity and dignity of the conditions of detention; rehabilitative purpose of the treatment; permeability of the prison, both involving the *civil society* in intramural activities (art. 17), as well as fostering inmates' contacts with the outside (arts. 18, 21, 28, 30). These external contacts were raised to a real pedagogical tool for the *re-educational treatment* (art. 15), together with work (art. 20), religion (art. 26) and the participation in cultural, recreational and sports activities (art. 27). The penitentiary institution is called upon to ensure the provision of appropriate equipment and environments (art. 12 par. 1), including the obligation to set up a library (with books and magazines), managed with the participation of the prisoners themselves (art. 12 pars. 2–3).

Education, understood as *cultural and professional training* (art. 19), has a prominent role: recalling that the obligation to establish courses of primary education and literacy was already provided for by L. n. 535/1958, the OP pays special attention to the secondary school and to higher education. In fact, par. 4 of art. 19 states that 'the attainment of university courses and equivalent must be fostered and the attendance at school courses by correspondence, radio and television must be favoured'.

The first Implementing Regulation of the OP (D.P.R. n. 431/1976) clarified that access to university is a right of all prisoners, both in execution of sentence and in custody. It provided that there were 'established the appropriate agreements with academic authorities to enable students to receive every possible help and to take the examinations' (art. 42). As can be noticed, the emerging pattern reflects the local autonomy model, but not without granting a national framework of incentives: the possibility of exemption from work 'in view of commitment and proved profit' (art. 42), the financial support for deserving students or economically disadvantaged (as reimbursement for fees and books) and an *award for academic performance* (art. 43).

Nevertheless, this first Regulation was silent on the concrete logistics (necessary complement to the theoretical affirmation of a right), thus severely limiting the access to higher education, providing no facilitation for the entry of university teachers and leaving the designation of educational spaces within the discretion of the management of prisons. In addition, university students could not take the exams or, even less, attend lessons in their respective faculties, since the permission to leave the prison was granted to inmates only for exceptional and grave circumstances (art. 30 of the OP). The amendment to par. 2 of art. 30 of the OP, by L. n. 450/1977, oriented the Judiciary Supervisory towards a wide interpretation of the rule while continuing to exclude the study-related reasons. Only after ten years (by L. n. 663/1986, that added the art. 30 *ter* to the OP), will the new *permission-prize* accord a momentary departure from the penitentiary in order, among other things, to cultivate cultural interests and study, this way allowing the convicted university students to take the examinations in a regular session.[4]

The new Implementing Regulation of the OP (D.P.R. n. 230/2000) introduced a number of significant changes on this issue: it states that the university students, as far as possible, are located 'in cells and wards adapted to study, also making available appropriate common rooms for them' and it provides permission to 'keep, in their cells and in other rooms, study books, publications and all the learning tools necessary in their study', including "computers, tape players and portable compact disc" (art. 44). Essentially, the Italian lawmaker finally recognised the important role played in the higher education field by learning and research tools on the one hand and, on the other, by environments suited to cooperation and confrontation (between student and teacher, as well as among learners).[5]

On the basis of the provisions of art. 44 of the new Implementing Regulation, since the early 2000s, numerous cooperation agreements between universities and prisons have been signed (Table 2), although the origin of the Prison University Poles (PUPs) is situated, as often happens, not in a law but in a spontaneous practice, in this case deeply marked by the contribution of voluntary work.[6] The PUPs, distributed fairly evenly throughout the country, usually guarantee the placement of the university students in

Table 2. The penitentiary university poles in Italy (1998–2015)

Denomination	Year	Involved prisons	Participating Universities	E-learn
PUP of Turin	1998	CC (*Casa Circondariale*: remand centre) of Turin	Università di Torino	
PUP of Tuscany	2000 2003 2010	Prisons in Tuscany	Università di Firenze/ Università di Pisa/ Università di Siena	
PUP of Bologna	2000 2013	CC di Bologna	Università di Bologna	X
PUP of Alessandria S. Michele/Pausania	2001 2008	CR (*Casa di Reclusione*: prison for sentence execution) of Alessandria	Università del Piemonte orientale A. Avogadro	X
SUP (University Prison System) of Lazio	2003 2008 2009	Prisons in Lazio	Università della Tuscia, Università di Cassino, Università La Sapienza, Università di Tor Vergata, Università di Roma Tre	X
PUP of Triveneto	2003	CR of Padova	Università di Padova	
Memorandum of undertaking DAP (Department of Penitentiary Administration) – University of Catania	2003	CC of Caltagirone	Università di Catania	X

Denomination	Year	Involved prisons	Participating Universities	E-learn
PUP of Calabria	2004	CC of Catanzaro	Università Magna Grecia di Catanzaro	
PUP of Lecce	2004	CC of Lecce	Università di Lecce	
PUP of Sardegna	2004 2007 2014	CC of Sassari/CC of Alghero/Prisons in Sardinia	Università di Sassari	
PUP of Abruzzo	2005	Prisons in Abruzzo and Molise	Università telematica L. da Vinci di Chieti	X
PUP of Reggio Emilia	2005	CC of Reggio Emilia	Università di Modena e Reggio Emilia	X
PUP of Brescia Verziano	2006	CR of Brescia Verziano	Università di Brescia	
PUP of Sulmona	2006	CR of Sulmona	Università dell'Aquila	
E-le@rning in carcere (proj.)[7]/PUP della Campania	2008 2013	CR-ICATT of Eboli/ Prisons in Campania	Università di Salerno/ Università Federico II di Napoli	X
Memorandum of undertaking DAP – University of Palermo	2009	CC Pagliarelli	Università di Palermo	
Metropolitan PUP of Milan	2013	Prisons in province of Milan	Università Bicocca di Milano	
PUP of Teramo	2014	CC of Teramo	Università di Teramo	
PUP of Ferrara	2014	CC of Ferrara	Università di Ferrara	
PUP of Umbria	2015	Prisons in Umbria	Università di Perugia	

Sources: Palmisano (2015); Pastore (2015); www.giustizia.it; www.ristretti.it

a special ward, supplied with individual cells, equipped with a common study room and subjected to a softer discipline. Universities, for their part, provide a range of services: the teaching (by mail, Internet or in presence, for students on probation); the examination boards (online and/or in presence, in prison and/or at the university); a certain amount (highly variable) of tutors, online and/or in presence, allowed access to the prisons (Pillera & González Monteagudo, 2016); additional economic benefits, provided for disadvantaged students or specifically agreed for inmates.

The Laws and the Actors in Spain

Spain, free of the Franco regime, rapidly produced a modern democratic legislation, approving, one year after the Constitution, its Penitentiary Act. Like the Italian one, the L.O. n. 1/1979 (henceforth LOGP: *Ley Orgánica General Penitenciaria*) is also based on the sources of international law and it is geared to the rehabilitation and social reintegration of the condemned (art. 1). Also in Spain the law allocates, jointly with work (considered as a right-duty), a key role to education and training (respectively: the 2nd chapter, arts. 26–35; and the 10th chapter, arts. 55–58): the obligation to establish a library in each prison is in force (art. 57)[8] along with the duty to provide school courses as similar as possible to those attended by students outside the prison (art. 55 par. 2); moreover, the principle of integration with the public system is implemented for the acknowledgement of qualifications and certifications (art. 56 par. 1). Finally, study is encouraged, allowing access to facilities to follow the related activities, both outside the institution, and, when this is not possible, inside the prison, by correspondence, radio and television (art. 55 par. 3).

The first Implementing Regulation (R.D. n. 1201/1981) decreed that university students have the right to communicate with their own teachers for study purposes and for the examinations (art. 168). Almost twenty years later, the second Regulation (R.D. n. 190/1996) adds at least two relevant details about university education: (a) special modifications to the penitentiary regime, due to the participation in educational programmes, can be obtained by inmates (art. 124 par. 3); (b) the possibility to keep in their cell, solely for educational or cultural purposes, personal computers without network connection and subjected to periodic inspections of the hard disk (art. 129).

Overall, the organisational model provided was not unlike the Italian one: although with vague directions, it allowed the free collaboration between prisons and universities. However, the developments and the results were significantly different compared to Italy, because the historical-cultural context where the phenomenon had its origin was very different. In Spain the conditions for university study in prison have ripened as a result of a broad movement against Franco in the late 60's (when Italy had been a democratic country for more than 10 years), in which university students played an active role. Indeed, in 1970, about 200 of them tasted political prison (Viedma Rojas, 2013). In spite of this, they continued to study, supported by the respective universities, and their choice became another form of opposition to the dictatorship. Until today, 'although nuanced and transformed, this spirit of resistance continues to form part of the interpretation of the action' (Viedma Rojas, 2013, p. 106), that can be read as a research of continuity and normality in the discontinuity represented by the experience of being imprisoned.

Indeed, in the early years of the Spanish transition, university study in prison vanished but, relatively quickly, at the end of the 70's it appeared again, among common inmates and especially among those from armed separatist movements (ETA, GRAPO, FRAP). Similarly, in Italy, in the same period but on a reduced scale, those condemned for terrorism were among the first convicts to take a degree (Migliori, 2004, p. 28).

In 1983, the first Spanish socialist government came to power and promoted an agreement between UNED (*Universidad Nacional de Educación a Distancia*), Ministry of Education, Ministry of Justice and Prison Administration, but this did not prevent the latter from signing several other agreements at the local level and thus involving various universities. The policy implemented by the socialists, marked by a cultural dynamisation of the prisons, allowed an extremely rapid increase in the number of university students among the imprisoned people (Viedma Rojas, 2013).

In the following years this number continued to increase, as, on the one hand, the role of UNED became consolidated,[9] while on the other, the contribution of the University of País Vasco (UPV) rapidly emerged and, in the late 90's, reached a student population among inmates close to that of UNED (Viedma Rojas, 2013). Unlike the latter, however, UPV always refused to sign any agreements with the Prison Administration (developing its work through the UNED Centre of Bergara); moreover, a great percentage of its imprisoned students were composed of members of the Basque separatist organisation, ETA. These elements sparked an inter-institutional conflict that brought about the legal expulsion of UPV from prisons in 2003, as a result of the amendment to art. 56 of LOGP, operated by L.O. n. 6/2003.[10] A second paragraph was added to the said article, specifying that: (a) the prison administration must sign the necessary agreements with the universities, ensuring conditions, rigour and quality appropriate to this type of study as well as the use of a methodology *adapted* to the prison context; (b) such agreements have to be established preferably with UNED, preserving, however, the possibility of accepting partnerships with other universities, in compliance with the previous rules.[11]

Consequently, a specialistic and centralised model was developed, managed entirely by UNED, in which, from the a.y. (academic year) 2003–2004, no public university took part or expressed interest in doing so, except UPV (Viedma Rojas, 2013). Of course, this chosen path reduces the diversification both in the curriculum and in the teaching methods. Nevertheless, UNED grants coverage throughout the country, thanks to its specialisation in distance learning as well as to the local support of its *Centros Asociados*, so enjoying rootedness and social legitimacy. Therefore, the Spanish model allows: the protection of the right of access to university, even with high spatial dispersion of the students; the extension of the provision to a wide variety of degree programmes, proposed with a flexible (andragogic and specific to prison) methodology; the guarantee of greater control and safety, as UNED shares with the prison system a direct dependence on the Central State Administration.

ICT FOR ACADEMIC STUDY IN ITALIAN AND SPANISH PRISONS

ICT has brought new tools for inclusive and active learning, particularly relevant to the contexts of isolation (geographical, physical, social or cultural), but the use of computers, and in particular the use of the internet, is heavily restricted in European prisons, when not totally forbidden, due to legal, practical and cultural problems. In spite of this, these technologies, used to support (to implement or to integrate) the treatment of prisoners, appear to represent a viable and increasingly practised methodological solution, especially in the UK, Scandinavia, Central Europe and Spain (Pillera, 2015). In Italy, e-learning has been used successfully, among others, in vocational training projects Trio (in Tuscany) and CISCO (at the CR of Bollate), as well as in the @URORA project, aimed at juvenile prisons (Suriano, 2011; Diana, 2013).

Furthermore, the use of e-learning in university education for prisoners is now documented in most of Europe, in the Anglo-Saxon world outside Europe and in South America (Costelloe et al., 2012; Hawley et al., 2013; Champion & Edgar, 2013; Czerwinski et al., 2014). This is due to the power and flexibility of ICT in education, in terms of the inherent characteristics of the new media (hypertext, multimedia, simulation, augmented reality, ubiquity), in strictly educational terms (individualisation of teaching, customisation of times, places and instruments, opportunities for remote cooperative learning, possibility to monitor the processes), and also in organisational and financial terms (flexibility, modularity, scalability, re-usability of the learning objects). In addition, e-learning appears effective in promoting continuity of an academic career for those entering or leaving prison.

As regards Italy, in Table 2 we have already indicated the PUPs in which there are e-learning resources for students (7 of 20).[12] In the hope and expectation that many more Italian universities develop structures and know-how related to de-materialised teaching and fulfil their third mission also entwining appropriate partnerships with (more or less distant) prisons, we would like to highlight the experience of the SUP (*Sistema Universitario Penitenziario*: University Penitentiary System) that was developed in Lazio using leading technologies and that had been proven effective as an organisational system. As elsewhere, the model adopted in Lazio is orchestrated on a regional basis but it appears extremely widespread in the territory. It consists of an institutional network that involves the PRAP (*Provveditorato Regionale dell'Amministrazione Penitenziaria*: Regional Superintendency of Penitentiary Administration); the 14 prisons in the region; the three Roman universities and those of Tuscia and Cassino; LazioDiSU (the regional institute for the provision of academic education); regional institutions and the regional Guarantor of detained persons, whose involvement in the project includes mediating in the management of paperwork and providing free textbooks and teaching materials (Garante, 2013).

As part of the experience of the SUP Lazio, the project "Teledidattica – Università in carcere", created in 2006 and designated as using best practices by the Ministry of Justice, consists of an operating agreement between the CC Rebibbia NC, the University of Tor Vergata, LazioDiSU and the telecommunications company Fastweb, with the coordination of the Guarantor (Garante, 2013). It makes available, within the Roman prison, three whole degree programmes (Humanities, Law, Economics), that currently account for about 40 of the 113 university students involved in the SUP (http://web.uniroma2.it). The lessons are progressively videotaped in their natural setting (using special lecture halls at University of Tor Vergata) and then uploaded onto a platform, that is accessible from two specifically equipped classrooms inside the prison of Rebibbia NC. Here the students can use computers, projectors, a multimedia library and a teleconferencing system, that is dedicated to the online tutoring and to examinations. The first is guaranteed, at least monthly, even in presence, by means of disciplinary tutors who have access to the prison; the second can be taken in presence (with the commission that goes to the prison or, vice versa, through the granting of a permit) or, when it is necessary for security reasons, directly online (through a conference call but with the presence in jail of a member of the examination board).[13]

In Spain, despite many universities offering degree courses or Masters' online for several years, UNED, as we saw earlier, is currently the only entity authorised to provide university education to the inmates, who are distributed throughout approximately 90 prisons (Viedma Rojas, 2013). The PEUCP (*Programas de Estudios Universitarios en Centros Penitenciarios*: University Study Programmes in Penitentiary Centres) of UNED offers to convicts: information, orientation and enrolment services; *in some prisons, exam simulations for access to Curso de Acceso Directo (Direct Access Course), reserved for people over 25 years old; support in the use of the e-learning platform aLF (www.innova.uned.es/servicios/alf); assistance from the closer Centro Asociado UNED, for students serving sentences in the open prison system (CIS)*[14] *or on probation or on parole* (http://portal.uned.es). Research has found several similarities between the main sociological variables recorded for jailed students and for the rest of the students at UNED, in particular with regard to the distribution by age (Bardisa Ruiz et al., 2003). Furthermore, the favourite degree programmes in the Spanish prison are practically the same as the rest of the UNED students but they coincide only partially with the preferred subjects among Italian inmates (Table 3), where we can notice a stronger (but diminishing) concentration of choices, probably due to the more limited degrees offered in Italian PUPs.

With the increasing use of ICT, the methodology of UNED has also evolved, first in the direction of the digitisation of contents, then towards their de-materialisation and delivery across the internet. However, these innovations have been adopted much more slowly in prisons (Callejo & Ramón Bautista, 2003): now ALF also services inmates for UNED's entire learning offer (only some degree courses that require laboratory practice are excluded from PEUCP), but not all prisons are yet equipped

Table 3. Six subject areas most selected by Italian and Spanish inmates studying on university programs

Spain (2010)		Italy (2010 and 2014)		
Law	21%	Humanities	24,6%	18.4%
Tourism	19.4%	Law	23.2%	24.2%
Psychology	8.4%	Politics and sociology	20.9%	29.5%
History	7.7%	Economics and Statistics	10%	3.1%
Business admin. and management	6.5%	Agricultural science	5.7%	4.8%
Social education	6.3%	Engineering	4.2%	3.6%
Others	30.7%	Others	7.2%	16.4%

Sources: www.giustizia.it for Italy; Gutiérrez Brito et al. (2010) for Spain and trained to maintain secure workstations and internet connections. In addition, some studies (Bardisa Ruiz et al., 2003; Vázquez Cano, 2013) identified serious weaknesses: primarily, a frequent total ban of electronic contacts between prisoner and teacher; at the same time, a strong limitation (in terms of time and contents) in accessing the computers, Internet and even ALF itself, to take advantage of interactive learning methods and to carry out the homework. Often, as a result, only the educators have access to the platform and they download the teaching materials, while the inmate experiences the online interaction exclusively as a bureaucratic channel.

CONCLUSIONS

In the interpretation of the reasons leading the prisoners to the decision to pursue university studies, the benefits provided for by law in Italy and in Spain often take on a certain importance. However, the appeal to interests and environments other than prison carries weight without doubt into a 'dynamic of awakening' that 'has to be harnessed so that it does not turn into frustration' (Margara in Migliori, 2004, p. 17). The theme of the learning experience as discontinuity, rupture and generative opportunity emerges once again and – on the flip side – so does the idea of the continuity of the intervention, with a strategy of accompaniment during post-detention, which is currently the most significant absent factor.

Concerning the reported evidence, the advantages and limitations of the two national models – the Spanish one, that could be called *centripetal*, and the Italian one, that can be defined as *territorial* – are summarised below, through a SWOT analysis grid (Table 4).

The two models of university education in Italian and Spanish prisons, dynamically adapting to the changes experienced both by the prison and society, have responded, in some way, to the major requirements emerging from the European regulations (equalisation of education and work, integration into the public system, specific resources and support materials), albeit with accents on different, probably complementary, aspects. The Italian PUP represents a rapidly spreading model, that offers to detainees an academic education networked with the local universities. On the other hand, in Spain, UNED has developed a remarkable work, at least for the breadth of the interested people and for the length of the experience, making use of special methodologies and resources. Nevertheless, in both countries, as noted by many researchers (Coralli, 2002; Bardisa Ruiz et al., 2003; Viedma Rojas, 2013), the discretion, which is granted to the individual prisons and their management, in the authorisation of support and facilitation for higher education, appears excessively wide, such that the transformative power of the learning is still subordinated to the requirements related to security, control and punishment. The legislative requirements, as well as the moral suasion of international organisations are contributing greatly to overcoming a culture of affliction and segregation throughout Europe, but not without difficulties and delays: after all, without a serious re-balance

Table 4. Comparative SWOT analysis between the Italian and Spanish characteristics of university education in prison

	Spanish centripetal model	Italian territorial model
Strengths	Historical tradition. Complete and homogeneous learning offer by UNED: possibility to study without being transferred. Methodological specialisation.	Specially equipped university centres in prison. Facilitated contacts between teachers and students and among students. Activation/enhancement of local resources. Horizontal integration with the public education system.
Weakness	Poorly equipped study areas, often lacking in computer stations. No access to in-presence learning for inmates in closed prisons. Strict security policy regarding Internet access.	Prison-based facilitations in access to university study (activation of PUP is delegated to local initiative). Discomfort in transferring to another prison. The Fragmentation of learning offer. Under-representation of foreigners among university students.
Opportunities	Activation/enhancement of local resources. Open prison (CIS): horizontal integration with the public education system and external attendance. Synergy with the territorial vocations.	Synergy with the territorial vocations. Improvements can come out from local experimentation. Emerging interest and trends: recent declaration of intent between the University of Padova and the Ministry of Justice; Circular of DAP about Internet access (note 11).
	Further development of distance learning through e-learning. Redoubling of the learning offer through MOOCs. Strengthening of the learning support to foreign detainees through web resources produced in their own countries. Networking of prison libraries with other public libraries.	
Threats	Security limitations in accessing online teaching and contacting UNED's teachers and tutors. Centralisation and vertical integration do not encourage innovation and experimentation.	To consider the university as a secondary issue when, in truth: (a) it express a great symbolic value as social redemption; (b) Spain demonstrates that the number of university students can substantially grow; (c) higher education impacts on placement and, consequently, on recidivism.
	No support policy in the post-detention period to facilitate the continuity of the learning careers.	

in resource allocation between security and treatment, obtaining a cultural change from a custodial to an osmotic model will remain an arduous challenge.

The movement between the categories of continuity and discontinuity, as shown, could help to read the non-linear evolution of the concept and practices of imprisonment: nowadays, to some extent, they are changing the relationship between the correctional institutions and the outside world, increasingly osmotic, as well as the image – always imbued with complex meanings – which the prison casts on society. There is still a lot of work on this front, especially in Italy; while Spain, with the introduction of the CIS, is initiating an experience that aligns itself with the northern European open prison model. Yet also in Italy there are positive signs – which can be partly interpreted as the results of the experiments undertaken under the PUPs – such as the recent ministerial directives on the encouragement of Internet access (note 11) and on the promotion of an open cell regime (Circular of DAP n. PU-0251644, issued on 13.7.2013, regarding guidelines for dynamic surveillance).

NOTES

[1] The US National Center for Education Statistics (NCES) found that 73% of all undergraduate students have at least one of the characteristics listed above (Choy, 2002). However, unlike the majority of prisoners, university students in jail do not seem to come from career failure in school, as reported by Spanish (Bardisa Ruiz et al., 2003) and English sources (Champion & Edgar, 2013).

[2] Nevertheless its limits and the increasing use of alternative measures to imprisonment, prison remains still the main option for penalty in many legal systems, involving almost 1.5 millions of people around the world in accordance with the World Prison Brief (www.prisonstudies.org).

[3] On a different but interrelated level of analysis, continuity and discontinuity can represent interpretive tools of prisoners' and staff's curricula, once within a horizon leading to the radical transformation of prisons, where the involved (old and new) professional cultures should engage in the search for difficult but necessary collaborations and mediations for the development of educational communities able to produce reintegration.

[4] Unlike the exceptional permit (art. 30 of the OP), the permission-prize (art. 30 ter of the OP), because its *pedagogical-propulsive* value, can only be obtained from prisoners under execution of sentence: to present the instance, the condemned must maintain a good conduct and must not represent a risk to society. Therefore, it has a preventive function on the one hand (helping to maintain and expand the affective, cultural and work interests of the convicted) and, on the other, an incentive function, through the mechanism of rewarding.

[5] The D.P.R. n. 230/2000 adds an indication, albeit bland, to guarantee the continuity of education: whenever possible, the convicts who are engaged in treatment activities (in particular work, education and vocational training) have to be excluded from the group transfers (art. 83 par. 9).

[6] Regarding the origins of the PUPs and the role of volunteers, that is remarkable until today, see: Coralli (2002), Migliori (2004), Palmisano (2015).

[7] On the e-learning experimental program (higher education and university) started at the CR-ICATT of Eboli, in collaboration with the University of Salerno, see: Diana (2013), Suriano (2011), Arcangeli et al. (2010). Both involved institutions have gained international experience through the European project Grundtvig 2009 "EEPP-E-Learning Education for prisoners and prisoners professionals".

[8] The library must be appropriate to the cultural and professional needs of the inmates, moreover the LOGP admits that they can take advantage of mobile libraries, established by the Penitentiary Administration or less (art. 57).

[9] In 1986, in accordance with a substantially unique model (in which only the financial participation of the signatory institutions varies), a series of agreements were stipulated between UNED and the *Departament de Justícia de la Generalitat de Catalunya* (which autonomously manages the prisons in Catalonia, under the R.D. n. 3482/1983), the *Ministerio de Defensa* (for the military prison of Alcala-Meco), the *Ministerio de Asuntos Exteriores* (to support the Spanish prisoners in foreign countries).

[10] The main facts of this legislative change were: the accusations of favouritism and academic irregularities by UPV in favour of ETA prisoners; the public declarations of a group of professors from UPV against the pressure from ETA on the University; the intensification and the extension of the fight against terrorism to other areas of the social network of the armed bands (Viedma Rojas, 2013, pp. 90–91).

[11] The LOGP clarifies that the methodology of intervention has to be adapted to the special circumstances of the prison (art. 56 par. 2), and not vice versa, thus identifying a distance learning model that, at the present day, not only UNED but also other universities are able to offer.

[12] Regarding the relationship among Italian universities, Italian prison and ICT, we report that, in 2007, an agreement was signed among the CR of Alessandria, the Department of Informatics at the University of Alessandria and the Faculty of SMFN (Mathematical, Physical and Natural Sciences) at the University of "Piemonte Orientale – Amedeo Avogadro", in order to commission the development of software to students in that prison. In addition, it is important to remark that the University of Padova, by signing a declaration of intent with the Ministry of Justice in 2013, has pledged to study the experiences, to promote the discussion and to gather proposals, in order to establish a national strategy for university within the prisons. *Among the first results of the work is the elaboration of some guidelines for the signing of new agreements between prisons and universities and the national conference of Padova "I Poli universitari in carcere"* (Palmisano, 2015). Finally, we have to underline that one of the latest Circulars of DAP (n. PU-0366755, issued on 02.11.2015) recognizes the importance of new media as a tool for personal growth and as a support to complex pathways of treatment; consequently, it announces the creation of a centralized infrastructure (managed through a white-list system) to allow a significant proportion of convicts to navigate a selected group of websites and it also regulates the access to these workstations.

[13] Data source: *Progetto Pilota di Teledidattica "Università in carcere"* (www.ristretti.it/areestudio/cultura/scuola). Within the SUP of Lazio, the use of e-learning is not limited to the CC of Rebibbia NC: in fact, the Department of Law of the University of "Roma Tre" has announced the creation of MOOCs to be put at the disposal of regional prisons; moreover, the agreement between de Guarantor and the online University "Unitelma Sapienza" allows every convict in Lazio to freely enrol on degree programs or to take single examinations (Palmisano, 2015).

[14] The Spanish CIS (*Centros de Inserción Social*: Social Integration Centres) were introduced by R.D. n. 190/1996.

REFERENCES

Arcangeli, B., Diana, P., Di Mieri, F., & Suriano, G. (2010). L'e-learning in carcere: una proposta. *Je-LKS, 6*(1), 91–99.

Bardisa Ruiz, T., Viedma Rojas, A., & Martín Pulido, P. (2003). *Proyecto abierto de investigación: "El alumnado de la UNED interno en centros penitenciarios"*. UNED-IUED. Retrieved from http://portal.uned.es

Callejo, J., & Ramón Bautista, J. (2003). Virtuales demandas sobre la virtualización de la enseñanza universitaria a distancia. *RIED, 6*(2), 77–93.

Champion, N., & Edgar, K. (2013). *Through the gateway: How computers can transform rehabilitation*. London: Prison Reform Trust.

Choy, S. (2002). *Nontraditional undergraduates*. Washington, DC: U.S. Department of Education, National Center for Education Statistics.

Coralli, M. (2002). *L'istruzione in carcere: aspetti giuridici e sociologici: L'altro diritto. Centro di documentazione su carcere, devianza e marginalità*. Retrieved from http://www.altrodiritto.unifi.it/ricerche/misure/coralli

Costelloe, A., Langelid, T., & Wilson, A. (2012). *Survey on prison education and training in Europe – final report*. Birmingham: GHK – European Commission.

Czerwinski, T., König, E., & Zaichenko, T. (Eds.). (2014). Youth and adult education in prisons. *Experiences from Central Asia, South America, North Africa and Europe: IPE – International Perspectives in Adult Education 69* (pp. 72–80). Retrieved from http://www.dvv-international.de/en/materials

Diana, P. (2013). L'e-learning in carcere. Esperienze, riflessioni, proposte. *Cambio III*, *6*, 261–271.
Hawley, J., Murphy, I., & Souto-Otero, M. (2013). *Prison education and training in Europe: Current state-of-play and challenges*. Birmingham: GHK – European Commission.
Garante delle persone sottoposte a misure restrittive della libertà personale. (2013). *Relazione attività anno 2013*. Retrieved from http://www.garantedetenutilazio.it
Gutiérrez Brito, J., Viedma Rojas, A., & Callejo Gallego, J. (2010). Estudios superiores en la educación penitenciaria española: un análisis empírico a partir de los actores. *Revista de Educación*, *353*, 443–468.
Migliori, S. (2004). *Lo studio e la pena. L'Università di Firenze nel carcere di Prato: rapporto triennale 2000–2003*. Firenze: Firenze University Press.
Ministerio del Interior. (2014). *Anuario Estadístico del Ministerio del Interior 2013*. Bilbao: Ministerio del Interior. Retrieved from http://publicacionesoficiales.boe.es
Palmisano, R. (2015). *Istruzione universitaria nelle strutture penitenziarie – Tema per Stati Generali dell'Esecuzione Penale – Tavolo 9*. DAP – Ufficio Studi Ricerche Legislazione e Rapporti Internazionali. Retrieved from http://www.giustizia.it
Pastore, G. (2015). Formazione e processi di inclusione sociale: il caso dei Poli universitari penitenziari. In M. A. Toscano & A. Cirillo (Eds.), *Xeni: Nuove sfide per l'integrazione sociale* (pp. 235–245). Milano: Franco Angeli.
Pillera, G. (2015, November 18–20). *E-literacy and access to Internet as inmate's right: European ICT frameworks in correctional education*. ICERI2015 8th annual International Conference of Education, Research and Innovation, Seville, Spain.
Pillera, G., & González Monteagudo, J. (2016). L'educatore penitenziario come tutor ed orientatore nelle carceri italiane e spagnole. In R. Biagioli (Ed.), *Il tutorato nei contesti formative* (pp. 69–92). Pisa: ETS.
SGIP. (2014). *El Sistema Penitenciario Español*. Bilbao: Ministerio del Interior – Secretaria General Técnica. Retrieved from http://publicacionesoficiales.boe.es
Suriano, G. (2011). E-learning in carcere: leva per il programma rieducativo trattamentale e per l'inserimento sociale dei detenuti ed ex detenuti. In T. Minerva & L. Colazzo (Eds.), *Connessi! Scenari di Innovazione nella Formazione e nella Comunicazione* (pp. 821–830). Milano: Ledizioni.
Vázquez Cano, E. (2013). Expectativas, obstáculos y hábitos de estudio de los internos que cursan enseñanzas universitarias en la UNED. *Un estudio de caso: centro penitenciario Madrid VII*. Revista de Educación, *360*(1), 162–188.
Viedma Rojas, A. (2013). *Universitarios en prisión. Experiencias y apariencias de sentido en el espacio penitenciario* (tesis doctoral). UNED, Madrid.

Giuseppe Pillera
University of Catania
Italy

PART 3

CONTINUITY AND DISCONTINUITY AROUND THE JOB MARKET

ANDREA GALIMBERTI AND EVA RATTI

7. CONTINUITY AND DISCONTINUITY AROUND ACADEMIA

The "Find Your Doctor" Project as a Space for Researching and Facilitating Learning Careers

"WE DON'T KNOW HOW TO DO ANYTHING ELSE":
A PERSONAL EXPERIENCE

In the summer of 2012, an Italian astrophysics graduate who is one of the authors of this article was completing her PhD in the Netherlands, and wondering what it was about her career situation that was making her unhappy. While sharing her doubts and thoughts with peers, she found herself listening to the personal career stories of other PhD candidates, post-docs and young researchers: gathering *de facto* a small but vibrant sample of experiences, impressions and viewpoints concerning career paths in research and related issues.

Although neither premeditated nor systematically conducted, these initial dialogues nonetheless offered valuable material for reflection. First, they suggested widespread insecurity about future employment possibilities and stability in public research, which the reader may recognise as a common concern for young academics across different disciplines and (Western) countries (Fumasoli et al., 2015). The second point of interest was that, despite their justified perception that there was little scope for them to develop a life-long career in science, the majority of these young researchers were not actively seeking out alternatives. On the contrary, they mostly intended to continue along the "post-doc-after-post-doc" path they anticipated for themselves, hoping that if they could withstand the pressure and, in some cases, homesickness for their native land, if they could deal with family issues, if they were good enough and strong enough, etcetera, some – as yet unforeseeable – solution would eventually turn up.

For a few of them, this choice was driven by a deep-set passion for research: they intended to go on doing and enjoying their dream job for as long as they possibly could. The majority, however, did not have such a strong sense that research was their one true calling: they did not dislike it, they appreciated its advantages, but were also acutely aware of its drawbacks. While the first group refused to imagine themselves "doing something else", the second group was more open to this possibility, but could not pinpoint a plausible "else". The overall conviction of this group of young academics was (and has since remained) that most of them would stay on in indefinitely in research because they could not identify a realistic alternative given what they knew – or thought they knew – about the world outside the academy.

"If I could turn back, I don't know if I would still choose this life" one young post-doc commented during an impromptu conversation at the front door of the research institute: "But I am fairly good at it and, let's face it, we don't know how to do anything else".

INSIDE/OUTSIDE OF THE ACADEMY: WHAT'S ON THE HORIZON FOR PHDS?

Surprisingly, in light of the growing interest in career prospects for PhDs displayed by many academic institutions, we were unable to find systematically collected international statistics on the percentages of annual PhD graduates that are expected to eventually achieve a permanent position in higher education. Although the situation can be depicted as tragic or not-so-tragic depending on the country and field of knowledge considered, it is reasonable to estimate that a PhD graduate's current chance of ultimately attaining a permanent position in public research is a few per cent on average, and may be even slimmer in certain geographical contexts.

For example, the 2013 European Science Foundation Report on research careers in Europe cites a study, based on annual reports filed by Finnish universities, indicating that roughly 10% of newly-qualified PhDs can expect to attain a professorship. In Italy, the situation is even worse: a recent study carried out by ADI – the national association of PhD students and PhD graduates – predicts that only 6.5% of current Post-doc researchers will obtain long-term academic positions (ADI, 2016). Van der Weijden and colleagues have outlined a similar situation in Dutch universities (Van der Weijden et al., 2015). The MORE 2 Higher Education Survey (2012) reported a decrease in long-term academic positions in favour of temporary contracts, in both the US and EU27, for those who had embarked on PhD programmes after 2006 as compared to those who had initiated their doctoral studies earlier.

The first decade of the 2000s saw a major increase in the number of PhDs granted globally each year, but this was not matched by an equivalent increase in permanent academic positions (OECD, 2011). Although the pattern may have changed over the last few years, for which international data have not yet been reported, it is reasonable to assume that this growth produced a large reservoir of professionals with research experience. Career data from the OECD Research and Development Statistics Database that included information on short-term contract employment, showed that in 2011, the business sector in the OECD area absorbed – on average – some 45% of researchers (OECD, 2011). If we also take into account non-researchers, that is to say, PhD holders who are currently not employed in research, the percentage employed by enterprise is likely to be even higher, particularly in the humanities in which fewer research positions are available compared to engineering and the hard sciences (Auriol, Misu, & Freeman, 2013).

There is also data to suggest that the broader jobs market is open to receiving PhD graduates, given that unemployment rates for the category remain below national averages and below equivalent rates for Master's degree holders (OECD, 2016). The European-level DOC-CAREERS project found that half of current PhDs hold research and non-research positions in the business, government, services and non-third-level education sectors (EUA, 2009, p. 7). So, why do PhD holders fail to identify future career options for themselves outside of academia? In our opinion, one of the reasons may be the lack of a suitable intermediary assisting PhD graduates (especially those moving to non-research positions) to make the transition to new professional settings. Doctoral graduates' typically poor awareness of the range of career paths available to them has been repeatedly been flagged as a crucial stumbling block in studies on the topic, as clearly stated by the European Science Foundation's (ESF) forum on research careers: "Information on research career perspectives", says the 2012 ESF report: "has focused on the academic career because systematic information is not readily available for the different career alternatives in other fields". And again: "the post-doctoral period is a critical stage for selecting a research career as a profession, but information about further research career prospects is not readily available in a structured way" (ESF, 2012, p. 5).

UNIVERSITY AND SOCIETY. THE TIMES THEY'RE A 'CHANGIN'?

The fact that PhD graduates are relatively uninformed about career possibilities outside the academy calls into question the role of universities in the so-called "knowledge economy" (Livingstone & Guile, 2012).

Over time, the academic world has modified its relationship with society by adapting its functions or missions (Scott, 2006). The two traditional tasks of universities, teaching and research, date back to the pre-modern era, prior to the birth of nation states. Today, the new activities demanded of higher education institutions by the knowledge society are referred to as their "third task" or "third stream" of activity, and imply changes in how universities are organised and design their curricula. Specifically, higher-education curricula are meant to provide for continuing professional development, thereby contributing to lifelong learning.

In this "age of supercomplexity" (Barnett, 2000), educational systems are continuously required to engage with new questions and new ideas about their relationship with knowledge. In the future, higher education's commitment to pursuing predominantly "formal" knowledge will increasingly be challenged, given the current politically- and market-led tendency to value the informal and non-formal dimensions of learning (Collini, 2012). Personal knowledge and transversal skills are becoming ever more important and this focus on competences implies the need for a different approach to teaching:

> The concept of competence involves two critical questions for formal education. First, how important and relevant is its academic content in relation to societal reproduction and diffusion of knowledge and skills? Second, how

effective are student-learning outcomes? Can people actually use in practice the knowledge and skills they have learned? (Olesen, 2013, p. 156)

These questions become salient as academic learning processes are increasingly drawn into dialogue with similar processes unfolding in non-university settings.

In the early stages of launching the European Research Area, a European Commission Communication noted that research is increasingly conducted in 'non-academic' institutions, such as companies, non-profit organizations and independent research centers and that researchers need to be trained and prepared to enter this wider job market. (EC, 2003, p. 14)

Enhancing the employability of university graduates (including PhD holders) will involve leveraging the developing relations between academic institutions and their new interlocutors. The changes underway entail new opportunities and new risks. One of the main risks derives from the idea that all universities need to do is adapt to market requirements. This assumption often underpins attempts to eliminate the distance between the academic sphere and the private sector via a sort of 'marketization' process (Collini, 2012). On the other hand, there is also the possibility that enriching new dialogues may take place. Attaining this second outcome is more challenging because it requires universities to pursue their academic mission in collaboration with other contexts and stakeholders, while maintaining their own distinct goals, interests and logics.

A key example of an "unconventional" interlocutor for universities is the world of small and medium enterprises. At both the formal and informal levels, the possible professional outlet for PhD graduates that is almost never mentioned is precisely the small and medium businesses sector, although it accounts for the greater part of European entrepreneurship. Small and medium companies are extensively present across all nations and potentially offer a broad range of working conditions, approaches and environments that may be matched with the individual values and needs of employees. Encouraging these companies to recruit researchers could significantly boost the choice of geographical locations and employment settings available to PhD holders. However, smaller businesses are more challenging interlocutors than large ones given their even greater cultural distance from the world of research, which has traditionally remained separate from the applied challenges of the market, business and production. Although (at least in Italy) a number of public and private initiatives aimed at facilitating contact between universities and companies have flourished in recent years, attempts to create links with small and medium businesses specifically, have met with little success to date. And this despite the fact that SMEs stand to benefit enormously from such a partnership. Broadly speaking, the main reason for this difficulty is the marked intrinsic difference between the goals, logics, timeframes and language of academia and those of small and medium-sized companies. However, if we shift from a model of organisation-to-organisation interaction to one of personal contact, the scope for convergence increases. An individual researcher's motivation to find a suitable career path can truly be paired with a company's specific needs for expertise, a spirit of innovation and solutions.

LOST IN TRANSLATION. THE FIND YOUR DOCTOR PROJECT

In an increasingly knowledge-based society, where innovation is depicted as a key goal for companies and the complexity and rapid diffusion of information makes the ability to organise and synthesise knowledge so crucial (Livingstone & Guile, 2012), it seems particularly wasteful that the very people who are trained in these skills remain stuck in an unnecessary contest for the few academic tenure positions available. On the other hand, there is a genuine risk that dialogue with the private sector will be perceived as frustrating if the distinctive characteristics of academic research experience fail to be recognised, integrated, and valued:

> Over-qualification and over-skilling lead to lower levels of productivity, lower job satisfaction and psychological stress, besides being on aggregate level a waste in terms of investment made in education. (Flisi et al., 2014, p. 11)

The ESF 2012 report emphasised the need for communication initiatives connecting universities and the private sector:

> As universities cannot be expected to provide jobs for a majority of researchers, funding programmes to support career opportunities in RPOs, industry and administration should be actively advertised. (ESF, 2012, p. 32)

Alongside the sustained, albeit debatably efforts of institutions and universities across Europe to enhance the employability of PhDs, we believe that initiatives involving both the academic and entrepreneurial worlds could make career options in industry more visible, and researchers' professional experiences more accessible. Such an initiative is the FindYourDoctor project, launched by an Italian consortium of private companies and operated by a team of professionals from both academic and business backgrounds. The aim of the project – which is run on a no-profit basis – is to provide a reference point for junior and less-junior PhD holders in all fields and of all nationalities, facilitating their contact with the entrepreneurial world, making their value accessible to broader society and challenging the idea that "researchers do not know how to do anything else".

In practice, FyD is based around a website (www.findyourdoc.org), which collates professional profiles of PhDs on the one hand and profiles of companies interested in recruiting researchers on the other. Indeed, the web – alongside informal networks – is increasingly being recommended to researchers as a resource for promoting their competences:

> Individual scientists may provide examples of their personal careers and different web portals are available. In interviews, doctoral researchers

themselves have reported positive experiences from their own network (of peers) for mentoring, coaching and career planning. (ESF, 2012, p. 5)

In our experience also, informal networks, advice from peers, and word-of-mouth via the web seem to be the most effective forms of support currently available to PhD graduates leaving higher education. The first-hand experience of the FindYourDoctor staff and careful analysis of web spaces, groups and forums on the topic suggest that the main online job-search portals and off-line job-placement agencies often provide little help, as they generally do not handle such high-level qualifications and niche areas of specialisation. Smaller initiatives exist in some countries: some are for-profit enterprises and related to particularly strategic market areas (e.g., big data analysis and strategic consultancy), while others are publicly funded, such as the interesting DocPro in France (www.mydocpro.org) which offers the most advanced discussion on the competences of PhD graduates that we have found to date.

Most current job-search instruments are largely based on keywords: online portals automatically filter applications for specific terms that conventionally do not feature in academic CVs, although the candidate may well possess the skills they denote. Similarly, the first level of the recruitment process via agencies is usually based on a list of schematic minimum requirements that are summarised in keywords, making it difficult for researchers' profiles to reach the desks of those who truly understand the requirements of the job to be filled and might be able to read between the lines of the PhD holder's experience.

We recently monitored an online discussion among researchers who were advising a recent PhD graduate in biology on the best way to write her CV to target a job in industry. Among many more or less reasonable suggestions, one in particular reflected a common misconception: "Keep it simple and let your research speak for itself". While this would be appropriate advice if one were applying for an academic position, in an initial screening process for a managerial position such as the case in hand, "letting the research speak for itself" would most likely come across to the recruiter as gibberish. Even when a researcher's CV is brought to the attention of someone with an in-depth understanding of the job requirements, as can happen in small companies with no structured recruitment offices, the highly specific expertise offered by a researcher may seem too much and too little at the same time. Vice versa, the requirements articulated in job-advertisements make many PhDs feel unfit because they feel that they cannot claim the expected labels.

Hence, job-search and job-placement procedures for researchers can be as effective as throwing two people that speak different languages into a room together and asking them to identify their common interests. In other words, the process cannot work, unless we introduce a translator.

TRANSLATION AND TRANSFERABLE SKILLS

Careful consideration of research training from an enterprise-oriented perspective reveals that many of the skills implicitly developed through research practices are required in a variety of positions of responsibility across a range of work environments (EUA, 2009). In the course of a good PhD programme, the student is trained to define, manage, and complete a multi-year project, locate the resources and expertise required to achieve each of the project goals, work on cross-national teams both as a coordinator and a team player, provide and accept feedback, and communicate and disseminate results in written and oral presentation format. We expect PhD graduates to be familiar with the methods of research, but in fact they have also learned to be proactive, driven and focused; and have received in-depth training in analytical thinking and problem solving, intellectual consistency, accuracy, deep and creative thinking, and an awareness of the novel, given that they have been working to push forward the frontiers of knowledge. All skills that are not easily found and that companies of different sizes seek and value in candidates for analytical positions and roles of responsibility. In a survey conducted in the UK, 60% of PhD graduates reported using the generic skills developed as research students in their everyday work (Vitae, 2010, pp. 34–37). However, unless a company's staff includes doctorate holders that are involved in the recruitment process, none of this will necessarily be extrapolated from a standard academic CV.

Research experience can be difficult for a potential employer to interpret, just as it is difficult for researchers themselves to discern what aspect of their experience may be of interest outside of their former work setting and on what grounds. Assessment processes may fail to shed light because the concept of competence itself has not been clearly enough defined. In fact:

> The term competence is sufficiently vague to be used by people in very different ways according to their particular assumptions and agendas. (Illeris, 2009, p. 8)

Multiple attempts have been made to define the key competences for knowledge-based economies (e.g., the European ESCO project). The outcomes are lists of abstract and "universal" skills. Particular emphasis is placed on so-called "soft", "transversal", "cross sector" or "transferable" skills, which are considered to be workers' best resource in an increasingly competitive economy based on "grey capital" (Field, 2006).

> Cross-sector skills and competences can be transferred from one occupation to another, thus enabling occupational mobility. They can be used in a number of similar occupations and sectors but might require additional training to be used in a new job and/or work environment. Cross-sector skills and competences are of growing importance all over Europe. (ESF, 2009, p. 47)

It is frequently claimed that workers in all sectors require competences that go beyond their own specific field and need to acquire transferable skills throughout their careers to enhance their professional prospects (EUA, 2010). Researchers are no exception to this rule:

Researchers today face new academic pathways and expanded opportunities to work in other sectors, as well as pressure to consider a wider variety of career paths and to use a wider variety of skills in their everyday work. To meet these challenges, researchers need skills that will allow them to work in and move between different sectors during their working lives and to cope with networked, interdisciplinary modes of work. (OECD, 2012, p. 16)

Increasing attention is being paid to the question of how researchers are trained in transferable skills: do they acquire such skills in the course of their studies? The EUA has suggested that researchers need to be more aware of the implicit acquisition of skills that takes place during their PhD programme and better able to convey it to potential employers (EUA, 2009, p. 93).

This kind of reflection often prompts attempts to devise formal and systematic training models with the explicit aim of creating suitable contexts for the teaching of transferable skills. Such models are intended to foster the development of transferable competences by leveraging the "informal" and tacit dimensions of learning processes. The results, to date, have generally been disappointing. Vitae (2009) found relatively high percentages of researchers who had undergone training in some area of personal and transferable skills but had not found it useful. Such unsatisfactory outcomes are likely related to the fact that the nature of transferable skills (as well as the concept of competence, see above) is problematic. Before analysing the best way to acquire them, it is crucial to examine the assumptions underlying the discourse on competences.

In general, the dominant discourse frames competences as commodifiable human abilities (Han, 2009), describing them as measurable and manageable. Some scholars see the notion of competence as fully embedded in the economic discourse (Olsen, Codd, & O'Neill, 2004). In fact the concept of competence as a 'tradable good' is based on a notion of invariance that is difficult to reconcile with concepts of situated performance or of knowledge as interwoven with practice and historical context:

The interest of political management in being able to measure and compare across countries requires a common and general descriptive system. Efforts have therefore been directed towards defining key competencies. The concept of competence contains a contradiction between that defined above and a notion of invariance. (Olesen, 2013, p. 156)

This is not the only flaw in the mainstream definition of skills and competencies as mere "things" to be exchanged in the marketplace:

If we view competences as mere 'things', we fail to see the processes they activate. We fail to reflect on how it may be possible to elicit competent behaviour. We fail to identify the dynamic processes implicated in developing, sustaining and modifying competences. (Cepollaro, 2008, p. 78)

The use of an instrumental metaphor (Lakoff & Johnson, 1980) to conceptualize competence has the drawback of obscuring its situated and relational nature: that is to say, the fact that competences are developed in specific settings, in the course of interaction, and through participation in complex professional activities. This consideration has a range of epistemological implications, concerning, for example, the role of tacit knowledge in acquiring situational understanding (Eraut, 2000) or whether practical knowledge that is embedded in specific activities and relations may be transferred to a different context. Relying on the instrumental definition can induce us to overlook the fact that transferring competences is not the same thing as transferring goods:

> Labour, it seems, is a remarkably 'sticky' factor of production. Many skills do not transfer easily from one setting to another, presumably because they are often embedded in dense networks of workplace relationships. (Field, 2006, p. 102)

Interpretive approaches invite us to consider worker and work as forming "one entity through the lived experience of work. Competence is thus seen as constituted by the meaning the work takes on for the worker in his or her experience of it" (Sandberg, 2000, p. 11). Complexity theories (Morin, 1995) describe competences as the result of contingent, provisional and contextual processes, as an emerging organisation dealing with order/disorder. From this perspective, it is of crucial importance to link our knowledge of a given element to our knowledge of the whole it belongs to; and to uphold the principle of distinction, rather than disjunction, between the object, or subject, and their environment.

These theoretical points of view introduce an alternative frame of reference that emphasises relational and contextual aspects. A change in frame of reference often raises new issues and new questions (Mezirow, 2009). The key question is no longer: "How can we acquire general and abstract skills that are transferable?", but: "What kind of transformation occurs when we move from one context to another?", and: "What kind of learning processes are activated by this move?"

Gregory Bateson proposed that information gleaned from relating different contexts to one another bears learning potential (see the concept of "deuterolearning" in Bateson, 1972). Moving to a different professional setting may be an opportunity to identify and revisit the roots (contexts, relationships, tacit learning) of one's own skills, and to uncover the frames of reference and assumptions that shaped the related learning processes.

The current project was designed and implemented based on these theoretical considerations.

THE STATE OF THE ART. WHAT DOES THE PROJECT INVOLVE?

A Successful Translation Initiative. Researchers Are Not Aliens after All

In the course of 2015 and 2016, we had the opportunity to test some of the ideas outlined above in collaboration with an association of small and medium enterprises that is interested in helping its members to innovate. We set out to verify whether the needs of these smaller companies and the skills offered by PhDs could be matched in practice, and whether it was possible for the two parties to work together successfully when an "interpreter" was provided.

In this case, given that we were operating locally, the translator was a physical person: Eva Ratti, the FyD project manager, whose academic background complemented her colleagues' corporate experience. We set up trials with twelve companies, mediating short-term consultancy services focused on solving highly specific problems. Such short-term consultancy arrangements, potentially leading to longer-term collaboration, turned out to be of extreme interest to small enterprises and an excellent opportunity to demonstrate that researchers can be a valuable resource when it comes to analysing and solving real-life, practical problems. Thirty-six young researchers were recruited from all over Italy to take part in the project: all were post-docs or PhD graduates in different branches of physics, engineering, and materials science. Our "translator" was present at all meetings with the participating companies, and also acted as coordinator of the teams that we put together ad hoc to work on the individual company projects. At the end of each trial, we asked for feedback from the company and the team of PhDs, obtaining an extremely positive response from both parties. As a result, a permanent cooperation agreement has been established between Find Your Doctor and the industrial association that facilitated the test phase.

"They [the researchers] are not aliens after all" commented the production manager of one of the companies we worked with, to peers potentially interested in trying out the consultancy service: "Once you really get down to discussing the issue, we *do* speak the same language".

"We expected that only somebody senior would be able to tackle a complex problem like ours" said another: "On the contrary, the [researchers] who came to us were young, but they asked the right questions, they listened to us and were very helpful".

Furthermore, the contribution of the FyD mediator was represented as crucial. "She got them to speak to one another" was the comment.

Such positive feedback lent support to our idea that the expertise offered by researchers can be of value to small businesses too, and we believe that this will also prove to be true in other contexts, such as local government institutions, organisations and associations who might benefit from drawing on the expertise of PhD graduates in the humanities and social sciences to address issues of social innovation. The organisations in question "only" need to become aware of PhDs as a resource.

Narratives and the Web. Beyond Standard CVs: The Potential Offered by a Narrative Approach

Although the basic structure of our website is very similar to existing job-search portals, with companies and researchers both registering and browsing through each other's profiles and adverts, FyD differs from the standard in many ways.

First and foremost, we direct our efforts towards devising the most effective possible presentation of the PhDs' profiles and customising the search engine used by the companies to browse through them.

Here, in fact, the translation problem described in the previous paragraphs manifests itself in force: how is it possible to narrow down one's search to a single entry in a database of hundreds? Keywords are required, but which are the most appropriate?

Of course, nothing can replace an interview, which is an indispensable part of any selection process. Indeed, our aim is to obtain interview opportunities for the PhDs, despite the apparent discrepancy between the experience outlined in their CVs and the needs of the average employer. This entails shifting the focus from labelling the candidate's experience to unpacking the actions required to produce it, and the attitudes and modes of thinking underpinning successful completion of the actions.

We may take a stock sentence from research resumes as an example: "I have published several papers in major peer-reviewed journals" is a meaningful statement when applying for an academic position but likely meaningless in most other contexts. "I am able to write accurate reports in English, work cooperatively with others – including remotely, and mediate among different points of view; in addition, I have learned to take and give feedback constructively" presents the same experience in an entirely different light.

Another key factor in determining the suitability of a given person for a certain role or context is his/her set of values. "I have worked as tutor and lecturer in university courses" is understandable *per se*, but still not particularly meaningful to prospective employers unless they know what teaching implies or happen to be looking for a trainer. "I liked teaching because I value the sharing of knowledge and enjoy contact with people" tells a far more interesting story.

Of course, we could directly teach researchers how best to write their CVs and indeed we are currently working towards offering such training via our network. Meanwhile, however, we have designed the website in such a way as to elicit a first step in the right direction, by guiding our subscribers through the creation of their profiles.

More specifically, we have devised sets of questions that invite researchers to reflect on their professional experience to date by getting them to focus on areas that frequently involve transversal skills (see Blomeke et al., 2013) such as creativity and innovation, rigour, managing risk and uncertainty, communication and networking. We have chosen to offer jobseekers a narrative space rather than measuring their competences via online tests (despite the growing popularity of the latter approach). Candidates' responses are fully viewable on their FyD profiles, making for better communication with potential employers. We next plan to analyse these narrative texts with a view to identifying categories for mapping researchers' learning experience. This might be viewed as reversing the typical paradigm whereby those seeking employment are asked to describe their professional selves by choosing among a predefined set of categories, whose meaning may be unclear or perceived as not readily applicable to certain kinds of experience. In contrast, because those registering on the FyD website are invited to freely answer open questions, their accounts of their work experience may be organised into categories, creating a language that we ourselves will have defined and is therefore unambiguous to us. We plan to build this set of categories a-posteriori, following the methods of "constructivist" Grounded Theory (Charmaz, 2006) and working with computer scientists who are currently developing an experimental tool that will use the categories to construct an individualised multidimensional professional profile for each subscriber.

CONCLUSIONS

FindYourDoctor is, first and foremost, an attempt to support and promote researchers outside the boundaries of academia, and so to address a critical issue for the contemporary labour market:

> In the last two to three decades, socio-economic changes such as increasing global competition, the skill-biased technological change or the ageing of population have resulted in a labour market situation where it is difficult to find the right people for the right jobs. Skill mismatch has become a major concern as it proves to be pervasive, widespread and persistent in developed economies resulting on real costs on individuals, businesses and society as a whole. (Flisi et al., 2014, p. 78)

While extending the employment options available to PhDs is one of our aims, we do not view FyD as a mere 'talent fishing' agency for companies. We also intend it to offer a space of self-reflection and learning for all those on research career paths who may have doubts about continuing, for motivational, personal, practical, philosophical or any other reasons. A place to reflect on one's strengths and options, reviewing past experience in the context of a broader range of future possibilities, so that the admirable and challenging decision to pursue an academic career may be consciously made and not adopted by default as a highly costly Plan B. An opportunity that may contribute to "unsticking" professional careers (Field & Lynch, 2015) perceived as blocked or interrupted. To further this objective we organise seminars both inside and outside the university setting, with the collaboration of PhD schools (currently at the universities of Milan and Turin) and PhD associations.

The project is also designed to become a research space in which the different learning career paths undertaken by participants will help us to explore professional transitions (Fenwick, 2013) between academic and other work contexts. In particular, we are interested in unpacking the transferable skills that can facilitate the transition process. As a variety of scholars have noted, competency is a "floating signifier", indicating nothing more than "whatever employers want" (Lafer, 2004, p. 118). This critique will inform an in-depth investigation of the experience and expectations of both researchers and private companies, aimed at uncovering the variety of specific meanings and practical scenarios associated with the notion of transferable skills.

Finally, we are aware that all labour market issues are embedded in politics and power relations (Sawchuck, 2008). Many authors have warned about the risk of new institutional forms of control via the colonisation of informal learning (Hager & Hallyday, 2008) and new forms of governmentality (Andersson & Fejes, 2005; Fejes & Dahlsted, 2013). For example, the risk of being excluded from the job market encourages forms of self-discipline whereby subjects are willing to expose private aspects of themselves in the hopes that this will increase their perceived value (Fejes & Dahlsted, 2013). In light of this danger, we deliberately invite researchers to explore and present their professional practices and learning processes while avoiding an undue focus on the 'self', an approach that is often associated with testing. In any case, ethical considerations such as these constantly inform our work and decisions concerning the key boundaries that we need to enforce in order to protect the integrity and private sphere of our interlocutors.

REFERENCES

ADI. (2016). *VI Indagine Adi su dottorato e Post-Doc*. Retrieved from https://dottorato.it/sites/default/files/survey/vi-indagine-adi-postdoc.pdf

Andersson, P., & Fejes, A. (2005). Recognition of prior learning as a technique for fabricating the adult learner: A genealogical analysis on Swedish adult education policy. *Journal of Education Policy, 20*, 595–613.

Auriol, L., Misu, M., & Freeman, R. A. (2013). *Careers of doctorate holders: Analysis of labour market and mobility indicators* (OECD Science, Technology and Industry Working Papers, 2013/04). Paris: OECD Publishing.

Barnett, R. (2000). *Realising the university in an age of supercomplexity*. Buckingam: Open University Press.

Batzson, G. (1972). *Steps to an ecology of mind*. New York, NY: Ballantine Books.

Blomeke, S., Zlatkin-Troitschanskaia, O., Kuhn, C., & Fege, J. (Eds.). (2013). *Modelling and measuring competencies in higher education. Tasks and challenges*. Rotterdam, The Netherlands: Sense Publishers.

Brown, P., Green, A., & Lauder, H. (2001). *High skills: Globalisation, competitiveness and skill formation*. Oxford: Oxford University Press.

Boreham, N. (2004). A theory of collective competence: Challenging the neo-liberal individualisation of performance at work. *British Journal of Educational Studies, 52*(1), 5–17.

Borrell-Damian, L. (2009). *Collaborative doctoral education: University-industry partnerships for enhancing knowledge exchange*. Brussels: EUA.

CEDEFOP. (2010). *The skill matching challenge: Analysing skill mismatch and policy implications*. Luxembourg: Publications Office of the European Union.

Charmaz, K. (2006). *Constructing grounded theory: A practical guide through qualitative analysis*. London: Sage Publications.

Coffield, F. (2000). Introduction: A critical analysis of the concept of learning society. In F. Coffield (Ed.), *Different visions of learning society*. Bristol: Policy Press.

Cepollaro, G. (2008). *Le competenze non sono cose. Lavoro apprendimento, gestione dei collaboratori*. Milano: Guerini.

Collini, S. (2012). *What are universities for?* London: Penguin Books.

Eraut, M. (2000). Non-formal learning and tacit knowledge in professional work. *British Journal of educational Psychology, 70*, 113–136.

EC (European Commission). (2003). *Researchers in the European research area: One profession, multiple careers, communication from the commission to the council and the European parliament.* Retrieved from http://eur-lex.europa.eu/legal-content/en/ALL/?uri=CELEX:52003DC0436

ESF (European Science Foundation). (2009). *Research careers in Europe: Landscapes and horizons: A report by the ESF member organisation forum on research careers.* Strasbourg: ESF.

ESF (European Science Foundation). (2012). *Developing research careers in and beyond Europe: enabling – observing – guiding and going global: A report by the ESF member organisation forum 'European alliance on research career development.* Strasbourg: ESF.

ESF (European Science Foundation). (2013). *Research careers in Europe. Landscapes and horizons. A report by the ESF member organisation forum on research careers.* Strasbourg: ESF.

Fejes, A., & Dahlstedt, M. (2013). *The confessing society: Foucault, confession and practices of lifelong learning.* Abingdon: Routledge.

Fenwick, T. (2013). Understanding transitions in professional practice and learning: Towards new questions for research. *Journal of Workplace Learning, 25*(6), 352–367.

Field, J., & Lynch, H. (2015). Getting stuck, becoming unstuck: Agency, identity and transition between learning contexts. *Journal of Adult and Continuing Education, 21*, 3–17.

Flisi, S., Goglio, V., Meroni, E., Caetano Rodrigues, J., Rodrigues Ferro, M., & Vera Toscano, E. (2014). *Occupational mismatch in Europe: Understanding overeducation and overskilling for policy making.* Brussels: Publications Office of the European Union.

Fumasoli, T., Goastellec, G., & Kehm, B. M. (2015). *Academic work and careers in Europe, trends, challenges, perspectives.* Dordrecht: Springer.

Gergen, K. (1999). *An invitation to social construction.* London: Sage Publications.

Hager, P., & Hallyday, J. (2008). *Recovering informal learning: Wisdom, judgment and community* (Lifelong Learning Book Series, Vol. 7). Dordrecht: Springer.

Han, S. (2009). Competence: Commodification of human ability. In K. Illeris (Ed.), *International perspectives on competence development.* London: Routledge.

Illeris, K. (2009). Competence, learning and education: How can competences be learned, and how can they be developed in formal education? In K. Illeris (Ed.), *International perspectives on competence development.* London: Routledge.

Lafer, G. (2004). What is 'skill'? Training for discipline in the low-wage labour market. In C. Warhurst, I. Grugulis, & E. Keep (Eds.), *The skills that matter.* London: Palgrave Macmillan.

Lakoff, G., & Johnson, M. (1980). *Metaphors we live by.* Chicago, IL: University of Chicago Press.

Livingstone, D. W., & Guile, D. (Eds.). (2012). *The knowledge economy and lifelong learning: A critical reader.* Rotterdam, The Netherlands: Sense Publishers.

Mezirow, J. (2009). Transformative learning theory. In J. Mezirow & E. Taylor (Eds.), *Transformative learning in practice.* San Francisco, CA: Jossey-Brass.

Morin, E. (1995). *Introduction à la pensèe complexe.* Paris: Seuil.

OECD. (2011). *Education at a glance: OECD indicators.* Paris: OECD Publishing.

OECD. (2012). *Transferable skills training for researchers. Supporting career development and research.* Paris: OECD Publishing.

OECD. (2013). *Skills outlook 2013: First results from the survey of adult skills.* Retrieved from http://dx.doi.org/10.1787/9789264204256-en

OECD. (2016). *Education at a glance: OECD indicators.* Paris: OECD Publishing.

Olesen, H. S. (2013). Beyond the current political economy of competence development. *European Journal for Research on the Education and Learning of Adults, 4*(2), 153–170.

Olsen, M., Codd, J., & O'Neill, A. M. (2004). *Education policy: Globalisation, citizenship and democracy.* London: Sage Publications.

Rodriguez, D., Patel, R., Bright, A., Gregory, D., & Gowing, M. K. (2002). Developing competency models to promote integrated human resource practices. *Human Resource Management, 41*(3), 309–324.

Sandberg, J. (2000). Understanding human competence at work: An interpretative approach. *Academy of Management Journal, 43*(1), 9–25.

Sawchuk, P. H. (2008). Labour perspectives on the new politics of skill and competency formation: International reflections. *Asia Pacific Education Review, 9*(1), 1–15.

Scott, J. C. (2006). The Mission of the university: Medieval to postmodern transformations. *The Journal of Higher Education, 77*(1), 1–39.
Van der Weijden, I., Teelken, C., Drost, M., & De Boer, M. (2015). Career satisfaction of postdoctoral researchers in relation to their expectations for the future. *Higher Education, 72*, 25–40.
Vieira, J. (2005). Skill mismatches and job satisfaction. *Economics Letters, 89*(1), 39–47.
VITAE. (2009). *What do researchers do? First destinations of doctoral graduates by subject.* Cambridge: The Careers Research and Advisory Centre (CRAC).
VITAE. (2010). *What do researchers do? Doctoral graduate destinations and impact three years on.* Cambridge: The Careers Research and Advisory Centre (CRAC).
Warhurst, C., Grugulis, I., & Keep, E. (2004). *The skills that matter.* London: Palgrave Macmillan.

Andrea Galimberti
Bicocca University
Milan, Italy

Eva Ratti
C2t Consortium
Italy

MONIKA KASTNER

8. STIMULATING EMPOWERMENT AND SUPPORTING ACCESS TO LEARNING FOR FORMALLY LOW-QUALIFIED ADULTS

Potentials of Work-Related Competency Assessment in Social Enterprises

INTRODUCTION[1]

Learning through work bears significant potential for formally low-qualified workers (Bolder & Hendrich, 2000). This contribution describes the development of a work-related competency assessment procedure to be used in Social Enterprises. The validation and recognition of learning outcomes is crucial for educationally disadvantaged adults with a biography in the world of work. Being identified as formally low-qualified does not necessarily mean being low-skilled. Fostering and facilitating work-related learning is key to job-related development (labour skills) and self-development (personal stabilisation and life skills) for this group at risk. Taking a close look at knowledge, skills and competences can stimulate empowerment and support access to learning. Referring to Honneth's Theory of Recognition (2003), the competency assessment procedure aims at improving disadvantageous learning preconditions in terms of developing a positive learning identity. Furthermore, it aims at providing formally low-qualified adults with a basic vocational qualification, which is aligned with the development of a National Qualifications Framework in Austria, referring to the potential of Qualifications Frameworks as a contribution to an equal and permeable society (Blings & Ruth, 2012; Büchter, Dehnbostel, & Hanf, 2012).

WORKING AND LEARNING IN SOCIAL ENTERPRISES

This chapter focuses on an educational intervention for educationally disadvantaged adults. It presents the results of the R&D project *Competency Amelioration through Competency Assessment* (German project acronym: KOMKOM), funded by the Austrian Federal Ministry of Education (September 2011 to March 2015).[2] The KOMKOM project focused on formally low-qualified employees working in government-funded Social Enterprises. Social Enterprises are part of the Austrian active employment policy. They aim at the (re-)integration of the long-term unemployed into the labour market via temporary employment (instructed work and work-related learning), counselling and guidance, and the provision of additional seminars (for instance on literacy or on German as a second language). Work instructors and personnel developers provide guidance and support, which facilitates work-related and therefore practical learning. They can be found in different business sectors, such as the food service, retail, agriculture/gardening, or technical/craft-based services. There are about 200 Social Enterprises in Austria (Arbeit Plus, 2016).

Temporary employment in Social Enterprises offers various possibilities for gaining evidence from work for competency assessment. The KOMKOM competency assessment procedure was developed in collaboration with Social Enterprises and their umbrella organisation *Arbeit Plus*. We pursued two objectives within the KOMKOM project. One was to develop a flexible tool for competency assessment of employees (the so-called transit workers) in Social Enterprises. Second, we aligned this tool with level 1 and level 2 (these are the lowest levels) of the Austrian National Qualifications Framework (NQF). This project approach aims at social inclusion and participation through adult education.

The KOMKOM project builds on two projects funded by the European Union (EU). *SYSCOM – Systematic Competency Documentation in Social Integration Enterprises* (2009 to 2010) produced two results: Various tools already exist to document learning outcomes and validate prior learning. Social Enterprises should participate in the implementation of National Qualifications Frameworks in order to support their target groups (European Network of Social Integration Enterprises [ENSIE], 2015). Within the context of the second project, *NQF inclusive – Accreditation and certification of basic vocational education for disadvantaged people* (2009 to 2011), vocational qualifications have been developed on NQF levels 1 and 2 for people with disabilities (NQF inclusive, 2011).[3]

The KOMKOM competency assessment procedure provides an example of a basic qualification for technical/craft-based services (prototype) on a fundamental and, therefore, easily achievable level. The tool consists of several learning areas with learning outcomes and identification traits. It is designed for self-assessment and for the assessment by others. A validation conversation follows the assessments. In this setting, the employee and work instructor/personnel developer compare and discuss the results and jointly consider the next steps for learning/development. This procedure helps to identify existing knowledge, skills and competences. It provides evidence and a basis for individual development via work-related learning. The KOMKOM qualification has a pronounced vocational education approach suitable for adults with a biography in the world of work. Furthermore, the learning outcomes cover the whole spectrum, and go (far) beyond labour market skills. The procedure is intended to empower the (often falsely and misleadingly so-called) 'low-skilled' workers. Taking a very close look at their knowledge, skills and competences makes them visible. As a secondary consequence, this approach supports the development of a positive learning career, by revealing the capabilities they already possess and those they have recently acquired. The KOMKOM competency assessment is aligned with the Austrian National Qualifications Framework, which is based on the European Qualifications Framework (EQF). Defined KOMKOM learning outcomes correspond with NQF descriptors on level 1 and 2, allowing an official qualification (certificate) to be awarded prospectively. Opportunities of gaining horizontal labour mobility can be expected and access to (formal) qualifications would be a possibility in the future. The focus of the R&D follow-up project (planning stage) will be on studying various impacts of this educational intervention.

LITERATURE REVIEW

Theoretical Background

Honneth's Theory of Recognition (2003) provides the theoretical foundations for the KOMKOM approach, both from an individual and a societal perspective. Honneth (Frankfurt school) defined three patterns of intersubjective recognition: Love, Justice and Solidarity. Educational disadvantage is closely related to power, recognition, and respect. The validation and recognition of prior learning is a matter of respect, fairness and solidarity towards groups at risk. Competency assessment is about making individual capabilities visible. The recognition of non-formal and informal learning outcomes is crucial for formally low-qualified adults. In this regard, we refer to Honneth's concept of Love by taking a close look at the knowledge, skills and competences of formally low-qualified adults on an individual basis and in an encouraging and appreciative way. We argue that this approach modifies disadvantageous learning preconditions in terms of developing a positive learning identity. This can be seen as a precondition for participating in lifelong learning activities. Opening non-traditional ways of gaining valuable certificates via NQF is a matter of power, because it empowers groups at risk. Furthermore, the NQF is a revolutionary undertaking for Austria, since the formal educational sector is very strong and key players are very powerful. Opening non-traditional ways for learners via the learning outcomes approach is more akin to a revolution (and not a reform) for the Austrian educational system. In this regard, we refer to Honneth's concept of Justice. Finally, we understand Honneth's concept of Solidarity as represented in the Social Enterprises themselves, because they aim at a just and sustainable society. They represent networks of solidarity with shared values. The KOMKOM approach aims at supporting the Social Enterprises' specific learning environments provided for educationally disadvantaged transit workers.

Dehnbostel (2011) described Qualifications Frameworks and validation processes as located between '*Bildung*' (education) and economy. He analysed the sharp distinction between pedagogical approaches to support self-development on the one hand and assessment procedures to match occupational requirements and employees on the other. Referring to Dehnbostel, KOMKOM aimed at developing a validation procedure, which equally supports self-development and empowerment as well as employability, by providing a basic vocational qualification. Within KOMKOM we referred to the scientific debate on social inclusion, participation and adult education (Kronauer, 2010; Burtscher et al., 2013). We understood NQF level 1 and NQF level 2 as an entry opportunity for the educationally disadvantaged. KOMKOM aimed at providing a basic qualification (official certificate) on a fundamental and therefore easily achievable level for formally low-qualified workers who do not hold a formal vocational qualification. KOMKOM aimed at providing this group at risk (formally low-qualified unemployed/long-term unemployed) with a basic vocational qualification. Referring to Reutter (2010), we understood this as a contribution to social inclusion provided by adult/continuing education. The validation of learning outcomes is the main key to making individual capabilities visible. Within KOMKOM we argued that our approach could support the development of a positive learning career. The procedure is intended to empower the transit workers. Opportunities of gaining horizontal labour mobility, which means finding a (better) job, can be expected. Access to (formal) qualifications on upper NQF levels, based on the basic KOMKOM qualification, would be a possibility in the future.

Empirical Background

In its recommendation on the validation of non-formal and informal learning the Council of the European Union (2012) stated that 'disadvantaged groups, including individuals who are unemployed and those at risk of unemployment, are particularly likely to benefit from the validation arrangements, since validation can increase their participation in lifelong learning and their access to the labour market'. This assumption also emerged from the SYSCOM project, which served, as previously mentioned, as an important foundation for the KOMKOM project. If KOMKOM competency assessment procedures were widely in use, this assumption could be examined and would hopefully prove true for the formally low-qualified workers in Social Enterprises. Here, we refer (red) to the scientific debate on the potential of Qualifications Frameworks as a contribution to a just/equal and permeable society (Blings & Ruth, 2012; Büchter, Dehnbostel, & Hanf, 2012; cf. recently Gutschow, 2014).

The KOMKOM approach aims at formally low-qualified, severely disadvantaged adults, working in Social Enterprises. So, what does educational disadvantage mean in Austria? For KOMKOM we focused on formally low-qualified adults who had – at best – completed compulsory school (9 years). This is the lowest formal qualification and it is a general education, not a vocational education. According to labour market data, people with a low formal qualification are at risk of becoming and remaining unemployed (there is a risk of 24 per cent for this group compared to a risk of 7 per cent for those with an apprenticeship qualification). People without a formal qualification beyond compulsory schooling make up almost half of those registered as unemployed (47 per cent) with the Public Employment Service (Arbeitsmarktservice [AMS], 2015).

Bolder and Hendrich (2000) presented a highly relevant finding in their book *Fremde Bildungswelten*, which can be translated as '*strange educational worlds*':

formally low-qualified adults tend to maintain a certain distance to formalised continuing education settings such as seminars and training courses. The authors identified a certain connectivity of this target group to workplace learning and therefore to practical learning. This empirical finding further strengthens the bond between working and learning, which enables individual competency amelioration through work (cf. also Dehnbostel, 2007, 2010). In Social Enterprises, practical learning and work-based learning are fostered through practical instructions and concrete guidance, supported by Human Resources Development (HRD) measures. The KOMKOM procedure offers an evidence-based foundation for those measures, which are already in use in Social Enterprises. Validation and recognition of prior learning is part of the European educational policy. CEDEFOP's (European Centre for the Development of Vocational Training) guidelines for validating non-formal and informal learning define several routes from learning outcomes to certification. When it comes to assessment methods, "simulation and evidence extracted from work" (CEDEFOP, 2009, p. 62) are described. The Social Enterprises offer various possibilities for gaining evidence from work, e.g. observations, interviews, feedback. These methods of gaining evidence are incorporated in the KOMKOM procedure as well.

A recent evaluation study (over a period from 2005 to 2012) on Social Enterprises concerning the formal educational background showed that 56 per cent of the transit workers hold the lowest formal qualification, which is compulsory (and thereby general education) on the lower secondary level (Eppel et al., 2014, p. v). Included in this group are approximately 8 per cent who have not completed any kind of formal qualification at all. So, more than half of all transit workers do not hold a formal vocational education/training qualification (vocational track involves apprenticeship qualification or vocational school qualification [VET]). The evaluation study showed that transit workers with a higher formal qualification are more successful at re-integrating into the labour market (effectiveness). The authors argued for developing suitable learning facilities for the formally low-qualified transit workers and strengthening the bond between working and learning in Social Enterprises (ibid., p. xxxix). There is strong evidence for the adequacy of the KOMKOM approach.

European and National Policies on Education

The Austrian policies on education refer to the EU's policies. The member states have been instructed to develop national strategies for lifelong learning. The Austrian strategy for lifelong learning (Republik Österreich, 2011) includes 10 goals. One task is concerned with promoting and facilitating workplace learning. Another task aims at valuing informal and non-formal learning outcomes. This task is linked to the development of the National Qualifications Framework in Austria. The EQF is a translation tool that facilitates communication and comparison between the qualification systems of the 28 member states. The eight European reference levels are described in terms of learning outcomes: knowledge, skills and competences.

This allows any national qualifications systems, national qualifications frameworks and qualifications in Europe to relate to the EQF levels. Learners, graduates, providers and employers can use these levels to understand and compare qualifications awarded in different countries and by different education and training systems (European Commission, 2015a).

Austria does not have a tradition of recognising non-formal and informal learning outcomes. Consequently, the EQF was a stimulus to develop a NQF in Austria, which meant quite a shift in the national educational system, especially for the institutions of formal learning (in terms of their self-conception). As part of the development of the Austrian NQF, the national EQF referencing report (Federal Ministry of Education, Arts and Culture [BMUKK] & Federal Ministry of Science and Research [BMWF], 2011) was published. Procedures for referencing qualifications to the NQF needed to be developed. It was divided into three 'corridors': formal qualifications in corridor 1 (K1), non-formal learning outcomes in corridor 2 (K2) and informal learning outcomes in corridor 3 (K3). As a first step, criteria for referencing formal qualifications (K1) to the NQF have been developed (Nationale Koordinierungsstelle für den NQR in Österreich [NKS], 2011). The KOMKOM qualification was selected to be referenced to the NQF as a qualification in the non-formal learning corridor (Tritscher-Archan et al., 2013). The KOMKOM qualification successfully passed through this national simulation procedure. The Austrian Federal Ministry of Education initiated a national consultation process on the validation of non-formal and informal learning, concerning goals, measures, organisational structures and standards for the validation of learning outcomes (Bundesministerium für Bildung und Frauen [BMBF], 2015). By the end of 2015, a legislative proposal on a federal law on the NQF has been published (Republik Österreich, 2015). The adoption of the NQF-Act by the National Council and Federal Council gave the NQF in Austria a legal foundation in March 2016. The act regulates the mapping process and enables further implementation of the NQF in Austria (Republik Österreich, 2016; NKS, 2016).

METHODS: DEVELOPING THE KOMKOM APPROACH

Guiding Principles

When it comes to educationally disadvantaged adults, or more precisely, formally low-qualified workers, the list of significant questions includes the following: Are these adults capable of MORE than their certificates (if they hold any at all) prove? What EXACTLY are they capable of? As noted above, more than half of all transit workers have only completed compulsory education at most, and have not gained a formal vocational qualification. Nevertheless, being seen or identified as formally low-qualified does not necessarily mean being low-skilled. Therefore, it is crucial to document any kind of knowledge, skills and competences. Temporary employment in Social Enterprises offers the possibility of competency assessment. The validation of learning outcomes is the main key to making individual capabilities visible. Qualifications Frameworks as described above provide the basis for this approach. The most important principle of the EQF is the learning outcomes approach. The learning outcomes approach shifts focus to what knowledge, skills and competences the learner has acquired by the end of the learning process (European Commission, 2015b). The references for the KOMKOM qualification are NQF levels 1 and 2. In the Austrian EQF Referencing Report those two levels are defined as in Figures 1 and 2 (BMUKK & BMWF, 2011).

A main principle guiding the definition of KOMKOM learning outcomes was the objective of *inclusion*. EVERY person working in a Social Enterprise would be able to reach level 1, so none would be in danger of being excluded. Level 1 was understood as an entry opportunity for the educationally disadvantaged, and this door needs to be wide open. The key to inclusion was encapsulated in the following statement, which expresses the expected amount of support and autonomy granted on level 1: "In his/her field of work or study he/she is able to deal with simple situations under given framework conditions and with corresponding assistance" (cf. Figure 1). With a sufficient amount of support and time, every single identification trait within the KOMKOM competency assessment is achievable by everyone. So ultimately, level 1 would really work as an entry into the Austrian NQF.

Within KOMKOM we aimed at providing an evidence-based foundation for daily work (e.g. work instructions and HRD) in Social Enterprises. Nota bene the KOMKOM qualification procedure works on a voluntary basis, it is meant to be an offer within the Social Enterprises. This corresponds fully with CEDEFOP's guidelines "that the process of making visible the full range of knowledge, skills and competences held by an individual is carried out in a way that remains voluntary and that the results of validation remain the property of the individual" (CEDEFOP, 2009, p. 50). When a new employee has her/his first interview in the Social Enterprise, she/he is provided with information about the possibility to participate in the KOMKOM assessment procedure. As such, the suggestion to participate is embedded within guidance and HRD measures.

During the national simulation procedure for the non-formal learning corridor (K2), the KOMKOM team consistently argued that the required knowledge- and skills-level on level 1 has been set too high in the Austrian EQF Referencing Report (see Figure 1), and individuals therefore could be excluded. Here, KOMKOM acted as an advocate for the formally low-qualified. Rethinking the descriptors on level 1 has been a learning drawn from the national simulation procedure, based on the KOMKOM input. However, the realisation of a possible redefinition of descriptors remains pending and is actually unlikely to come to fruition.

One crucial aspect is the required fundamental knowledge of reading, writing, arithmetic and use of modern information and communication technologies, especially on level 1 (that should work as an easily achievable entry into the NQF).

	EQF descriptors	NQF descriptors
KNOWLEDGE	Basic general knowledge	He/she has • elementary-level general education, including fundamental knowledge of reading, writing, arithmetic and use of modern information and communication technologies • knowledge about social norms and values • knowledge about the accepted and common ways of behaving in everyday situations • an insight into the world of work and occupations, which enables him/her to make a decision on the educational and professional career • the ability to acquire available knowledge independently • knowledge which enables transfer to further school-based education or training at the upper secondary level
SKILLS	Basic skills required to carry out simple tasks	In his/her field of work or study he/she is able to • communicate properly using language, participate in discussions and share his/her views • deal with simple everyday activities under given framework conditions with the use of literacy and numeracy skills • look for different possible solutions to simple problems, select the appropriate solution and use this to carry out the task • gather basic information about simple themes from common, including computer-aided sources, form a subject-related and value-oriented opinion and take up a corresponding stance • develop his/her own position on issues which affect him/her using social norms and values as a basis • take part in social events and find his/her own role within a community
COMPETE	Work or study under direct supervision in a structured context	In his/her field of work or study he/she is able to • deal with simple situations under given framework conditions and with corresponding assistance

Figure 1. Austrian NQF descriptors level 1 (ibid., p. 55)

STIMULATING EMPOWERMENT AND SUPPORTING ACCESS TO LEARNING

		He/she has
KNOWLEDGE	Basic factual knowledge of a field of work or study	• a sound general education • knowledge of fundamental business connections • basic knowledge of the structure of the labour market and how it works • elementary-level previous professional qualifications in a specific field • knowledge which enables transfer to further school-based or vocational education or training
SKILLS	Basic cognitive and practical skills required to use relevant information in order to carry out tasks and to solve routine problems using simple rules and tools	In his/her field of work or study he/she is able to • use given instruments, methods and procedures appropriately • cope with simple routine tasks autonomously • deal with simple standard challenges independently • develop certain independent and logical thought • actively take part in discussions on familiar themes and take up his/her own viewpoint • understand and use information to fulfil his/her tasks from given sources • present facts and circumstances from his/her experience orally and in writing using the correct standard language
COMPETENCE	Work or study under supervision with some autonomy	In his/her field of work or study he/she is able to • act autonomously in simple situations • cope with simple challenges under given framework conditions and with a certain amount of assistance • successfully deal with new, more specific activities with corresponding support and guidance in order to develop the self-confidence required to take on more extensive tasks

Figure 2. Austrian NQF descriptors level 2 (ibid., p. 55)

Possessing this 'fundamental' amount of knowledge cannot be seen as given, as the PIAAC results (Programme for the International Assessment of Adult Competencies) for Austria revealed (Organisation for Economic Co-operation and Development [OECD], 2013). Showing a low proficiency in literacy, numeracy, and problem solving in technology-rich environments is closely related with holding the formal lowest qualification (compulsory education at most), but low proficiency is also found within the group that has gained an apprenticeship certification (Kastner & Schlögl, 2014). Within the KOMKOM assessment procedure, basic skills (reading, writing, numeracy, and ICT skills) have been included as work-related skills and life skills, which deserve and need to be developed.

As mentioned above, practical, work-related learning is seen as suitable for educationally disadvantaged adults. Their learning experiences are closely connected with school, and (quite often) with painful or unpleasant memories. Such conditions do not support a positive attitude towards further learning. Within the KOMKOM assessment procedure, 'learning to learn' is therefore included as a learning outcome. The aim is to help to develop a positive learning career, and gain self-esteem with respect to learning. The KOMKOM procedure aims at building capacities.

Research-Based Development

The KOMKOM competency assessment procedure was developed in collaboration with several Social Enterprises and their umbrella organisation *Arbeit Plus*. Different research methods and development methods were applied:

- Literature study on the state of the art regarding competency discourses and on assessment procedures for the disadvantaged, mainly for people with disabilities
- Questionnaires sent out to Social Enterprises: which tools are already in use and what are the requirements concerning a new tool for competency assessment
- Working groups with invited experts: discussions of facts and approaches (for instance with P. Dehnbostel)
- Observations in several Social Enterprises: workplaces, requirements, instructions
- Definition of learning outcomes and identification traits according to the NQF descriptors ('translating' these requirements) and based on the preliminary work (various prototypes/redefinition)
- Testing of prototypes with learners and work instructors/personnel developers in several Social Enterprises
- Focus groups with relevant stakeholders
- Presentations of steps and findings in relevant groups (learners, work instructors/personnel developers)
- Presentation of steps and findings at conferences and in publications, using both channels for science-to-science communication and those for science-to-professionals communication

RESULTS: THE KOMKOM PROCEDURE

The KOMKOM Assessment: Tool and Process

The KOMKOM procedure can be used at least twice during a period of temporary employment (six to twelve months). First, at the beginning of the employment, in order to assess the starting point in terms of documentation of existing capabilities. A second time at the end, in order to assess the competency amelioration, while an optional third assessment can be scheduled sometime around the middle of the employment period (in terms of assessing recently developed knowledge, skills and competences, and of documenting progress). The assessment procedure consists of self-assessment and assessment by the work instructors/personnel developers, followed by a validation conversation. The aim is to provide evidence for further work-related development and self-development. Individual development achieved during the employment becomes visible and provides a valid basis for further steps, e.g. concrete work instructions, HRD measures, and suitable seminars (if required).

The prototype assessment tool for the technical/craft-based services consists of 70 learning outcomes based on approximately 200 identification traits. The learning outcomes are defined for 14 areas, which are assigned to the three main competences:

Professional and method competence: vocational knowledge and skills; profession-related arithmetic; basic and work-related ICT competence; work-related literacy (oral expression, writing); knowledge and skills for dealing with working life & labour market requirements;

Social and communicative competence: knowledge and skills for teamwork, communication, and participation; ability to handle and express criticism; diversity competence;

Personal competence: ability to accept responsibility; organizational competence; ability to deal with work-related problems and every-day-life challenges; learning to learn.

Assessment involves the rating of identification traits. The wording in the four different answer categories depends on the wording in the identification traits (knowing, doing something). In general, the categorisation works as follows:

Table 1. Rating categories

Major learning need	NQF level 1	NQF level 2	Beyond NQF level 2
I still have to learn this.	With a lot of support, I am able to …	With a little support, I am able to …	No support necessary, I am perfectly able to …

The employees use the tool for self-assessment. It runs on a tablet computer. The tool uses Easy-to-Read language. There is a voice output in German for those who like to listen and prefer not to read, which also works as a support for improving reading skills in German. The categorisation of the identification traits works by answering by selecting buttons with icons (rating). The four rating categories make learning needs visible. The tool provides a colour guidance system, and it shows information about the progress.

The work instructors/personnel developers perform the assessments of the employees on a PC. Each learning outcome is furnished with its identification traits as a reminder of what exactly is covered by each learning outcome during the rating.

A validation conversation follows the self-assessment and the assessment by others. The tool produces a comparison document, where the employee's rating and employer's rating are printed side by side. This is the pedagogical moment, where self-assessment results and the work instructor's/personnel developer's view are put together and discussed in an encouraging way. This is the place to compare the two views regarding the employee's knowledge, skills and competences. Understanding differing results can be seen as a contribution to developing a realistic and positive self-concept, because over-estimation (and more likely) under-estimation can be indicative of a weak self-concept. The focus during the validation conversation is on the individual's strengths and achievements, and on potential for (further) improvement and development. The identification traits help to specify work instructions and HRD measures: where exactly is the learning need, what exactly needs to be trained to achieve this learning outcome in terms of agreeing upon future steps to take. We suppose that all in all the documentation of existing capabilities and recently developed learning outcomes is a positive learning experience.

The KOMKOM Qualification: NQF Certificate and Its Supplement

As it stands at the moment, the KOMKOM assessment tool provides a basic qualification for technical/craft-based services (prototype). The assessed learning outcomes are the foundations for awarding a NQF certificate, in the best scenario for NQF level 2. The aim is that, within a period of temporary employment, an employee would be able to develop her/his knowledge, skills and competences up to NQF level 2 (or even better in some learning areas). The decision about whether to gain a NQF certificate or not is accompanied and guided by the work instructors and personnel developers. It should not be awarded automatically.

If an employee wants to acquire a NQF certificate, the ultimate assessment by others is carried out by two work instructors/personnel developers (double verification principle). Again, a concluding validation conversation follows self-assessment and assessment by others. Finally, a NQF certificate with detailed information and the personalised supplement can be printed. The NQF certificate and its supplement name the qualification (for the prototype: basic qualification for technical/craft-based services), and a summary of the learning outcomes within the 14 learning areas is listed and described, and references to the particular NQF level are specified. Learning areas with high scores (beyond NQF level 2) are placed at the top of the supplement, followed by the learning areas where level 2 was achieved, (if relevant) followed by the learning areas where level 1 was achieved. The certificate also provides information about the Austrian NQF (level 1 to level 4).

Prospectively, a NQF certificate would be an official qualification for technical/craft-based services (and others to follow), which is referenced to the NQF. This certificate documents learning outcomes, and could therefore work as a link to continuing education and the formal VET system, given that lifelong guidance for the educationally disadvantaged is thus (further) improved in Austria. In the meantime, the document works as a valid and conclusive certificate of employment and serves as a detailed job reference.

CONCLUSION & FUTURE PROSPECTS

Findings so far and future prospects are closely connected. A follow-up R&D project is in preparation. In the meantime, a Social Enterprise included the KOMKOM procedure within a new project for formally low-qualified adults (offering training for building and repair service). In 2017, this cooperation will provide the opportunity to evaluate the KOMKOM procedure and it will enable to answer some of the following questions.[4]

Future Project Steps

The follow-up project includes different work packages.

- A training course for work instructors and personnel developers in Social Enterprises is to be developed. The KOMKOM tool is expandable and adjustable, which means that learning outcomes and identification traits can be adapted (to a certain extent) to the particular Social Enterprise. The definition of learning outcomes that refer to the NQF correctly requires training. Furthermore, the training course aims at improving adult educational professionalisation. Participants learn to conduct the validation conversation, e.g. name and discuss strengths and learning needs, and to agree upon future work-related steps to take. Of course, all of this is based on prevailing guidance principles for the educationally disadvantaged (Gieseke, 2014).
- Learning outcomes for agriculture/gardening, based on the KOMKOM prototype, have been defined already, and further learning outcomes for other occupational fields are to be defined (service sector: food service, retail). The KOMKOM approach could be suitable for other occupational fields, where work-related learning takes place, e.g. sheltered employment for people with disabilities or employment/learning facilities in prisons.
- The KOMKOM qualification for technical/craft-based services needs to be developed for NQF level 3. This is the missing link to an apprenticeship qualification (NQF level 4; cf. BMUKK & BMWF, 2011, p. 58). An apprenticeship qualification is a significant formal vocational qualification, and there are currently almost 200 different apprenticeships in Austria. Level 3 needs more profound

vocational differentiation within the learning outcomes. It has to be defined with a more strategic direction towards one or more apprenticeships to secure a certain amount of connectivity towards an extraordinary apprenticeship examination.
- Furthermore, there are plans to provide the users not only with the voice output in German to support reading skills in German. Voice output in other languages, which are widely in use in Austria because of immigration would also be necessary.
- A main work package of this follow-up is to test and improve the KOMKOM assessment procedure (evaluation). We need to know how useful the KOMKOM procedure is for the work instructors and personnel developers in their daily work in Social Enterprises. How good is the usability? Is it a valid procedure? Does it provide personnel with a valid basis for identifying appropriate measures?

Studying the Impacts of KOMKOM

We need to study the various impacts of the KOMKOM procedure as an educational intervention. The framework for this accompanying research will be the findings presented as the theoretical and empirical backgrounds of the KOMKOM R&D project (see above). Main research questions will be the following:

- We assume that the assessment procedure provides the employees with positive learning experiences and enables the development of a positive learning career (empowering the ability to learn, building capacities). The procedure could therefore help to select and engage in continuing education.
- We assume that the assessment procedure helps individuals to cope (better and more successfully) with job interviews, because (future) employees are able to name individual and work-related knowledge, skills and competences, based on identification traits and learning outcomes they became used to talking about in the validation conversations. Reporting about past learning progress and strengths in a structured way could be helpful in job-application situations.
- We assume that educationally disadvantaged groups will welcome an official NQF-related certificate. Schools on the lower secondary level place emphasis on general education. Meanwhile, the KOMKOM qualification has a pronounced vocational education approach, which is more suitable for adults with many years of experience of life, including work. Furthermore, within the KOMKOM target group, there are adults who have attended a special needs school or who have left compulsory education with a negative final report. Presenting such reports in job interviews is degrading and insulting. Furthermore, within the KOMKOM target group there are adults who have completed a prevocational school (one year to fulfil compulsory education), but this certificate is not highly esteemed. A neutral and basic vocational qualification via the NQF could be helpful for those who lack valuable certificates.
- We need to know how (future) employers assess the KOMKOM qualification (NQF certificate and supplement). Do they appreciate the learning outcomes approach and regard the detailed certificate as helpful in job interviews? Does a

KOMKOM certificate provide sufficient information about managing future job requirements successfully? Is the KOMKOM certificate seen as a positive signal within the labour market?
- Finally, regarding the KOMKOM approach, which means using the NQF for inclusion (Kastner, 2016), we need to study if the Austrian NQF has the potential to include the educationally disadvantaged via validation and recognition of learning outcomes acquired outside the formal educational system.

NOTES

[1] A slightly different version of this topic was presented at the 9th International Conference on Researching Work & Learning, 8–12 December 2015 in Singapore, entitled *Promoting learning through work for formally low-qualified workers*.
[2] R&D made possible thanks to the Federal Ministry of Education, Department of Adult Education. Special thanks go to Gabriela Khannoussi-Gangoly for her unwavering interest in the KOMKOM project.
[3] The KOMKOM project was developed and carried out by the Austrian SYSCOM coordinator Hedwig Presch, psychologist and expert for labour market/work and learning; the NQF inclusive lead Marion Bock, educationalist, project developer and manager at 'Chance B', a provider of social services; Irmgard Kaufmann-Kreutler, expert for adult literacy, low-threshold adult education, and technical vocational training for women; Monika Kastner, educationalist and education researcher (KOMKOM lead). Many thanks go to my KOMKOM colleagues Marion, Irmgard and Hedwig, for it is always a pleasure to work with you and learn from you.
[4] Information can be retrieved from www.komkom.at (currently only available in German).

REFERENCES

Note: Internet references most recently retrieved and verified on December 22, 2016.

AMS. (2015). *Arbeitsmarkt & Bildung. Jahr 2014*. Retrieved from http://www.ams.at/_docs/001_am_bildungJahr2014.pdf

Arbeit Plus. (2016). *Association of social enterprises in Austria: A network of social entrepreneurs*. Retrieved from http://arbeitplus.at/english/

Blings, J., & Ruth, K. (Eds.). (2012). *Transparenz und Durchlässigkeit durch den EQR? Perspektiven zur Implementierung*. Bielefeld: Bertelsmann.

BMBF. (2015). *Konsultationsdokument. Validierung nicht-formalen und informellen Lernens. Entwicklung einer nationalen Strategie zur Umsetzung der Ratsempfehlung vom 20.12.2012 (2012/C/398/01)*. Retrieved from http://www.bildung.erasmusplus.at/fileadmin/lll/dateien/lebenslanges_lernen_pdf_word_xls/nqr/EQF_Advisory_Group_Meetings/Validierung_non_formalen_und_informellen_Lernens/Konsultationspapier__Beilage.pdf

BMUKK & BMWF. (2011). *Austrian EQF referencing report*. Retrieved from https://ec.europa.eu/ploteus/documentation#documentation_73

Bolder, A., & Hendrich, W. (2000). *Fremde Bildungswelten. Alternative Strategien lebenslangen Lernens*. Opladen: Leske+Budrich.

Burtscher, R., Ditschek, E. J., Ackermann, K.-E., Kil, M., & Kronauer, M. (Eds.). (2013). *Zugänge zu Inklusion. Erwachsenenbildung, Behindertenpädagogik und Soziologie im Dialog*. Bielefeld: Bertelsmann.

Büchter, K., Dehnbostel, P., & Hanf, G. (Eds.). (2012). *Der Deutsche Qualifikationsrahmen (DQR). Ein Konzept zur Erhöhung von Durchlässigkeit und Chancengleichheit im Bildungssystem?* Bielefeld: Bertelsmann.

CEDEFOP. (2009). *European guidelines for validating non-formal and informal learning*. Luxembourg: Office for Official Publications of the European Communities.

Council of the European Union. (2012). *Council recommendation of 20 December 2012 on the validation of non-formal and informal learning (2012/C 398)*. Retrieved from http://eur-lex.europa.eu/legal-content/EN/TXT/?uri=CELEX:32012H1222(01)
Dehnbostel, P. (2007). *Lernen im Prozess der Arbeit*. Münster: Waxmann.
Dehnbostel, P. (2010). *Betriebliche Bildungsarbeit. Kompetenzbasierte Aus- und Weiterbildung im Betrieb*. Baltmannsweiler: Schneider Verlag Hohengehren.
Dehnbostel, P. (2011). Qualifikationsrahmen: Lernergebnisorientierung und Outcomeorientierung zwischen Bildung und Ökonomie. *Magazin erwachsenenbildung.at. Das Fachmedium für Forschung, Praxis und Diskurs, 14*, 05-1–05-11 (E-Journal). Retrieved from http://erwachsenenbildung.at/magazin/archiv_artikel.php?mid=5847&aid=5850
ENSIE. (2015). *SYSCOM: Systematic competency documentation in social integration enterprises*. Retrieved from http://www.ensie.org/syscom
Eppel, R., Horvath, T., Lackner, M., Mahringer, H., Hausegger, T., Hager, I., Reidl, C., Reiter, A., Scheiflinger, S., & Friedl-Schafferhans, M. (2014). *Evaluierung von Sozialen Unternehmen im Kontext neuer Herausforderungen. Evaluierung im Auftrag des Bundesministeriums für Arbeit, Soziales und Konsumentenschutz durch WIFO – Österreichisches Institut für Wirtschaftsforschung und prospect Unternehmensberatung GesmbH*. Retrieved from http://www.wifo.ac.at/publikationen?detail-view=yes&publikation_id=50690
European Commission. (2015a). *Learning opportunities and qualifications in Europa: Find information on the EQF, NQF's*. Retrieved from https://ec.europa.eu/ploteus/search/site?f[0] =im_field_entity_type%3A97#
European Commission. (2015b). *How does the EQF work?* Retrieved from https://ec.europa.eu/ploteus/content/how-does-eqf-work
Gieseke, W. (2014). Konzept- und Strukturanforderungen für die Beratung von gering Qualifizierten. In Projektträger im DLR (Ed.), *Kompetenzen von gering Qualifizierten. Befunde und Konzepte* (pp. 89–100). Bielefeld: Bertelsmann.
Gutschow, K. (2014). Chancen der Kompetenzanerkennung für gering Qualifizierte. In Projektträger im DLR (Ed.), *Kompetenzen von gering Qualifizierten. Befunde und Konzepte* (pp. 33–46). Bielefeld: Bertelsmann.
Honneth, A. (2003). *Kampf um Anerkennung. Zur moralischen Grammatik sozialer Konflikte*. Frankfurt am Main: Suhrkamp.
Kastner, M. (2016). Inklusion durch Erwachsenenbildung – mehr als nur eine utopische Hoffnung? Eine Bildungsintervention für formal gering qualifizierte Erwachsene im Kontext des Nationalen Qualifikationsrahmens. *bwp@ Berufs- und Wirtschaftspädagogik Online*, Ausgabe 30 (E-Journal). Retrieved from http://www.bwpat.de/ausgabe30/kastner_bwpat30.pdf
Kastner, M., & Schlögl, P. (2014). Fundamente gesellschaftlicher Teilhabe. Neues empirisches Wissen aus der PIAAC-Erhebung zu den unteren Kompetenzniveaus. In Statistik Austria (Ed.), *Schlüsselkompetenzen von Erwachsenen. Vertiefende Analysen der PIAAC-Erhebung 2011/12* (pp. 256–278). Wien: Statistik Austria.
Kronauer, M. (Ed.). (2010). *Inklusion und Weiterbildung. Reflexionen zur gesellschaftlichen Teilhabe in der Gegenwart*. Bielefeld: Bertelsmann.
NKS. (2011). *Handbuch für die Zuordnung von formalen Qualifikationen zum Nationalen Qualifikationsrahmen (NQR) – Kriterien*. Wien: Nationale Koordinierungsstelle für den NQR in Österreich (NKS).
NKS. (2016). *Development of the NQF in Austria*. Retrieved from https://www.qualifikationsregister.at/public/Entwicklung#
NQF inclusive. (2011). *Accreditation and certification of basic vocational education for disadvantaged people via NQF*. Retrieved from http://www.nqfinclusive.org/index.php?l=1
OECD. (2013). *OECD skills outlook 2013: First results from the survey of adult skills*. Paris: OECD Publishing.
Republik Österreich. (2011). *LLL:2020. Strategie zum lebensbegleitenden Lernen in Österreich*. Retrieved from http://www.esf.at/esf/wp-content/uploads/LLL-Strategiepapier_20111.pdf

Republik Österreich. (2015). *Ministerialentwurf betreffend ein Bundesgesetz über den Nationalen Qualifikationsrahmen (NQR-Gesetz)*. Retrieved from http://www.parlament.gv.at/PAKT/VHG/XXV/ME/ME_00152/index.shtml

Republik Österreich. (2016). *Bundesgesetz über den Nationalen Qualifikationsrahmen (NQR-Gesetz)*. Retrieved from https://www.ris.bka.gv.at/GeltendeFassung.wxe?Abfrage=Bundesnormen&Gesetzesnummer=20009496

Reutter, G. (2010). Inklusion durch Weiterbildung – für Langzeitarbeitslose eine utopische Hoffnung? In M. Kronauer (Ed.), *Inklusion und Weiterbildung. Reflexionen zur gesellschaftlichen Teilhabe in der Gegenwart* (pp. 59–101). Bielefeld: Bertelsmann.

Tritscher-Archan, S. et al. (2013). *NQR K2-Simulationsphase. Provisorische QVS und wissenschaftliche Begleitung, im Auftrag des Bundesministeriums für Unterricht, Kunst und Kultur* (unpublished).

Monika Kastner
Alpen-Adria-Universität Klagenfurt
Austria

CAMILLA THUNBORG AND AGNIESZKA BRON

9. POLICIES FOR EQUALITY AND EMPLOYABILITY

Consequences for Non-Traditional Students in Sweden

The general picture in Sweden, as elsewhere, is that higher education (HE) graduates have better chances to become employed than people with a lower educational level. Sweden has had a long tradition of including non-traditional students into HE by widening access, building new higher education institutions, and upgrading post-secondary education to tertiary education (SOU, 2015; Thunborg & Bron, 2012). The number of HE graduates has increased dramatically as a result of these changes.

During the recent decade, and in accordance with EU and national policies, issues of employability have become politically important. Fejes (2010) claims, that the shift from employment to employability means a shift in responsibility from society and the labour market towards the individual. HE institutions (HEI) are also seen as responsible for enhancing or developing the appropriate competencies of individual students (SOU, 2015). The match between the supply of educational graduates and the requirements and demands of the labour market has thereby become a market model for measuring HE effects. The policy for widening access of non-traditional students and the policy of employability can, on the one hand, be regarded as two strategies for enhancing social mobility. But, on the other hand, the two policies do not seem to be related to each other. For example, when studying policy documents, we cannot find any special concern for non-traditional students in relation to employability.

Thus, in this article we want to address the relation between issues of equality and employability, especially regarding their consequences for Swedish non-traditional students. Our interest in this question derives from our involvement in the European Erasmus+ project called EMPLOY Enhancing the Employability of Non-Traditional Students in HE in which six countries are taking part (2014-1-UK01-KA203-001842-TP).

By non-traditional students we mean, in the broadest sense, under-represented groups participating in HE (Bron & Lönnheden, 2004). In this chapter as elsewhere (Finnegan, Merrill, & Thunborg, 2014), when writing about non-traditional students we refer to mature as well as young adult students that are the first in their family to enter HE in Sweden (see Thunborg, Bron, & Edström, 2012). However, in this text we focus particularly on social class and ethnicity. When writing about social class we refer to parents' educational level as used in Swedish official statistics. When using ethnicity, we refer to, on the one hand, students born outside Sweden or with both parents born outside Sweden, which in official statistics are called students with an international background. On the other hand, and in comparison, students with a Swedish background are defined as students born in Sweden or with at least one parent born in Sweden.

In this chapter we present firstly the Swedish policies for both widening access as well as employability. Secondly, we map the participation of non-traditional students in HE with regard to social class and ethnicity based on the official Swedish statistics. Thirdly, we describe the demand and supply for the labour market, and finally analyse the employability from the perspective of non-traditional students.

The way to approach our inquiry and be able to discuss, on the one hand, the match between students' demands and patterns of participation in HE, and on the other, the requirements and demands of the labour market and society, we rely on official Swedish statistics from the Swedish Higher Education Authority for HE (UKÄ, 2013, 2014, 2015) and policy documents from the State authorities (Utbildningsdepartementet, 2012, 2014, 2015).

SWEDISH HIGHER EDUCATION POLICIES CONCERNING WIDENING ACCESS AND EMPLOYABILITY

In the European comparative reports two perspectives of employability are used for analysing policies of employability in different countries; a competence-based and an employment-based perspective. Employability in Sweden according to these reports is defined from a competence-based perspective, focusing on students' skills in relation to the needs of the labour market and society (Eurydice, 2014; Yorke, 2006). There is, however, no clear definition of employability presented by the UKÄ which is executing the state's policies for HE (formulated by the Ministry of Higher Education). In the UKÄ reports, one way of measuring employability is related to students' establishment in the labour market one to two years after the award of qualifications within the area for the graduate degree (UKÄ, 2013).

From the political point of view, HE is seen as a means for both securing employment opportunities for graduates as well as making society more equal by widening participation. The tradition of widening access for non-traditional students in HE is still a central goal, together with a new emphasis on making HE graduates employable in the labour market. Reforms aiming to widen access began in the 1950, but became a central issue in policy reforms from 1977, 1993 and 2007 (SOU, 2015).

According to the Ministry of Higher Education the supply of HE programmes should be related to both student demands and the needs of the labour market (Utbilningsdepartementet: U2012/6996SAM). Thus, new programmes created by HEIs need to take these two aspects into consideration. In line with this, the Swedish government set up a committee to investigate whether the supply of educational programmes are well matched in relation to the demands for quality, from students' perspective and the needs of the labour market, as well as society (Utbildningsdepartementet: Kommittédirektiv, diarienummer: 2014, p. 54). A year later the Government Official Report was ready and named *Higher education under twenty years* (SOU, 2015, p. 70). An overall conclusion in this report is that the match between students' choices of educational programmes and the needs of the labour market is sufficient, with teacher education as an exception. The report, however, is not covering issues regarding non-traditional students.

INEQUALITIES CONCERNING SOCIAL CLASS AND PARTICIPATION IN HIGHER EDUCATION IN SWEDEN

Despite the reforms for widening participation in HE, inequalities concerning social class persist. According to UKÄ (2014) students, with parents without third cycle education, are less represented in HE than other students. According to UKÄ (2015):

> A total of 44 per cent of those born in 1988 had begun to study in higher education by the age of 25. But for those with at least one parent with a research qualification (licentiate or doctoral degree) the initial participation rate was considerably higher – 84 per cent. In comparison, a mere 22 per cent of those whose parents had only completed lower-secondary education had begun higher education studies. (UKÄ, 2015, p. 26)

Moreover, there are still social differences relating to the choices of educational programmes (ibid):

> A larger proportion of those whose parents have advanced educational qualifications choose long programmes. Some examples are programmes in medicine (where 70 per cent of HE entrants in the academic year of 2011/2012 had parents with advanced educational qualifications, Bachelor's programmes in law (55 per cent) and Master's programmes in engineering (54 per cent). In programmes leading to the award of general qualifications students whose parents have advanced educational qualifications are more likely to study for a Master's degree (50 per cent in the academic year of 2011/2012). (UKÄ, 2014, p. 25)

It is, thus, interesting to find out what programmes students with parents having lower educational level, choose. According to UKÄ (2015) vocational teacher training is considered to have the highest degree of students having parents with a low educational level, namely 47 per cent of the students. Even pre-school teacher training has a high proportion of students with parents having a low educational level, thus 41 per cent.

However, it should be added that vocational teachers are already non-traditional as they worked as craftsman and skill workers before applying to HE.

C. THUNBORG & A. BRON

INEQUALITIES CONCERNING ETHNICIY REGARDING PARTICIPATIION IN HIGHER EDUCATION IN SWEDEN

From our analysis of national statistics concerning ethnicity, it appears that the number of students from an international background has increased in the last ten years. The overall differences concerning ethnicity is according to UKÄ (2015) small with 41 per cent of those with an international background, i.e. students born in another country than Sweden or with both parents born outside Sweden, compared to 44 per cent of students born in Sweden and with both or at least one parent born in Sweden. However, in an earlier report we claimed that there are differences between ethnic groups where 55 per cent of the Iranians and 21 per cent of the Somalis had entered HE 2011/2012 (Bron, Thunborg, & Edström, 2014, p. 63). Thus, ethnicity cannot be regarded as a general category.

When considering the participation rate of students with an international background the dental and health care sector appears to be the common choice for students with an international background. 59 per cent of the students studying dental hygiene, 55 per cent of the dentist students and 49 per cent of the students studying biomedical laboratory science have another ethnical background than Swedish (UKÄ, 2015, p. 8). However, there are few students with an international background in programmes for becoming physiotherapists (5 per cent), economists (10 per cent), lawyers (11 per cent), psychologists (11 per cent), and architects (12 per cent) (SOU, 2015, p. 106).

THE MATCH BETWEEN SUPPLY AND DEMANDS FOR THE LABOUR MARKET AND SOCIETY

According to the overall figures concerning unemployment in Sweden, HE graduates have better chances to become employed than people with a lower educational level. The unemployment rate amongst people with higher education level is 5 per cent compared to 7, 5 per cent of those with upper secondary school and almost 21 per cent of people lacking an exam from upper secondary school (www.ekonomifakta.se). In the statistics provided by the UKÄ (2014), 78 per cent of those graduating from HE 2009/10 had established themselves in the labour market in 2011. One question that could be asked is whether the graduates from HE match the demands of the labour market.

UKÄ (2015) presents a prognosis concerning the relation between demands and supply in different occupational areas and claims that there seems to be needs within the health care sector, educational sector and the engineering sector in the future. There are, however different reasons, according to UKÄ, for these shortages (2013):

> In a number of these programmes, mainly in the health sector, the shortage is due to a lack of places on offer. Other programmes have places for more students but there are not enough interested applicants. The shortage of many different kinds of qualified teachers is likely to persist, unless more students choose these programmes. (ibid, p. 4)

Art, journalism, humanities, human resources (HR) and behaviour science, natural science and economics are according to UKÄ (2015) educational areas where there are too many students in relation to labour market needs. There are probably two reasons for that. Firstly, the labour market is not valuing, art and humanities. Secondly, journalism, HR and behavioural science as well as economics are popular educational programmes and thereby have too many applicants.

A conclusion about the match between supply and demands of the labour market is that non-traditional students are applying for educational programmes with good prognosis of getting employment. Thereby they are going to have good chances on the labour market and be able to fill the gaps between demand and supply on the labour market in the future.

DISCUSSION

In this chapter we have addressed the relation between issues of equality and employability, especially regarding their consequences for Swedish non-traditional students.

By relying on the official statistics and policy documents, we have discussed the employability of non-traditional students in Swedish higher education with a special interest relating to social class and ethnicity. Still, our interest has been focused on the match between patterns of participation for non-traditional students in HE, and the needs and demands of the labour market and society.

On the one hand, and in the overall picture, stated in HE policies as well as national official statistics, the market model built on the match between students' choices of educational programmes and the needs of the labour market is seen as sufficient with a few exceptions. Non-traditional students to a larger extent also seem to help to fill the gap and fulfil the labour market needs by choosing HE programmes related to the education and health care sectors. On the other hand, though, and as a result of our analysis, it seems like HE is becoming a means for a segregated labour market rather than an arena for equality and social mobility. Students having parents with higher education level to a larger extent participate in high status educational programmes such as medicine, engineering and law. However, they also to a larger extent participate in general academic programmes, both at Bachelor and Master levels for getting a unique individual competence to compete on the labour market. They, thereby, enhance their own employability which is in accordance with the new demands claimed in the shift towards employability (Fejes, 2010). Non-traditional students become gap-fillers on the labour market, where students with parents having low educational level chose to become pre-school teachers and vocational teachers and students with international background health and dental care workers. Despite widening access to higher education there are still inequalities in regards to participation. That non-traditional students choose programmes highly demanded by the labour market, could be a consequence of wanting to secure their employment, but at the same time also contributing to a lack of social mobility among non-traditional graduates.

What happened then to the policy of equality in Swedish higher education? It seems like the market forces have taken over the policy of equality. In accordance with the concept of employability, individuals are responsible for their own choices, and unconsciously choose such areas that contribute to segregation on the labour market and in society at large. Moreover, non-traditional students prepare themselves to stay at the lower social stratification level despite gaining higher education graduation, thus not contributing to advance their own social mobility. Fine professions and general programmes are still chosen by the middle and upper classes, while these which have lower demand and lower social status still by socially disadvantaged. This is a paradox of opening access to HE when the market forces steer students' choices, and not only in relation to employment.

A NEED FOR MORE RESEARCH

Even if there are studies concerning students' employability in Sweden, and their transition between HE and working life generally (see Nyström, Abrandt Dahlgren, & Dahlgren, 2010; Reid, Dahlgren, Petocz, & Abrandt-Dahlgren, 2008; Johansson, Hård af Segerstad, Hult, Abrandt Dahlgren, & Dahlgren, 2007; Johansson, Kopciewicz, & Dahlgren, 2008; Nilsson & Nyström, 2013; Haake & Löfgren Martinsson, 2009; Johansson, 2008; Ohlsson, 2009) there seems to be a lack of studies interested in non-traditional students specifically. In a previous European project (RANLHE) we were concerned with the access and retention of non-traditional students but without looking at the issues of employability (Bron, Thunborg, & Edström, 2014; Thunborg, Bron, & Edström, 2012; Edström, 2009). There is, thus, a need for further studies regarding the employability of non-traditional students in higher education and their experiences of the transition to the labour market. We hope that the EMPLOY project will help to contribute to research concerning the employability of non-traditional students and graduates.

REFERENCES

Bron, A., & Lönnheden, C. (2004). Higher education for non-traditional students in Sweden: A matter of inclusion. *Journal of Adult and Continuing Education, 7*, 175–188.
Bron, A., & Thunborg, C. (2015). *Sweden: State of the art in regards to employability of non-traditional students and graduates* (EMPLOY report).
Bron, A., Thunborg, C., & Edström, E. (2014). Ethnicity and class matters: Experiences in Swedish higher education. In F. Finnegan, B. Merrill, & C. Thunborg (Eds.), *Student voices on inequalities in European higher education* (pp. 63–73). London: Routledge.
Edström, E. (2009, April 22–24). *Wanting to become something: About forming identities in higher education*. Paper presented at the third Nordic Conference on adult learning: Communication, collaboration and creativity, University of Southern Denmark, Odense. Retrieved from http://www.ekonomifakta.se/sv/Fakta/Arbetsmarknad/Arbetsloshet/Arbetsloshet-efter-utbildningsniva/
Eurydice Report. (2014). *Modernisation of higher education in Europe: Access, retention and employability*. Brussels: EC.
Fejes, A. (2010). Discourses on employability: Constituting the responsible citizen. *Studies in Continuing Education, 32*(2), 89–102.

Finnegan, F., Merrill, B., & Thunborg, C. (Eds.). (2014). *Student voices on inequalities in European higher education: Challenges for theory, policy and practice in a time of change*. London: Routledge.
Haake, U., & Löfgren Martinsson, M. (2009). Mellan verktygslåda och kritísk reflektion. Om personalvetares anställningsbarhet. In G. Berglund & A. Fejes (Eds.), *Anställningsbarhet: perspektiv från utbildning och arbetsliv*. Lund: Studentlitteratur.
Higher Education Act. (1977). *Högskolelagen* (SFS 1977:218). Stockholm: Utbildningsdepartementet.
Högskoleförordningen. (2014). 2014:1096.
Johansson, K., Hård af Segerstad, H., Hult, H., Abrandt Dahlgren, M., & Dahlgren, L.-O. (2007). The two faces of political science studies – junior and senior students' thoughts about their education and their future profession. *Higher Education, 55*, 623–636.
Johansson, K., Kopciewicz, L., & Dahlgren, L.-O. (2008). Learning for an unknown context: A comparative case study on some Swedish and polish political science student' experiences of the transition from university to working life. *Compare, 38*(2), 219–231.
Nilsson, S., & Nyström, S. (2013). Adult learning, education, and the labour market in the employability regime. *European Journal for Research on the Education and Learning of Adults, 4*(2), 171–187.
Nyström, S., Abrandt Dahlgren, M., & Dahlgren, L.-O. (2010). A winding road – professional trajectories from higher education to working life: A case study of political science and psychology graduates. *Studies in Continuing Education, 30*(3), 215–229.
Ohlsson, U. (2009). *Vägen in i ett yrke: en studie av lärande och kunskapsutveckling hos nyutbildade sjuksköterskor* (Doctoral dissertation). Örebro University, Örebro.
Proposition (2004/05:162). Ny värld – ny högskola [New world – New Higher Education]. Government Bill, Swedish Government, 2004/05:162.
Proposition (2009/10:139). Fokus på kunskap – kvalitet I den högre utbildningen [Focusing knowledge – Quality in higher education]. Government Bill, Swedish Government, 2009/10:139.
Reid, A., Dahlgren, L.-O., Petocz, P., & Abrandt Dahlgren, M. (2008). Identity and engagement for professional formation. *Studies in Higher Education, 33*(6), 729–742.
SOU. (2015). *Högre utbildning under tjugo år. Betänkande av Utredningen om högskolans utbildningsutbud. 2015:70*. Stockholm: Regeringskansliet.
Thunborg, C., & Bron, A. (2012). Higher education and lifelong learning in Sweden. In H. Schutze & M. Slowey (Eds.), *Higher education and lifelong learning*. London: Routledge.
Thunborg, C., Bron, A., & Edström, E. (2012). Forming learning identities in higher education in Sweden. *Studies for the Learning Society, 2*(2–3), 23–34.
UKÄ. (2013). *Higher education in Sweden* (2013 Statatus report. Report 2013:3). Stockholm: Swedish Higher Education Authority.
UKÄ. (2014). *Higher education in Sweden* (Report 2014:10). Stockholm: Swedish Higher Education Authority.
UKÄ. (2015). *Universitet och högskolor* (University and University Colleges. Årsrapport 2015:8). Stockholm: Swedish Higher Education Authority.
Utbildningsdepartementet. (2012). U2012/6996SAM.
Utbildningsdepartementet. (2014). Kommittédirektiv, diarienummer: 2014:54.
Utbildningsdepartementet. (2015). *Promemoria, U2015/1626UH*. Retrieved from http://www.ekonomifakta.se
Yorke, M. (2006). *Employability in higher education: What it is – what it is not*. York: The Higher Education Academy.

Camilla Thunborg
Stockholm University
Sweden

Agnieszka Bron
Stockholm University
Sweden

MARÍA A. TENORIO-RODRÍGUEZ, TERESA PADILLA-CARMONA
AND JOSÉ GONZÁLEZ-MONTEAGUDO

10. LEARNING CAREERS OF NON-TRADITIONAL STUDENTS ON EMPLOYABILITY SKILLS

INTRODUCTION

The employability of graduates is a key aim of the Bologna process. Although university graduates are more likely to find a job than non-graduates, the current economic crisis has had an effect on the employability situation of graduates in Spain (Edvardsson et al., 2010; Tholen, 2012). Research indicates that non-traditional students have specific difficulties in achieving a smooth transition into the labour market (Brown & Hesketh, 2004). University graduates often face a lack of concordance between their university degrees and the demands of the labour market. This problem is exacerbated for non-traditional students who generally need more time than "traditional" students to find highly qualified jobs (Purcell, Wilton, & Elias, 2007). Furthermore, they are more likely to come across jobs which are below their qualification level and that are, therefore, less interesting and have lower salaries. There is also a mismatch between the graduates' competences and employers' expectations or needs.

This study takes place within the EMPLOY project: a European research project in which six universities are taking part with the aim of improving the employability of non-traditional university students and graduates (youths and adults) in order to foster a smoother transition into the labour market.

Research has, until now, been about the general topics of accessing the job market, and the experiences of non-traditional students who move from university to the labour market have been mostly ignored. This is why it is essential to gather opinions, experiences and perceptions of non-traditional students which take into account their points of view and subjective perspectives. To do so, we present the process and results of a qualitative analysis developed from biographical interviews with non-traditional students. This enables us to acquire new knowledge and perspectives concerning the employability of these students, as well as identifying if higher education institutions are responding to these students needs and endowing them with the competences necessary to carry out a successful transition to a qualified graduate level job.

NON-TRADITIONAL LEARNERS IN UNIVERSITY AND THEIR EMPLOYABILITY

The changes in the general state of the economy and the job market are the most significant determinants of work opportunities. A person's employment perspectives are, however, influenced by many factors. This means that not all graduates have similar job opportunities despite having received the same education. These factors include the mode of study (full time or part time), location and mobility, graduates who have previous work experience, as well as their age, gender, race and social class (Harvey, 2001). Regarding the latter series of factors, the discriminatory practices which these graduates could face in the job market are often overlooked in discussions about employability (Morley, 2001).

There are no statistics which shed light on the employability of non-traditional graduate students. All the studies point to the process of integration into the labour market being more satisfactory and successful for university graduates in comparison to the rest of the population. Both, if we speak about work participation and the probability of unemployment, work stability or salary incomes, people with a university degree benefit from better conditions.

However, some of the characteristics linked to non-traditional students (disability, mature age, ethnic origin, low socio-economic capital, etc.) could aggravate the situation of this group with respect to their employability. The level of employability of those with new degrees is going to be determined by various factors related to both the economic situation and some personal and social determining factors. It is therefore necessary to investigate what the starting point is in Spain in terms of the statistics and policies of employability for university graduates and to what extent these statistics and strategic lines consider the differential aspects which characterise the population of non-traditional students and graduates.

The research carried out in Spain by Pastor and Peraita (2014) with data from 2007 to 2013 shows that employment prospects have been destroyed for people at all educational levels (including short university cycles), with the exception of graduates, where there has even been a certain growth. Nonetheless, in the samples of these studies the set of characteristics which can affect the probability of having a job (gender, age, nationality, level of studies, the branch of these studies and even the region of residence) are controlled. This is why we lack information precisely concerning if these work benefits can affect non-traditional graduates to the same extent or not.

Another report about the employability of university graduates in Spain comes from the Ministry of Education, Culture and Sport (2015). It compiles statistics about the work integration of university students based on the rate of registration for Social Security[1] for the cohort of graduates for the academic year 2009–2010, for which information is facilitated from 2011 (one year after the students finished their studies), 2012, 2013 and 2014. Working on Social Security registration we can obtain certain information about the quality of the employment (if it is permanent, temporary, full-time and in keeping with their educational level) of the university students.

The first data which we have is that employment increases with the passing of time. Of the university graduates of the 2009–2010 course, 43.4% (42.9% of the women; 44.3% of the men) are registered for Social Security one year after finishing their studies, 55.6% are registered two years after, 58.6% three years later and 64.4% four years after (64.1% of women; 64.9% of men).

These results vary according to the age section (see Table 1). Those who got their degrees when they were younger (under 30 years old) have registration rates lower in the first year than those who are over 31. Yet this data could be due to the fact that in the higher age sections it is frequent for students to already be in the job market before finishing their studies. This is why it is necessary to add that as time passes the graduates who finished their studies when they were between 25 and 40 years old are those who attain higher registration rates, while those who finished them when they were over 40 are delayed, their registration rate hardly varying with respect to those who have recently graduated.

Table 1. Social security registration rates in the first and fourth year after graduation according to age group (MECD, 2015)

	2011 (first year after graduation)	2014 (fourth year after graduation)
Total	43.4%	64.4%
Less than 25 years old	33.1%	63.8%
25–30 years old	48.6%	64.9%
31–40 years old	63.1%	66.6%
Over 40 years old	61.4%	61.3%

In addition to this, the transition from university to the labour market is an area explored in several Spanish publications. Calvo and Fernández (2013) studied the programmes of "first young employment" and Alonso (2010) focused on different career patterns, creating several typologies about the ways of navigating from higher education to work. Some studies researched on factors that hinder and enhance good working itineraries (ANECA, 2009; Pastor & Peraita, 2014).

Nevertheless, we lack research which goes thoroughly into the competences of employability and transitions to the job market of non-traditional university graduates. The viewpoint which underlies this absence of a specific focus is that once in higher education there is equality among students, irrespective of their social or family background (Monteagudo & Ballesteros, 2011). Consequently, we also expect that the university degree will itself eliminate the disadvantageous background which some students have.

AIMS

The capacity of universities to provide their students and graduates with employability cannot be precisely evaluated by using uniquely "objective" indicators, such as job and salary perspectives. This data needs to be supplemented by information which sheds light more directly on the graduates' capacities. That is to say, on their competences, paying special attention to non-traditional students.

Our study aims to contribute to improving this situation by increasing the information available concerning the employability of non-traditional students. To do so, we draw on their experiences. These are our research aims:

- To analyse the university education received concerning employability.
- To understand employability from the perspective of non-traditional students.
- To identify the factors which foster or hinder the employability of non-traditional students.

METHOD

The methodological options emerge from our main aim: to understand the employability of non-traditional students. To do this we have followed a qualitative approach in order to analyse these students' perspective of employability. We identify their relation with university education and the factors which foster or hinder it. We have opted to carry out biographical interviews in which the narrator and researcher have gone deeply into those aspects which are deemed necessary. In this context, the biographical interview is the key axis for the information gathering process.

We have centred on working with a few subjects (seven) whose series of specific characteristics can provide us with a view of the problem which is broad and selected enough. The choosing of the participants was carried out based on a series of criteria which we established as relevant for our study: to be in the last year of the degree course at the University of Seville and to correspond to one or more characteristics of the typical non-traditional profile.

We have managed to represent diverse profiles. We had three women and four men, each from a different knowledge area (Arts and Humanities, Sciences, Health Sciences, Engineering, Architecture, Social Sciences and Law) – except from the latter, as we had an easier access to these students in the other fields. After gathering the data through biographical interviews, we carried out an analysis of their content. During this process we have kept the aims and questions with which we began the research very much in mind. Given the characteristics of the questions, it seemed appropriate to undertake a qualitative analysis of the content of the answers based on the identifying of categories. Hence, after an independent reading of the interviews, the different category sets were extracted. These sets fall into three dimensions: a valuation of the university education, the factors which influence job placement and conceptions of employability.

RESULTS

Now we present the results of the analysis carried out about the three previously-formulated dimensions: a valuation of university education, the factors which influence job placement and conceptions concerning employability.

Valuation of University Education

First and foremost, the students perceive that the contents of the study plans are not proportionate with the time allocated. Furthermore, they highlight the lack of transversal subjects which deviate from the specific competences of the degree and study in greater depth other generic competences, mainly concerning emotional and social skills.

> The competences are in social skills. Because today's world does not require a degree, although it seems to do so, it demands an interest in doing things, in progressing. (Boti)

> Well, I think what most needs to be improved in the healthcare degree is the human aspect, humanistic, I don't know what's the exact term (…) I've missed this a lot, them teaching you to empathise and to deal with people and to deal with them well, a bit of psychology or I don't know what it could be, but I miss it. (Botico)

Regarding the subjects, there is an almost unanimous wish to broaden the practical contents and set up a stronger relation with the theoretical contents.

> There's too much theory without practice so they don't combine, it's like nothing. (Gracia)

> What's bad about the engineering degree is it's all theoretical, you don't do anything practical there, nothing, what you do in practice is to hang out. (…) I think it should be more centred on practice, I think that is important. (José Antonio)

A general approval is given to incorporating internships into the study plans, even for those students who belong to degrees in which this is not obligatory or not included in their study plans.

> In the biology degree we don't have internships, I think having them would be positive because it helps you to work in other areas, not only in the university and you get more involved I think. (Bio)

We however find some complaints referring to the mismatch between the tasks carried out in internships and the reality of work, others which describe how those students doing internships are abused by employers and others concerning their time programming and the content of the previous workshops.

> There's an important shortfall in the subject of internships. Firms normally use pedagogues to do other duties which are not really what a pedagogue should do. (…) The faculty's internships ought to be the reality of what you're going to come across after or of what you're supposedly going to come across after and it's not like that. (Boti)

> There are some who take advantage of the students, some or most. In the interview they told me: "we're going to train you" (…) and they also said this to some colleagues who they interviewed but it was a sham. (José Antonio)

The students went against their traditional profile of the methodology based on data transmission and theoretical contents. Alternatives are proposed to foster significant learning, such as carrying out debates, presentations, group work and a greater participation in class. Also, to favour the crossover to the job market a greater relation between the university and employers was proposed, including the latter in the classrooms.

> Only one teacher took us to a pharmacist, to an inspector of chemists at a national level and another at a regional level, people who had devoted themselves to orthopaedics, people who had set up a herbalist's shop but who had a pharmacist's degree. (Botico)

> With the group discussions we rebutted the teacher-student idea a bit, that hierarchy which is at times adverse to education. (Alejandro)

> We did few presentations, little group work (…), so I think there should be a lot more for the students to come out of their shells. (Gracia)

> It also helps to work in a group because really when you leave here, in the world of work you're going to have to work with all kinds of people, you're going to have to fit in with all kinds of people. (Bio)

Conceptions about Employability

The conceptions about employability vary among the students belonging to the field of pure sciences and health sciences, and those of social sciences and humanities. The former stress the specific competences which are characteristic of the degree and having skills to profit from, and to produce in the least time possible.

> I think you have to have something that is a bit different that the firm needs (…) for example, if you have to model in 3D you need computer programme knowledge like Catia V5. (José Antonio)

> A person who develops their mind to do things more easily is sure to suit my firm more than another person (…). If a job can be done in five ways you must know how to develop it in the easiest way. (José Antonio)

However, the students who belong to the field of social sciences and humanities highlight the generic competences referring to personal attributes. They specify emotional, social and communication skills, having a vocation and proactive attitude, as well as the ability to be self-taught and self-sufficient when acquiring education. Regardless of the degree, they all valued competences in languages and having experiences of mobility.

> Languages are obviously essential, whether we like it or not, it's like that and it's going to be like that. If you don't have a second language you're going to be almost illiterate because the world is increasingly more globalised and it's going to be like that (…). For example, of course, experiences of mobility, that is how it has to be. (Boti)

Factors Which Influence Employability

One of the most influential job-seeking factors is to have work experience. Having it becomes a facilitating factor (an advantage for mature students) and not having it is a hindrance. Also, most of the interviewees coincide in stating that not having contacts which facilitate employability becomes a barrier.

> I don't have many contacts, often it's much easier to find a job through a contact with someone who gives you an opportunity. (Alejandro)

> Something which makes looking for a job difficult … perhaps it's not what it's about but pulling strings (…) what I don't understand is there being five candidates and one, who's somebody's niece, well they choose her even though the other four have twenty times more knowledge about the job than her. (José Antonio)

Not having a variety of degrees, knowledge of languages or experience abroad is added to the list of factors which hinder employability. This situation is made worse by not having the economic resources to overcome them. It is specified that the university where you are from can also become a barrier if a comparison is made with students belonging to other, more prestigious universities.

For some of those interviewed, having a "non-traditional" profile is considered to be an additional problem. Examples are immigrants, those who have a low socio-economic level, being a woman and mature students; although the latter do, nevertheless, have the advantage of their greater resources for self-employment.

> Because of being an immigrant there will be certain things, certain stereotypes that in some way you go to a firm and they say: "oh, those no", but I think that the work you do speaks for itself. (Gracia)

> Sadly the weak point is age. I don't know why, don't ask me why but it's age, I don't understand it. (Boti)

> I know that out there I'm a person who's at risk of exclusion (…) because I'm a woman, I'm over forty-five and I'm middle class, though I'm educated the social class still counts. (Justa)

> To overcome the subject of age the easiest thing is to make up your own story. Self-employment because it's easier for me than for youngsters, I've more resources for that, I've more friends, I know more people, and other ways. (Boti)

As external factors, they point out our country's current crisis; not only the economic crisis but also certain policies and few career opportunities, especially in the field of humanities. Work conditions, particularly those with respect to schedules, can become a problem because of having to reconcile them with another job, with education or with the family. Family support is vital when making the move into the labour market.

> There are people who don't care about working in the afternoon or in the morning and others who do, but the fact of going one week in the afternoon, one week in the morning of course complicates you being able to enrich yourself or being able to continue developing something else in parallel. (Alejandro)

> Yes, I've got a family environment which I'm getting support from (…). I'm here thanks to them, when I've been desperate they've given me encouragement. (Justa)

> In Spain for philosophy (…) it seems we only want to fabricate teachers who're going to fabricate future teachers continuing a cycle, I don't know where it's going to end up (…). Nor, for better or for worse, is the panorama very good for these fields in Spain. (Alejandro)

CONCLUSIONS

Yorke (2006) differentiates two approaches to employability: one centred on employment boosted by those factors which enable people to move into, make progress in or stay in employment; and another whose focus is on competences and skills which higher education students acquire during their studies. To understand employability from the students' perspective, we can conclude that all the students interviewed have a concept of employability based on competences and not on employment.

The competences of employability which the participants highlight vary according to the field of knowledge to which they belong. Some students who are doing a degree in pure science or health sciences underscore specific competences (Teichler, 2011), namely those related with particular professions. However, the students who belong to the field of social sciences and humanities emphasise generic competences (communication, emotional and social skills, teamwork, etc.).

In line with the contributions of Harvey (2001), in our study we have noted factors which influence a person's employability: previous experience (which is an advantage to have and a hindrance to not have), his/her age, gender, race and social class. That is to say, the profile of a "non-traditional" student is also considered as a barrier given that, as Purcell, Wilton & Elias, 2007 pointed out, they need more time to find jobs than "traditional" students. Only the possibility of self-employment is noted as a factor in their favour.

It has also been demonstrated that, as Bermejo (2011) indicated, these kinds of students have trouble combining their studies with work or with other family responsibilities. This is the reason why they come across limitations of availability in their work schedules and conditions. Not having economic resources to broaden their education, gaining in knowledge of languages or having experiences of mobility are added to this list of obstacles, as well as not having the contacts which facilitate the transition into work.

As Monteagudo and Ballesteros (2011) noted, it is sometimes assumed that after having begun higher education there is equality among students, irrespective of their social or family backgrounds. Yet we have found out in this study that there are other factors which are overlooked by higher education policies and institutions.

NOTE

[1] The Social Security registration is measured with a fixed date of March 23rd. of the calendar years following the conclusion of university studies.

REFERENCES

Agencia Nacional de Evaluación de la Calidad y Acreditación. (2009). *Los procesos de inserción laboral de los titulados universitarios en Españ. Factores de facilitación y de obstaculización*. Madrid: ANECA.

Alonso, M. A. (2010). Evaluación del potencial de inserción laboral y patrones de carrera. *Revista de Educación, 351*, 409–434.

Ballesteros, M. A., & Monteagudo, J. (2011, April). *Social and cultural dimensions of higher education as context to understand non-traditional students*. Paper presented at RANLHE Conference on Access and Retention: Experiences of non-traditional learners in Higher Education, Seville, Spain. Retrieved from http://www.dsw.edu.pl/fileadmin/www-ranlhe/files/Monteagudo_Ballesteros.pdf

Bermejo, L. (2011). *Aprendizaje a lo largo de toda la vida*. Madrid: IMSERSO.

Brown, P., & Hesketh, A. (2004). *The mismanagement of talent: Employability and jobs in the knowledge economy*. Oxford: Oxford University Press.

Calvo, F. J., & Fernández, M. F. (2013). El contrato de 'primer empleo joven'. In M. F. Fernández & F. J. Calvo (Eds.), *La estrategia de emprendimiento y empleo joven en la ley 11/2013: desempleo, empleo y ocupación juvenil*. Albacete: Editorial Bomarzo.

Edvardsoon, B., Gerbauer, H., & Bjurko, M. (2010). The impact of service orientation in corporate culture on business performance in manufacturing companies. *Journal of Service Management, 21*(2), 237–259.

Harvey, L. (2001). Defining and measuring employability. *Quality in Higher Education, 7*(2), 97–109.

Ministry for Education, Culture and Sport. (2015). *Datos y cifras del sistema universitario español. Curso 2014–2015*. Madrid: Secretaría General Técnica del MECD. Retrieved from http://www.mecd.gob.es/dms/mecd/educacion-mecd/areas-educacion/universidades/estadisticas-informes/datos-cifras/Datos-y-Cifras-del-SUE-Curso-2014-2015.pdf

Morley, L. (2001). Producing new workers: Quality, equality and employability in higher education. *Quality in Higher Education, 7*(2), 131–138.

Pastor, J. M., & Peraita, C. (2014). La inserción laboral de los universitarios españoles. *Revista de la Asociación de Sociología de la Educación, 7*(1), 252–266.

Purcell, K., Wilton, N., & Elias, P. (2007). Hard lessons for life-long learners? Age and experience in the graduate labour market. *Higher Education Quarterly, 61*(1), 57–82.

Teichler, U. (2011). International dimensions of higher education and graduate employment. In J. Allen & R. van der Velden (Eds.), *The flexible professional in the knowledge society: New challenges for higher education.* Dordrecht: Springer.

Tholen, G. (2012). Graduate employability and educational context: A comparison between Great Britain and the Netherlands. *British Educational Research Journal, 40*(1), 1–17.

Yorke, M. (2006). *Employability in higher education: What it is-what it is not learning and employability.* York: Higher Education Academy.

María A. Tenorio-Rodríguez
University of Seville
Spain

Teresa Padilla-Carmona
University of Seville
Spain

José González-Monteagudo
University of Seville
Spain

ANA SILVA, MARIA DE LOURDES DIONÍSIO
AND JULIANA CUNHA

11. LITERACY PRACTICES IN ADULT LEARNING BIOGRAPHIES

Possibilities and Constraints

LITERACY CHALLENGES

The answer to the social and economic challenges is assumed to be literacy (or its lack). Consequently, the developed countries are deeply concerned with the problem and all governments, particularly those of the OECD area, have created public policies in relation to this challenge. In recent decades, these concerns have given rise to several and varied monitoring devices, initiatives and programmes for (mainly) reading development, thus putting a major stress on education. UNESCO (2006, p. 6), for instance, assumes that the challenge of literacy can only be met by raising the quality of primary and secondary education and intensifying programmes explicitly oriented towards youth and adult literacy. In Portugal, this concern has also been echoed in public reforms that aimed at "the increasing of schooling, extending the hours in pre-schools, reducing early drop out, increasing secondary education completion rates, as well as the overall improvement of the access to higher education" (Data Angel Policy Research Incorporated, 2009, p. 65).

One of the most representative cases of such initiatives was the programme New Opportunities (NO), and its process of Recognition, Validation and Certification of Competencies (RVCC), which was targeted at adults over the age 18, who had not concluded the current ninth grade of (compulsory) pre-secondary schooling. This New Opportunities programme aimed at the promotion of the inclusion of adults in formal education (OECD, 2008, p. 136). Although there are no explicit references to literacy in the normative documents of the NO and RVCC, one may say that literacy is indeed one of their goals, as it assumes – in the case of RVCC – a particular status: the end and the means of learning. In fact, the entire certification process is mediated by language practices that are considered essential for self-reflection about the personal experience of individuals; namely, life stories, interviews, portfolios, among others. All of which are written products to serve simultaneously, as evidence and as development of the skills acquired throughout life. Ultimately, as in previous policy measures, the educational goal of the process is:

> to ensure all adults living in Portugal [...] an easy access to specific learning modalities, that may enable them to learn to read and write, to achieve a

> basic literacy level and to get an equivalent degree to the current compulsory education. (Melo et al., 1998, p. 16)

This hypothesis about the role of literacy in the process is also confirmed in the implementation processes which, as it has been observed, institute literacy as a priority area of action (Castro & Laranjeira, 2009; Gomes, 2006).

In the sense that they allow the study of the ways certain groups relate with writing and with knowledge (Charlot, 2000), these 'new opportunities" for learning are ideal situations for understanding how participation in these processes acts in the transformation of the literate identities of people and how, in their life trajectories, it reflects opportunities and constraints impacting on the ways they use, access and value texts (Barton, Hamilton, & Ivanic, 2000; Barton, Ivanic, Appleby, Hodge, & Tusting, 2007).

"Challenging representations" about the position in the community of adults without or with scarce schooling, which tend sometimes to be considered in a "mistaken view" (Freire, 1980, p. 73), as "socially excluded" (Hamilton & Pitt, 2011, p. 350) and suffering from the disease of "illiteracy" (Lahire, 1999), the goals of this text are, first of all, to contribute with empirical data to the deeper comprehension of the individual life story of adults that voluntarily or compulsorily had to go back to school. Secondly, we intend to identify and characterise some social and personal factors that tend to promote or inhibit access to the written world, to knowledge and to lifelong learning after the completion of the RVCC process.

From the combination of data gathered for two different studies (Cunha, 2012 and another one, still in progress), we can characterise the learning trajectories and the literacy narratives of four adults that completed the Basic Level of the RVCC process. Besides the specificities of the reading and writing practices of the adults, particularly regarding the whats, whys and wherefores and under what circumstances they read and write, ultimately we are expecting to understand why they will keep, or not, reading and writing throughout their lives.

PATHS TO LITERACY: PERSONAL NEEDS AND SOCIAL IMPOSITION

The data regarding the four adults that we will discuss are related, as it has been said, to two different studies: a case study of two adults with distinct motivational profiles (Study 1) and one larger study (Study 2), which involved 30 adults and which, in addition to interviews and documentary analysis, used other methodological procedures; namely, reading and writing tasks and questionnaires.

In Study 2 in order to understand how the learning process contributed to other kinds of involvement with texts in the various fields of life including more formal situations, the adults were interviewed before starting the RVCC process and then again six months after concluding their certification. As in Study 1 in which the data were collected at the end of the process, the underlying goal of the interviews was the need to build a solid understanding of the factors involved in the ways adults continue – or not – to participate in formal learning events and the extent they kept (or not) being involved in more socially recognised literacy practices.

The four adults ('Pedro', 42 years old, and 'Inês', 30, from the Study 1 and 'Jorge', 58, and 'Marta', 49 years, from the Study 2 are from the district of Braga in Portugal and they completed the RVCC for the Basic Skills Level Certification in 2012. The criteria for the constitution of this particular sample were the representativeness of gender and school experience of the adults. These adults represented a population that, living with the phenomenon of unemployment, had at the start of the RVCC process, low academic qualifications. They also represented different paths through education and literacy. Marta and Inês, voluntarily enrolled in the process to complete the third cycle of Basic Education, while Pedro and Jorge "were forced" to enrol, due to the imposition of the State and within a legislative framework for employment support, as they keep stressing during their interviews:

> I did not sign up voluntarily, I was forced. I had no chance, I was forced. (…) for me it will not change anything at all (…) This (…) only goes to make me waste time walking back and forth, nothing else. (Jorge)

> I did not go there with many expectations. (…) No, because, as far as the employing companies, they do not see this as an improvement (…) and they knew that I was in that place, so that the Portuguese statistics would not increase, so as not to have so much school dropout. (Pedro)

Although the educational background of these two adults had not been enough for them to complete the nine years of compulsory education, Jorge (with five years of pre-secondary schooling) and Pedro (with seven), throughout their lives had held relevant professional positions. Before becoming unemployed, Jorge was a successful commercial agent in the area of sales and finance for several years and Pedro was a talented sales manager in a family food trade company:

> Until a few years ago, I really played choosing the jobs I wanted. That's why now forcing me to do the ninth grade, the ninth grade … For God's sake! (…) Note that I already worked in the Post Office; I was a civil employee (…), in the express mail (…). I also worked with finances (…) no one without the 12th grade could get the job, but I did. (Jorge)

> I can say what I wanted, it was a job that would fulfil me, because, as I already mentioned, it was a family business. (Pedro)

By that reason both believed that their attendance at such a process would not bring them any added value; namely, the development of their reading and writing skills. They were certain that during their professional trajectories they had had the opportunity to acquire and develop literacy practices similar to those valued by the school system, such as writing reports or formal letters. On the other hand, they did not believe that the school diploma could bring them more advantages for a successful job quest. Jorge had a professional past that he used to reinforce this argument. For these two men, then, the RVCC process was – from the beginning – a kind of downgrading and disregard for their literate identities (Dionísio, Castro, & Arqueiro, 2013) forged through engagement in multiple and diversified life contexts.

As for the women, Marta and Inês, their views on the importance of the RVCC both for their learning and their professional careers were totally different. With very short school trajectories – Marta only completed the fourth grade and Inês the sixth of compulsory education – due to severe money difficulties of their families, the possibility of going back to school to get a certificate appeared as a dream that was going to be true, a kind of late "divine justice:"

> I hope that this dream that I idealised in my head becomes true (…). That's what I really expect. (Marta)

> I returned to study, not only to obtain more schooling, but to learn a little more and in this way to have studies equivalent to compulsory education. (Inês)

Marta and Inês expected that – with attendance of the RVCC and the certificate of Basic Education – they could, more easily, be more active professionally again and, with that, have better life conditions. Until starting the certification process these two women had been mainly seamstresses in textile factories. Because of these professional roles, unlike the two men, they did not have opportunities for the development of reading and writing skills, as well as being involved in more culturally valid reading and writing practices. According to these women they should have had these practices to really be *insiders* of the dominant groups (Gee, 1996) and maybe to be considered as holders of references shared by the literate world and, consequently, to feel authorised to say: 'I make part of it'. Sharing such views, Marta and Inês had a "devalued vision of themselves" (Charlot, 2000; Freire, 1987), thus aspiring to become literate persons only after the obtaining of their certificates:

> You know, miss, I wanted to know more. I wanted to know more! (…) I hope, when I finish the process, I hope to get a job, to work with which I am learning in the course and later to be able to write on the computer. To be faster in everything. Given this current modern stuff, to be able to follow these technologies. Because, for us, me for instance, it is everything with the ball pen, right? For now. Whereas, if I can, then I will be able to do things by myself. Do you understand? (Marta)

Therefore, and although they read frequently, for instance, magazines and marketing brochures and even write not only SMS but also poetry, this did not seem enough to them to be taken as "literate persons".

LITERACY IDENTITIES: OUTSIDERS AND INSIDERS

A social perspective of literacy sees the use of texts as human actions of a social nature. In this sense, reading and writing includes everything that people do with texts in their diverse modes and formats and in the different social events in which they engage daily. Thus, taking this into consideration – in such events – the way one uses texts varies, due to the multiplicity of purposes of reading and writing. Consequently, literacy does not have then the same features in all life domains. In fact, in order to acquire, learn and exhibit the social languages and identities which are proper of those domains (Gee, 1996), people need to be socialised in several spheres according to their norms and ideologies. Then, it is with participation in several events of literacy that the shaping of the literate identity occurs.

Looking at what happened to these four adults after having participated in the RVCC, a formal learning context, which was characterised by specialised reading and writing practices that were unfamiliar mainly to Marta and Inês, it is possible to conclude, in fact, that there have been more or less significant changes in the ways they viewed and engaged with texts and – in the cases of the two women – also in the ways they thought about their social identity. Besides the frequent reading and writing practices that already had a presence in the lives of these adults, after the RVCC new literacy practices became part of their daily life, mainly as a cause of their participation in new social domains.

In the case of Marta, whose reading and writing practices, before the certification process, were mainly of a private nature; namely, the reading of popular and love magazines, as well as poetry and diary writing, for instance, they were a means of filling spare time. After the RVCC, besides the reinforcement of these same practices, others of a more formal nature gained an important space in her life. Due to her new religion, she started reading quite often the Bible and other religious books. She also began to take on the duty of writing about what she read in order to share her learning with others of the religious group:

> I often go to the Bible and I read books, but related to the Bible. (…) I write summaries when I have the Bible study group. (Marta)

Although attendance at the certification process had not played a significant role in the decision to belong to a new social group, the certificate and the literacy skills she developed gave her confidence to participate more actively within it and for the community. It is worth noting that the literacy events of this new domain were in several aspects very similar to those Marta learned during the RVCC, as she stresses:

> We look for texts in the Bible, then we have books which have Bible texts, with note calls, they have those explanations and after we go to the Bible to confirm that what is said is really correct and things like this (…) Because they then ask me questions and I have to know how to answer them without going to see the book, without copying. (Marta)

As for Inês, her confidence and autonomy regarding literacy were also positively affected after certification. She made clear that reading and writing activities became much more present in her daily life; namely, those valued by the educational context, such as literary reading:

> Indeed, since we talked the other day I managed to read a book to the end (…) Burnt Alive. It's a story… a little bit … even tragic. I do not know if you know the story. (Inês)

If the textual worlds of Marta and Inês became larger, the same cannot be said in the cases of Jorge and Pedro. For these two men, the compulsory 'schooling' did not bring the same changes. In fact, taking into account the past of Jorge, as text user, the literacy practices that characterised his daily life – for instance, book, journal and newspaper reading or the writing of formal letters and texts about archaeological artefacts – maintained the same space that they already had in his life, except for the difference that some of those reading and writing practices became associated with the use of the computer and the internet:

> I use [the computer] to do things such … things like [written texts on topics that interest me]. Look, now I use Skype to talk to my daughter, who went to London (…) And I use that and I also use the internet to do, to search things and whatever more is necessary. (Jorge)

> Mainly through the newspapers, Internet, I still continue … one or other book that now comes with the newspapers …. (Pedro)

To a certain extent, then, the RVCC had the merit of introducing Jorge to new literacy technologies – a fact that he does not seem to value. In fact, both for Jorge and for Pedro, their reading and writing skills, that they have always perceived as specialised and sophisticated, perfectly serve their professional, social and personal goals:

> I do not know any other person that reads as well as I do, I mean, well, on a daily basis, I read very well. I also write very well (…) I fully understand what is written, everything I read'. (Jorge)

For Pedro and Jorge the time spent on the RVCC was a waste and without any consequence for them:

> To be honest, I did not learn anything new. (Pedro)

> That (the training) was useless! I always said and felt that, since the beginning (…) didn't affect me at all for good or for bad. It only made me waste my time and to spend fuel. (Jorge)

This negative impact was felt from the beginning, when these men were treated almost as outsiders, and in a very inhuman way put outside the social system (Freire, 1980), because they did not possess a certificate. In the case of Jorge it is possible to think that his disbelief about the RVCC was reinforced when he had to declare to the RVCC professional that he had no certificate:

> – I do not have certificate of competence, I said. "So what now? Do I put zero here?" she said with arrogance (…). I did not even reply. (Jorge)

Although, as Freire (1980) says, these persons without certificates "are not at the margins ... they are not outside ... consequently the solution to their problem is not to force them to become inner beings" (pp. 74–75). Jorge and Pedro, because once they had been full citizens and suddenly they were made redundant, felt the process as an aggression. In the case of Jorge this aggression was exacerbated by the discourse of the RVCC professional. In another position were the women that did not perceive themselves, as someone who "knows" or as someone that possessed some kind of knowledge. They did not believe in themselves, thereby embodying the devalued vision they made of their literacy identities (Freire, 1987, p. 50).

LEARNING AND LITERACY LIVES: INTERRUPTION AND REDISCOVERY

The data discussed until now showed us a clear variation in the ways the men and women regarded learning and literacy before and after the RVCC process. Since Jorge and Pedro once had been successful insiders of the literate culture, had engaged daily with literacy practices that were – to a certain extent – similar to the "dominant/ school like" ones, their engagement in literacy or more specifically in learning that they foresaw after the RVCC was not expected to have changed greatly or almost certainly it was not likely to continue. What seems to have really happened was an improvement in the competencies that they already possessed; namely, of those that were more standardised and formal. On the other hand, although they were not able to identify changes, it is impossible to deny the change, because it can be said that there is always:

> a sense in which 'doing' anything, engaging in any social practice, always means 'learning' in the broad sense. Each time someone engages in a practice, whether that practice is brand new to them or whether they have done it many times before, there is some 'learning' going on, because each time you engage in a practice, you reinforce your expertise in it, and also have the possibility to change it slightly. (Barton, Ivanic, Appleby, Hodge, & Tusting, 2007, p. 25)

The opposite situation is that of Marta and Inês who after completing the RVCC have been seen participating with self confidence in literacy events that demand the features of the dominant and legitimate reading and writing practices. Special life circumstances dictated this. Marta, because she became involved with a religious group, and Inês, because she had recently become a mother and, according to her, to be a good mother was synonymous with being able to carry out school-certified literacy practices. In the case of the women, it is indeed the overvaluation of the school-like reading and writing practices associated with the positive experience that the RVCC represented for them that made Marta and Inês develop willingness to give continuity to their learning trajectories by keep being involved in other education situations:

> Look, listen to this, I even signed up for an animation course ... for seniors. But not here, you know, it was in another place. And for children, for children. Something like this. (Marta)

> In a near future, I would like to complete the ninth grade, learn how to use the computer in order to conclude the twelfth grade. (Inês)

With respect to Jore and Pedro, the fact that the RVCC had been seen by them as a discrediting of their literacy identities, as well as an hindrance to their lives, which had been interrupted in order to learn what they already knew but which they could not prove, led to not wanting to participate any more in formal learning events:

> [About his possible engagement with other training] No way! (...) One thing I like to do it is to make a good use of my time. And that was lost time (...) A waste of time. (Jorge)

However, the break with the RVCC processes does not necessarily lead to a total discontinuity in the learning career of these adults. Taking into consideration these adults literacy biographies, it is almost certain that their lifelong learning careers certainly will continue, albeit informally, in other contexts of their lives.

Looking at the life trajectories of these adults, we see how literacy lives can, of course, follow different paths. Such paths crossing, at some point, formal learning contexts, such as the RVCC, may or may not have continuity, due to factors such as life circumstances and personal future prospects, as well as personal views towards the value of the written culture in the different social spheres in which these persons operate. The perception that each one has of himself/herself, while text users and knowledge personas, is also invaluable for these continuities and discontinuities. The social roles that one has in the community may also determine the future learning path.

Indeed, for the men of these studies, who did not have in their future projects the return to school and whose personal and professional involvement with textual worlds was notable and sufficient to allow continuous learning for personal, social and institutional purposes, the RVCC process was clearly understood, as a threat to their literate identities, an interruption or even a regression in their already sophisticated ways of using the written word.

The opposite was found in the biographies of the women. Because they were guided by the dream of being able to continue their educational background, and because they were aware of their scarce and undervalued way of engaging with texts, the attendance at the RVCC represented both one opportunity to have a better life and the beginning of learning careers that will certainly go far, albeit with distinct contours, in the everyday life of each one.

As we have seen, it is almost certain that attendance at these processes, although for disparate reasons and under different circumstances, helped to add to the identity kits of these four adults features and values that the literate communities attach to reading and writing.

REFERENCES

Barton, D., Hamilton, M., & Ivanic, R. (2000). *Situated literacies: Reading and writing in context.* London: Routledge.
Barton, D., Ivanic, R., Appleby, Y., Hodge, R., & Tusting, K. (2007). *Literacy, lives and learning.* London & New York, NY: Routledge.
Castro, R., & Laranjeira, R. (2009). Educação e formação de adultos em Portugal: Concepções de literacia no discurso pedagógico oficial. *Fórum, 42–43*, 95–110.
Charlot, B. (2000). *Da relação com o saber.* Porto Alegre: Artes Médicas.
Cunha, J. (2012). *Trajetos de literacia de adultos em processos de RVCC – um estudo de ca*so (Dissertação de mestrado em Educação, Ensino do Português, não publicada). Universidade do Minho, Portugal.
Data Angel Policy Research Incorporated. (2009). *A Dimensão Económica da Literacia em Portugal: uma análise.* Lisboa: GEPE.
Dionísio, M. L., Castro, R. V., & Arqueiro, A. S. (2013). Literacies in the workplace: Social conditions, practices and meanings. In D. Masny (Ed.), *Cartographies of becoming in education: A Deleuze-Guattari perspective* (pp. 111–125). Roterdam, The Netherlands: Sense Publishers.
Freire, P. (1980). *Conscientização: Teoria e prática da libertação.* São Paulo: Cortez e Moraes.
Freire, P. (1987). *Pedagogia do oprimido.* Rio de Janeiro: Paz e Terra.
Gee, J. P. (1996). *Social linguistics and literacies: Ideology in discourses.* London: Taylor & Francis.
Hamilton, M., & Pitt, K. (2011). Challenging representations: Constructing the adult literacy learner over 30 years of policy and practice in the United Kingdom. *Reading Research Quarterly, 46*(4), 350–373.
Lahire, B. (1999). *L'invention de l'illettrisme: rhétorique publique, éthique et stigmates.* Paris: La Découverte.
Melo, A., Queirós, A. M., Silva, A. S., Salgado, L., Rothes, L., & Ribeiro, M. (1998). *Uma Aposta Educativa na Participação de Todos. Documento de Estratégia para o Desenvolvimento da Educação de Adultos.* Portugal: Ministério da Educação, Secretaria de Estado da Educação e da Inovação.
OECD. (2008). *OECD economic surveys: Portugal.* Paris: OECD.
UNESCO. (2006). *Education for all: Literacy for life* (EFA Global Monitoring Report). Paris: UNESCO.

Ana Silva
University of Minho
Portugal

Maria de Lourdes Dionísio
University of Minho
Portugal

Juliana Cunha
University of Minho
Portugal

PART 4

CONTINUITY AND DISCONTINUITY IN PROFESSIONAL CONTEXTS

PASCAL ROQUET

12. ADULTS' LEARNING AND CAREER TEMPORALITIES IN THE ANALYSIS OF PROFESSIONALISATION AND PROFESSIONAL IDENTITY CONSTRUCTION

Adults develop experiential learning (Kolb, 1984) in private and professional contexts and situations that are increasingly diverse and mobile. Thus, the related identity construction processes are marked by articulations but also, and mainly, by tensions between on the one hand, the short temporalities defined by urgency and by the acceleration of the requirements for performance and career success, and, on the other hand, the longer temporalities that foster professional or personal development. These individual temporalities intersect with institutional ones that are affected as well by the cult of urgency, of quick solutions (Aubert, 2003), but also by the necessity of sustainability, of durable constructions and of long term institutional programmes (Dubet, 2002). This conflictuality between short term and long term temporal rhythms and perspectives is key to the understanding of the identity construction processes of adults engaged in learning and professionalisation journeys.

Within this framework, we will develop a reflection on macro, meso and micro temporal positions, and their articulation to professionalisation. Then, we will explain how our conception of *temps vécu*, which is lived-time, can clarify the comprehension of the temporal processes that are inscribed in the professional and learning pathways of adults. Finally, three analyses taken from our research work, covering three professional groups, French engineers, physiotherapists and junior community mediators, will identify two distinct processes of temporal construction of professionalisation and reveal their effects on the construction of the professional identities of those three professional groups.

TEMPORAL POSITIONS OF PROFESSIONALISATION

Temporalities concern all the activities of traditional, modern and post-modern societies and contribute to the fact that every society, every individual, can experience time (Hall, 1983). The power of programmatic time and the domination of clock time characterise modernity (Sue, 1994) and fit into the organised and streamlined time of work organisations and institutions in industrial societies (Sennett, 2006). This type of time equally organises nature (seasons), companies (rationalisation of economic, social and educational times, etc.) and individuals (careers, life cycles, etc.); it is a specific feature of the Western civilisation of the 19th and 20th centuries. But the time of clocks, a concept that refers to *Chronos*, the physical, objective time of real-word event sequence, has eventually expelled kairological time (Urry, 2000), the time of change and movement, the time of the emergence of forms and opportunities, the form of time that we feel when we are actively seeking new phenomena. This conception of *Kairos*, of discontinuous and creative time, is found in the post-modern and hypermodern approaches that place the development of individualism at the heart of major mutations. This relationship to time can then be understood as a series of empty rooms that one could explore in a given period. Individuals thus inscribe themselves in multiple temporalities that may be restrictive or emancipative (family, professional or learning temporalities). The question then arises to define the temporal positions along which these temporalities can unfold. These multifaceted temporal processes involve private and public activities as well as professional activities. Specific forms of temporality can be identified in individual life course, around several nonlinear sequences.

Temporalities are multiple and diverse. They relate to forms of temporal experience that affect differentiated levels of human life. The classical macro/meso/micro differentiation, is based on the distinction defined by Braudel (1949) on the plurality of social time and its tiered temporalities: firstly, the base of long duration, secondly, conjuncture, and finally the short term of the event. This differentiation enables us to think temporalities as being in direct contact with social and cultural processes in both individual and collective dimensions. Locating these processes on separate temporal positions does not prevent from 'watching them live' in constant interaction, within individual temporal experiences and dynamics.

Macro Temporality: A Historical Depth

Macro temporality pertains to long-term historical time. It generates identifiable and dated temporal figures belonging to defined space-times. This temporality remains on a human scale, it is the result of a specific historiality, specific to each culture and to each society. What it produces is a temporal configuration (Elias, 1996), a regime of historicity (Koselleck, 1990; Hartog, 2003) that favours specific relationships between past, present and future, or even between the field of experience (past to present relationship) and the horizon of expectations (future to present relationship). In connection with professionalisation, it is the historical construction of professional models, especially for the professions as in the case of engineers. Understanding the historical process is essential to grasping the genesis of the dynamics of professionalisation, for the professions but also for occupations in the process of recognition, or for emerging ones, as well as for occupations that are considered non-organised. The links between education or training and professionalisation define articulations between different types of knowledge. At the macro level, construction and exploitation of knowledge can be identified in the three following forms of knowledge: the theoretical one which is transmitted academically, the professional and empirical one, which is acquired through experience, and action-knowledge which is acquired through specific formative and professional activities. They can exist separately or form combinations, resulting in formalised modes within education curricula, or in more informal modes of knowledge transmission (e.g., self-study, peer learning). This trilogy both refers to the transmission of the specific learning modes of a professional activity and to the integration of this type of transmission into the mode of organisatio7n of the corresponding professional group. In fact, it refers to the production of educational and formative processes that underpin the legitimacy of the practice of a professional activity through the production of professionalisms, and of professional paths and careers. Without this historical depth, professionalisation become a momentary social stake, whose fulcrums and temporal frameworks are not sufficiently established for the situations and actors concerned.

Meso Temporality: An Institutional Translation

Meso temporality is a form of temporal mediation that is materialised by the production of collective temporal experiences, primarily through institutional and organisational forms. Historical temporal regimes get translated into temporal schemes that are anchored in specific socio-cultural contexts. This temporality is part of a contemporaneity, a present that is palpable for each individual. It aims at a present, social, political issue, located at a time 't' in a historical configuration. Its most visible shape can be found in the temporalities of institutions and organisations in our modern and post-modern societies. On this level, the professionalisation that has been built on a macro level is translated into a professional education curriculum, a training apparatus or a professional curriculum. This translation is often defined in 'an institutional programme', i.e. a socialisation mode of actors in learning or professional situations. Schools, universities, training curricula, professionalisation frameworks, define institutional programmes that fit or do not fit in previous historical models. As Dubet wrote it, an institutional programme:

> (1) considers that working on others is a mediation between universal values and specific individuals; (2) affirms that the activity of socialisation is a vocation because it is directly founded on values; (3) is based on the belief that socialisation is aimed at inculcating norms that shape individuals and, at the same time make them autonomous and free. (2002, pp. 13–14)

Transmitted knowledge, articulation between forms of knowledge, professionality building are social constructs that participate in this translation process.

The distinct training apparatuses then play a socialising role, they are the translation of modes of relation to others that value a type of normalisation between the universal values of a profession or trade, and their transmission to individuals wishing to practice an activity which is defined in specific areas of autonomy.

Whatever their nature or construction may be, apparatuses meet social requirements. Their continuity and transformation over time, their short existence, or even their disappearance, appear to be mediating elements between historical professional models and individuals inscribed in heterogeneous social and personal trajectories.

Micro Temporality: Lived Temporalities

Finally, the micro temporal level directly affects individuals and individual temporalities; it consists in temporal experiences that are specific to each person, that are heterogeneous, based on spaces of biographical continuity and/or rupture, including the differentiated movements and rhythms of life. It refers to the 'professionalisation pathways' embedded in diversified biographical journeys. These temporalities are identifiable in life cycles, in individual biographies but also in the time connections which are experienced and built by individuals. They may not be disjointed from historical temporalities and from institutional temporalities, because they reflect social representations and express the actual experience of individual and collective temporalities (Boutinet, 2004). At the same time, they give meaning to the various forms of temporalities and reflect the true-life dimension of temporality experience in everyone's daily life. They incorporate stabilisation processes as well as change processes in the fragmented modern temporalities. Thus, the micro level questions macro and meso temporalities in return. In this perspective, it is essential to grasp the diversity and singularity of these structures in the specific temporal plurality of every human being. The professionalisation processes get materialised in individual dynamics of knowledge production within lifelong differentiated learning, training and working activities (transformative learning, professional retraining, and so on). The lived experience of professionalisation is built on combinations of established educational and professional models and by training modes created by individuals (self-training, on the job training, peer-training) which respect individual temporalities and root professionalisation trajectories in individual itineraries.

How Temporal Positions Connect

Temporalities may therefore diversify, generate different speeds (Virillo, 1995, 2005), and also stagnate, stabilise, accelerate, slow down, split into forms of disruption-discontinuity-continuity, and affect individual temporalities as well as institutional temporalities. They only exist through these movements, these rhythms, which are the expression of continuities and discontinuities inherent in any social or individual process. Thus, a 'deprogramming', a break-up of the established models seems to oppose the rationalising frameworks of the modern era, of the industrial society, which were made of linear temporalities (life-lasting family and job) as they now seem to split into a variety of institutional and individual bricolages. Moreover, the continuity/discontinuity distinction is no more thoroughly clear-cut. Continuity may be seen in the resistance of institutional frameworks to the heterogeneity of individual situations (planning and scheduling time frames are still up-to-date), but also in individual constructions, such as the models of boundaryless careers (mobility can be a form of continuity through professional success). Discontinuity can be considered through the more and more frequent rupture processes taking place in private and professional lives, but also in the managerial modes of institutions increasingly faced with permanent changes.

These dynamics are embedded in the forms of time which individuals experience and construct both in their own trajectories and their experiential contexts. These dynamics can take the aspect of continuity, but also of ruptures, where representations of the past and projection in the future articulate. What we call temporal positions (macro, meso and micro) are successive layers of temporalities which can be used to grasp these representations, at a specific time 't', linking them so that they gain meaning in individual and social reality. They correspond to experiential and therefore human states of lived-time, rebuilt *a posteriori* by individuals and, modelled, necessarily later, by researchers.

Thus, the conceptual framework of temporalities allows to think professionalisation processes as constantly intersecting, in the distinct temporal dynamics that punctuate the life cycles of individuals. These processes occur both in collective contexts (work organisations, professional organisations) and in individual contexts. These processes take place in collective configurations, namely occupational groups, or through individuals who perform a similar occupation. The acceleration of temporal rhythms emphasises the tensions between individual and institutional rhythms of professionalisation: the gap widens between the long-term timescale, which is necessary to the construction of professionalism, and the urgent time frame required by institutional professionalisation.

THE EXPRESSION OF LIVED-TIME

Our interest therefore lies in biographical material, in the one that gives an account of life course, and, more specifically, of the life sequences linked to the formative and professional activities. This approach merges into a comprehensive conception of experienced time: 'historical time models' have no existence in themselves, if they are not relayed by, or do not integrate, social and individual conceptions, which are the representations that actors build in their biographical and temporal trajectories. These articulations are inscribed in processes that have differentiated durations and rhythms within the individual experience of time. They provide the ability of connecting temporal positions, not only on hierarchical temporal registers, but on an identical time line experienced individually and socially. This posture and this perspective do not refer to a concept of *Chronos*, the linear programmed time, but to the concept of *temps vécu* or, in English, *lived-time*, developed by Minkowski (1933), and therefore to intercalary interspersed recursive processes which connect different levels of temporalities. Minkowski's conception of time provides an adequate framework to the comprehension of lived temporalities. Time is considered, on the one hand, as an irrational phenomenon, refractory to any conceptual formula, but on the other hand, as soon as we try to represent it, it quite naturally takes the appearance of a straight line. To reduce this tension, phenomena intercalate and spread between these two extreme aspects of time, by enabling the passage from one to the other. These phenomena constitute articulations between temporal positions, thus creating the sense of many individual, social and professional activities.

These processes are embedded in the *lived-times* (Roquet, 2013) built by individuals both in their own singular trajectories and experiential contexts of continuity, but also in situations of rupture linking representation of the past, present itself, and projection into the future. Links are built in the past/present/future relation, thus giving meaning to the experiences of individuals. Walter Benjamin's (1982) analysis helps us identify a dissociation between the space of experience and the horizon of expectations. This dynamic creates an accelerated, but not cumulative, succession of isolated episodes of experience that juxtapose and result in a transformation of the structure of subjective temporal experience. Differentiated rhythms generate meaning in this organisation of lived-time and touch upon the understanding of the processes of professionalisation. They contribute to the setting in motion and to the recognition of the professionalities of the subjects within their career paths.

Thus, in the employment/training trajectories of adults, professionalisation is permanently questioned. Professionalisation incorporates a dimension of individual lived-time; it is a lifelong construction which can be realised under differentiated experiential forms. The professionalisation of the subject refers to a combination of, on the one hand, identifiable existing educational and professional models and, on the other hand, new professionalities requiring the intervention of appropriate training modes. These models do not consist in 'planned' paths, but in paths that include the contingencies, opportunities and hazards which allow the construction of professionalisation strategies that are contextualised in educational and professional situations identifiable in the biographical trajectory. They result in identity constructions considered as socialisation processes and contributing to the production of professionalisation dynamics.

THE TEMPORAL CONTINUITY AND DISCONTINUITY OF PROFESSIONALISATION: DIFFERENTIATED FORMS OF IDENTITY CONSTRUCTION

This reflection on the temporalities of professionalisation highlights the links between the formative and professional identity constructions of adults in specific temporal positions and reveal how they result in various forms of professionalisation. In this regard, we will take three examples from our research work to illustrate our point of view and show how temporal continuity and discontinuity produce differentiated forms of identity construction.

As far as temporal continuity is concerned, we can identify two differentiated forms of identity construction in engineers and physiotherapists: the professionalisation process of engineers rests on a historical depth and on an identity offer that have both been built over more than 200 years, whereas the more recent professionalisation of physiotherapists is marked by the search for a specific identity.

Engineers: Sustainable Professionalisation, Temporalities of Continuity

The numerous historical and sociological research studies on the occupational group of engineers in France insist on the hierarchical and segmented aspect of this group regarding its reproduction and transformations modes over two centuries (Grelon, 1989; Picon & Chatzis, 1992). The traditional characteristics of this professional group are the emblematic figure of the engineer graduated from the *grandes écoles*, that are elite higher education institutions,[1] and the traditional polarisation between the academically qualified engineers and the technicians who gained their qualification thanks to promotion. This situation can be explained by the constitution of educational and professional engineer models over a long historical period; it refers to a sustainable professionalisation process articulated to characteristic engineer figures (Roquet, 2000). Neither the profession nor its representation are unified, but the historical dynamics of the training modes of engineers have given meaning to the identity construction of this professional group. Professional models range from the central segment of the engineer graduated from a *grande école* to the minority one of the autodidact, who is generally called *ingénieur maison*[2] (Roquet, 2000). A third intermediate segment developed more recently due to the creation of university curricula, of "second-rank" *écoles d'ingénieurs*; these new engineer schools delivered academic education but were less selective than the *grandes écoles* and were more open to the productive system. Thus, three engineer models (*grandes écoles* engineer, production engineer, promoted engineer) developed in relation to the sociohistorical evolution. The forms of temporalities induced in this long process of professionalisation alternate: a historical time long enough to define the models of the engineering profession, the time of institutionalisation of these models through the creation of permanent and recognised training apparatuses (engineer schools, initial education, continuing education, apprenticeship) and the individual biographical temporalities which permanently allow to anchor and transform these models into professional, social and individual life cycles. These three professional models constitute identity offers organised in relation to different professional segments. The recruitment channels, the training apparatuses, the learning modes of the distinct academic and professional forms of knowledge and the professionalities contribute to the identity definition of the segments and to their differentiation. A basic process such as professionalisation overlaps with authentication and transformation mechanisms that redefine existing identities. In relation to historical periods, the segments are recomposed, but at the same time maintain professional models, in a permanent movement of identity construction-deconstruction-reconstruction of the professional figures of the engineer. Somehow, these are biographical temporal forms (how do I identify myself as an engineer?) and institutional temporal forms (how am I recognised as an engineer?) of identity construction which give meaning to the existence of this professional group. We can then put forward the following proposal: the three professional models of the engineer (*grandes écoles* engineer, production engineer and promoted engineer) only come to life in the biographical stories of the engineers and in the speech of the actors. These (micro level) biographical temporalities give meaning to the existence of these models, which are translated into social and professional representations and into modes of acquisition of knowledge. The central segment and the intermediate segment are linked to forms of temporalities of continuity, and to recognised and established models of self-identification, whereas the minority segment coincides with transitional temporalities more related to biographical courses that are embedded in continuing education. There is absolutely no temporal linearity, but we rather observe the stabilisation of a process of professionalisation in individual trajectories.

French Physiotherapists: Identity Construction Within a Temporal Continuity

In the historical context of the practice of physiotherapy, or more precisely of *masso-kinesitherapie* in France, it took the First World War and its many mutilated victims to see the creation of a group of new professionals responsible for physical therapy. Then, the definition of the activity of physiotherapists became clearer with the creation of the State diploma of *infirmier-masseur*[3] in 1923, and then the degree of *professeur de culture physique médicale*[4] (1932), the *diplôme d'Etat de moniteur de gymnastique médicale*[5] (1942) and finally the degree of *masseur médical*[6] (1943). In 1946, it is the fusion of these trades that gave birth to the French profession of physiotherapists. In relation to the development of their professional practices, physiotherapists have established their group as a professional group, seeking to differentiate themselves from other health professionals.

Indeed, the results of a recent study (Roquet, Gatto, & Vincent, 2015) show that physiotherapy is a profession in France, and that it is serves patients as well as society. It meets the professionalism criteria defined by Wilensky (1964):

> the profession is exercised full time; it is regulated by a legal framework, which is here composed of the French code of public health, and the French penal and civil codes; it has a specialised training curriculum and specific schools, possesses professional organisations (here, a professional order and several trade unions), its monopoly is legally protected, and it has established a code of ethics.

However this recent professionalisation process is linked to the development of professional stakes that are more and more visible.

The results of this research allowed us to define the contours of several social roles that physiotherapists have acquired through experience in a long-term temporal construction and as a result of adaptation and adjustment dynamics balancing their various societal demands with the needs and demands of patients and society. Some of these new roles are not yet recognised by the French administration in the definition of the professional practice of physiotherapy. Identified social roles appear in different categories:

- Physiotherapy diagnosis
- Physiotherapy diagnosis of exclusion.
- Differential physiotherapy diagnosis.
- Physiotherapy diagnosis of orientation.
- Direct access care.
- Autonomous therapeutic decision-making with the patient as a partner.
- Answers to the patient's implicit and explicit needs and requirements (quality).
- The relational, educational and communicational activities concurrent with rehabilitation activities.
- Inventiveness, creativity, conceptualisation, decision-making (singular activities resulting from the patient's requests, using disciplinary knowledge, associated know-how and experience of physiotherapy).
- Conceptual and technical innovation within professional practice.
- Prevention, patient and caregiver education.
- Care from birth to the end of life.
- Advice.
- Alternative to hospitalisation.
- Home support.
- Holistic patient-environment care approach in accordance with the logic of the current health care system.

The results have also led to demonstrate that the professional identities of French physiotherapists were both constructed around a common dimension, in which these healthcare professionals could all root their identification (the vocation/profession relationship), and around the differentiation between three identity logics that are respectively development, expertise and vocation. This double perspective defines the professional identity of French physiotherapists and constitutes the core of their profession. This identity construction allows French physiotherapists to define themselves and to be recognised in their activity; it also allows a collective construction around a common platform thanks to which they can be recognised by other occupational groups (doctors, healthcare professions and occupations, etc.) and by patients as well. After an analysis identifying professional situations experienced by French physiotherapists, a second analysis also identified two axes through the biographic, and sometimes reflective, narrative of those interviewed.

The first axis which founds the identification of each physiotherapist (stability of self-representation, meaning given to activities, stabilisation of practices) connects, sometimes in tension, the vocational origin of the activity of physiotherapy with the professional practice of French physiotherapists. Vocation corresponds to the values of universality, humanity, human relationships, and so on. Profession corresponds to professional roles (e.g., expert, communicator, and instructor) and social roles (such as patient's education and physiotherapy diagnosis). This link between vocation and profession constitutes a stable component of the professional identity of French physiotherapists. It is at the heart of the meaning of their professional activity and of their social and professional recognition. It is the common point of the identity construction of the profession, an identity in which any physical therapist will personally recognise himself. This construction belongs to the long-term level of professionalisation that articulates the past and the present of a profession in a temporal continuity.

The second level of analysis also allowed us to define three differentiated logics of identity-building that are involved in the collective identity construction of French physiotherapists. The basis of this differentiation lies in the processes of the personal, social and professional recognition of their activities. The cross-references made between the professional situations encountered by the interviewed French physiotherapists and their past and present career trajectories reveal that three identificatory models of the profession, both common and differentiated, can be identified in their professional careers: one of them is articulated by an identity logic of vocation, another one by an identity logic of development, and another one by an identity logic of expertise.

The identity logic of vocation relies on the affirmation process of a personal identity but also on the search for appropriate social roles (for example, for a care mission). Reflexivity on the practices, professionalisation construction through the use of experience and knowledge contribute to explore the personal part of identity while seeking, in different stages of career, several modes of recognition (others, institutions, etc.).

The identity logic of development fits into career dynamics that are generally oriented upwards, allowing to integrate different statuses (self-employed or not) as well as distinct positions and functions, but also enabling to develop different forms of expertise (e.g. scientific and technical) while seeking paths of professional development especially through continuing education. Occupational mobility is "the ingredient of this dynamic".

The identity logic of expertise rather lies in a process of identity differentiation. As experts, or as artists, French physiotherapists express themselves through the creation of new technologies and knowledge that fit into an art which is recognised in different socio-professional worlds (high performance sport, for example). Thus, the issue of recognition is competence singularity, which can therefore become visible in their distinctness from other professionals or colleagues.

These three identity forms are also found in a long-term form of professionalisation that more specifically articulates present and future types of professional career construction.

ADULTS' LEARNING AND CAREER TEMPORALITIES IN THE ANALYSIS

The processes of identity construction of engineers and physiotherapists were built in differentiated time frames. If the engineers could quickly find their professional autonomy through the specificity of their professional activity, the physiotherapists have had to define their scope of activities by comparing them to the doctors' and had to adapt their professional practices more quickly. These identity construction processes of working adults reveal how experience is built and valued thanks to the use of forms of reflexivity (Dewey, 1934). For the individuals, these structures of professionalisation belong to long-term temporal configurations. This long-term time scale, time of durability, is built on a set of events, of ordeals, that solidify the career paths of individuals into forms of recognition. This long-term time scale provides a form of continuity in the professionalisation of French physiotherapists.

Emploi Jeunes Junior Community Mediators: Temporalities of Discontinuity

The objective of the youth employment promotion programme called *Nouveaux services – Emplois Jeunes* (1999–2005) was to enable young people to quickly access employment in new forms of activities such as social mediation, thanks to subsidised contracts that could last up to five years. During this period the inputs and outputs of the programme were highly variable. The objective of activity creation determined the finality of access to employment for young people, thus professionalisation became an intervention category of youth employment policy. The temporal dimension was associated with this process: the professionalisation of the youth was being built in sequenced temporalities (when they entered the programme, during the programme and after the programme). It operated as a transition path or professional socialisation route for a large part of the target population. The *Emplois Jeune* programme belonged to an ephemeral temporality which ran counter to job sustainability and professionalisation process. Numerous training courses were created but they mainly only resulted in setting fuzzy future time horizons, instead of building professional models of activity and knowledge for the youth. The young workers had to develop, legitimise and assert their skills by themselves within their learning and professional journeys. The construction of their professional identities thus relied on fragmented processes of activity autonomisation, in occupations devoid of established or recognised professional models; the young people in the programme were in charge of the promotion and legitimation of their own activities, including those related to social mediation. Professional models were too few or absent, and *Emplois Jeunes* junior community mediators could not either rely on the professionalisation models of their activities: there were no established professional frameworks. These frameworks are temporal constructions that allow individuals to integrate, or not to integrate, the spaces of opportunity in their own professionalisation trajectory. This possibility refers to intentionality, to *agency*, i.e. the ability of individuals to be or to become active agents in their own lives.

So, as those professional models did not exist, new forms of professionalism were built within heterogeneous biographical journeys, in continuity/discontinuity.

The biographical temporalities of these young people were more marked by unstable constructions characterised by 'moments' of professional recognition of their activities and experience. The biographical and experiential framework set in various temporalities was then put forth without having so far been recognised or consolidated by the institutional framework. In this configuration, we could only identify forms of permanent transaction between life sequences, inscribed in trajectories and patterns of professionalisation occurring with occupational groups, peers, work collectives or organisations (companies, institutions, etc.). These transactions underlie the construction of professional identities (Dubar, 2000) and give an experiential meaning to 'professionalisation paths" marked by both temporal continuity and ruptures.

The professionalisation of *Emplois Jeunes* junior community mediators contributed to this adaptation and adjustment process by coming closer to common professional and formative models, or through the invention of training modes (self-training) that respected individual temporalities and rooted professionalisation journeys in individual itineraries. The hypothesis of a prescriptive or programmed route designed by institutional actors in the traditional descriptive and classificatory model of job-training courses is refuted by a comprehensive approach of individual trajectories. On the contrary, a multiplicity of contingencies, opportunities, risks and accidents can build professionalisation strategies, contextualised in identifiable formative and professional situations. Then the professionalisation time model of the *Emplois Jeunes* junior community mediators was built through diversified experiential learning configurations that allowed individuals to develop various skills (relational skills, resourcefulness) in multiple forms of identity construction, with no established model. Fragmented and discontinuous forms of individual temporalities have built unique and singular professionalities for the young people enrolled in the *Emploi Jeunes* programme.

CONCLUSION: THE SHORT-TIME/LONG-TIME OPPOSITION OF PROFESSIONALISATION

The three identity construction processes of French physiotherapists and *Emplois Jeunes* junior community mediators belong to differentiated professionalisation dynamics that have distinctive temporalities. Individual trajectories are inscribed in different temporal sequences: continuity, discontinuity, rupture, project, etc., which permanently structure educational and professional paths. These temporal forms expressed in biographical narratives, do not dissociate from institutional time forms that mark and punctuate individual routes, as exemplified in landmarks such as the beginning of training or of professionalisation programmes, or in the successive steps of socio-professional recognition. The well-structured time of the professionalisation of engineers, inscribed in a system of identity dynamics that are stabilised, and of French physiotherapists, whose identities are stabilising, is opposed to the discontinuous professionalisation time model of the *Emplois Jeunes* junior community mediators whose identity forms are uncertain. The proposed identity offers developed in differentiated space-time and socio-historical contexts which secure, which fix, the references of professional self-identification that are marked by the variation of professional models. These three forms of temporal dynamics affect the life-courses of adults engaged in professionalisation paths that are becoming increasingly complex nowadays. The historical time required for any perpetuation and recognition of a professional activity is overlapped by the shorter times of professional socialisation. In other words, the long-term time scale, necessary to all forms of professional recognition, opposes the short-term time scale of immediate activity, often little socially recognised. Moreover, the lived-time of professionalisation, i.e. biographical time, on the micro level, is embedded in professional contexts pertaining to the meso level, but sustains transitions towards significant differences in recognition and therefore in sustainability, consequently to the existence or lack of stable and established professional models, inscribed in the macro level.

NOTES

[1] In France, the *grandes écoles* ("grand schools") such as the prestigious *Ecole polytechnique* or *Ecole centrale* are higher education establishments outside the university system. Some of them were created several centuries ago. These schools are state-run and state-funded, and are famous for the quality of their teaching and research. Unlike in universities, admission is based on a selection process. The *Diplôme d'ingénieur*, i.e. engineer diploma, awarded by the *grandes écoles* generally after five years of studies after high school, is still a reference for engineership today.
[2] "Home-trained engineers" or "company-trained engineers".
[3] "Masseur-nurse".
[4] "Teacher of medical physical culture".
[5] "State diploma of medical gymnastics teacher".
[6] "Medical masseur".

REFERENCES

Aubert, N. (2003). *Le culte de l'urgence. La société malade du temps*. Paris: Flammarion.
Benjamin, W. (1982). *Charles Baudelaire. Un poète lyrique à l'apogée du capitalisme*. Paris: Payot.
Boutinet, J.-P. (2004). *Vers une société des agendas. Une mutation des temporalités*. Paris: PUF.
Braudel, F. (1949). *La Méditerranée et le monde méditerranéen à l'époque de Philippe II*. Paris: Armand Collin.
Dewey, J. (1968). *Expérience et Éducation* (M.-A. Carroi, Trans.). Paris: Armand Colin. (Original Edition, 1934)
Dubar, C. (2000). *La crise des identités*. Paris: PUF.
Dubet, F. (2002). *Le déclin de l'institution*. Paris: Le Seuil.
Elias, N. (1996). *Du temps* (M. Hulin, Trans.). Paris: Fayard. (Original Edition, 1984)
Grelon, A. (1989). Les universités et la formation des ingénieurs en France (1870–1914). *Formation Emploi, 70*, 31–42.
Hall, E. T. (1983). *The dance of life: The other dimension of time*. New York, NY: Anchor Press/Doubleday.
Hartog, F. (2003). *Régimes d'historicité : Présentisme et expériences du temps*. Paris: Le Seuil.
Kolb, D. (1984). *Experiential learning as the science of learning and development*. Englewood Cliffs, NJ: Prentice Hall.

Koselleck, R. (1990). *Le Futur passé. Contribution à la sémantique des temps historiques* (J. Hoock & M.-J. Hoock, Trans.). Paris: EHESS Ed. (Original Edition, 1979)
Minkowski, E. (1933). *Le temps vécu. Etude phénoménologique et psychopathologique* (1ère ed.). Neufchâtel: Delachaux et Nestlé.
Picon, A., & Chatzis, K. (1992). La formation des ingénieurs au siècle dernier. Débats, polémiques et conflits. *L'orientation scolaire et professionnelle, 21*(3), 227–243.
Roquet, P. (2000). *Les Nouvelles Formations d'Ingénieurs: une approche sociologique*. Villeneuve d'Ascq: PU Septentrion.
Roquet, P. (2004). Temporalités biographiques et temporalités institutionnelles: la construction identitaire de l'ingénieur promu. *Savoirs, 4*, 99–121.
Roquet, P. (2013). Temporalités et temps vécu. In P. Roquet, M.-J. Gonçalves, L. Roger, & V. Caetano (Pys.), *Temps, temporalités, et complexité dans les activités éducatives et formatives*. Paris: L'Harmattan.
Roquet, P., Gatto, F., & Vincent, S. (2015). *L'identification et la reconnaissance des rôles et des identités des masseurs-kinésithérapeutes*. Essonee: Centre de Recherche sur la Formation, CNAM.
Sennett, R. (2006). *La culture du nouveau capitalisme* (P.-E. Dauzat, Trans.). Paris: Albin Michel. (Original Edition, 2006)
Sue, E. (1994). *Temps et ordre social*. Paris: PUF.
Virillo, P. (1995). *La vitesse de libération*. Paris: Galilée.
Virillo, P. (2005). *L'accident originel*. Paris: Galilée.
Urry, J. (2005). *Sociologie des mobilités* (N. Burch, Trans.). Paris: Armand Colin. (Original Edition, 2000)
Wilensky, H. (1964). The professionalisation of everyone? *American Journal of Sociology, 2*, 137–158.

Pascal Roquet
Conservatoire National des Arts et Métiers
Paris, France

CATARINA PAULOS

13. WAYS OF LEARNING OF ADULT EDUCATORS IN UNCERTAIN PROFESSIONAL CONTEXTS

INTRODUCTION

Considering that adult education is an educational practice field and simultaneously a field of reflection and research (Canário, 2008; Barbier, 2009), this research focused on a particular category of adult educators, on a field also specific to adult education which is the Recognition of Prior Learning (RPL). Canário (2008) stated that the dissemination of educational practices aimed at adults is accompanied by a process of internal differentiation and complexity of the adult education field itself, which is notable at three levels; firstly on the level of educational practices in terms of purposes, ways and target groups; secondly, in terms of the diversity of the institutions involved; and lastly, in terms of the new concern with the professionalisation of adult educators (Canário, 2008).

In Portugal the concern with adult education increased with the transition to a democracy, which occurred with the revolution on the 25th of April, 1974. Until then, adult education 'as a specific social field had practically no past in Portugal' (Rothes, 2004, p. 62) and training directed at adult educators did not exist. Despite the strengthening of the interest after the democratisation process of the country, adult education has been a field full of discontinuities. As mentioned by Lima (2008), over the past three decades adult education was marked by discontinuous educational policies, characterised by the absence of a plan of continuity. Adult education policies are characterised by discontinuity in the last decades. Similarly adult educators' pathways have been marked by discontinuous patterns. In Portugal, after the end of the 1990s, RPL was launched and integrated with adult education public policies. Due to the New Opportunities Initiative, between 2006 and 2010, there were an increasing number of both adult learners and adult educators involved in RPL. But after 2011, RPL suffered a strong disinvestment by the Government and thus adult education and training policy was suspended. Between 2012 and 2013 all RPL centres were closed. After that, the majority of adult educators involved in RPL became unemployed. After 2014, RPL has been implemented, but involves fewer number of adult educators. Additionally, adult educators involved in adult education provision have been hired and fired according to national programmes underdevelopment or suspended programmes. When programmes are under development, they are positive as adult educators but when programmes are suspended they assume other professional identities.

Social actors who have dedicated themselves to adult education are thus hostages of the changes in policies in this area. With the emergence of new educational practices in the field of adult education, there have been new actors to perform newly created professional activities. On the one hand, we have adult educators who have moved from other professional activities belonging to the education field and are therefore already familiar with issues related to education. On the other hand, we have adult educators who, for the first time, have or don't have professional experience in other knowledge areas. The design of adult educators´ training systems takes into account a broad concept of adult education (Castro, Guimarães, & Sancho, 2007). Adult educators should be able to act in a wide range of educational activities, and they must be able to achieve different goals, and to work with different target groups and in several educational contexts. Loureiro (2012) highlighted the need to study 'more continuously' (p. 127) the new educational contexts that have been emerging and the actors who are working in this field of practices.

The aim of this chapter is to discuss the ways of learning of adult educators in a changing world. Considering that learning is an activity of knowledge appropriation that one does not possess (Charlot, 2000), but whose existence is in objects, places and people, the current study has the intention of providing input into the adult educators' learning ways in a changing professional context. This chapter focuses on a specific category of adult educators named RPL (Recognition of Prior Learning), professionals who had an important role in the implementation and development of RPL. Firstly, I will discuss how adult educators who had worked in RPL learned to do their job. Secondly, I will discuss how adult educators coped with the uncertainty of their professional pathways in the adult education field.

WAYS OF LEARNING IN ADULT EDUCATION

Charlot (2000) stated that human beings have an obligation to learn, this duty is conferred with the act of birth. According to the author, learning has the aim of self-forming the individual, in a way that the individual becomes someone, becomes a unique example of someone and becomes a member of a community, sharing its values and occupying a place in it. The individual has the need to learn to live in society 'to appropriate the world' (Charlot, 2000, p. 53). Learning is thus a dual process in which the individual builds himself/herself and is constructed by others, in a dialectical relationship.

In everyday life, humans establish relationships with others, and with the external environment and the social world. When an individual relates with the world, he/she acts over it, producing changes on a physical, mental and social level, giving meaning and assigning meaning to the acts and the environment in which these take place. Barbier (2009) stated that the activity of the individual is both a 'world transformation process and a process of transformation of himself/herself transforming the world' (p. 122). When the individual acts, he/she has a transformative action on the world, a result of the involvement with the physical, social and mental environment.

Through interactions with others and with the world in general, individuals acquire a set of knowledge, skills and competences that will promote a better individual environment and adjustment, facilitating appropriate answers to the demands of everyday life. Learning that is a result of this interaction may have been produced in formal, non-formal and informal contexts, and may have more or less permanent effects. Learning promotes the construction, by the individual, of a world view, that is, a view of himself/herself, of the relationship with others and the social reality. This world vision becomes concrete in a system of representations that works simultaneously to read the reality on a confirmatory way or as a reference point to build new world views (Canário, 2008).

Experience has received a growing valorisation in adult education, namely in professional life, being seen as a source of learning (Zeitler, Guérin, & Barbier, 2012). The concepts of experience and learning from experience can have several meanings as Charlier, Roussel, and Boucenna (2013) stated, experience can be cognitive and affective, individual or collective, and refers to the professional or personal life. The concept of experience has two meanings: one characterised by the orientation towards the future, and the other referring to the past (Villers, 1991). In the first sense, experience is linked to an attempt, to the action to test something which the outcome is not totally unknown, existing data that may point out possible outcomes. According to the second meaning, the action has already taken place and it has already been experienced by the individual. In this second formulation, experience is a way by which a person gains knowledge. That is the reason why experience can have learning value.

According to Zeitler, Guérin, and Barbier (2012), experience can designate an activity, the understanding about certain life situations and the process that derives from these situations. Experience is what underlies being an active part of several individual situations in different contexts, and the products that are derived from this process. Bondía (2002) believed that experience is the 'possibility that something happens to us or touches us" (p. 24) and requires time to observe, listen, think and reflect. According to this author, the knowledge of experience results from the development "of the sense or the nonsense of what happens to us' (p. 27).

Lived situations are the base of experience (Charlier, Roussel, & Boucenna, 2013), although they are not an *a priori* experience. An experience presupposes, on the one hand, a link to a lived situation, and on the other hand a detachment from the situation, which allows the construction of meaning. For an experienced situation to acquire meaning and become significant, it must be thought about by the individual; it has to undergo a reflective process. Reflection allows experienced situations to acquire a meaning for the individual. Experience leads to 'a reconstruction of the meaning' (Charlier, Roussel, & Boucenna, 2013, p. 11) of lived situations. Canário (2008) pointed out that the assignment of importance to the experience in the learning process assumes that it is seen as an internal process of the individual, functioning as a process of self-development along the life path.

Kolb, an author who was influenced by Dewey, saw the experience as a source of learning and development (Jarvis, 2006). Kolb (1984) presented experiential learning as a cycle, which consists of four stages: concrete experience, reflective observation, abstract conceptualisation and active experimentation. The concrete experience is the basis for observations and reflections. Reflections are assimilated and transformed into abstract concepts, that is, into thoughts, from which are generated new implications for action. Experiential learning is a process of construction of knowledge that involves a tension between the four ways of learning. This process is represented by a circle or spiral, in which the individual will go through each one of the steps that constitute it – experience, reflection, thinking and action – in a continuous process, which would result in a learning situation. Experiential learning is thus a process in which knowledge is created from the transformation of experience.

According to Josso (1991, 2002), to have learning value, an experience needs to be reflected on and thought about by the individual, in order to extract knowledge and know-how. Josso (2008) referred to all learning as experiential, insofar as the experience requires reflection about what was experienced by the individual. If learning is not experiential, there is transmission of information, but there is no learning. Learning involves the existence of an awareness process, learning from lived experiences and reflection about them. Learning involves a process of change by the individual in a learning context, of transition from one state to another state of knowledge. Josso (2008) also pointed out that there were 'temporalities in the learning processes' (p. 124), that is, the individual learns according to a certain rhythm which the learning process should respect.

Pineau (1991) stated that experiential learning results from direct contact with the action without the intervention of mediators such as educators, curricula and training programmes, or documentation, and it takes place immediately. In order for an experience to acquire learning value, it must be reflected on. The individual needs to reorganise and reconstruct the elements which compose an experience, to give them a sense, in the light of previous lived situations and the way he/she is projected in the future. Pineau (2009) pointed out that learning can be of three types: self-directed learning (*autoformation*), hetero-learning (*hétéroformation*) and eco-learning (*écoformation*). According to this theory, self-directed learning is the mechanism by which the individual appropriates experiences and interactions from daily life. Hetero-learning is about the learning done with people, watching their behaviours, asking them questions and arguing about work procedures and guidelines. Eco-learning focuses on the learning from contact with the environment and its context. Learning is the result of the interaction between the individual and other people, in professional, social and personal contexts. There is learning that derives from the individual's interaction with others and with the environment, and it also may result from the mobilisation of personal resources, in an attitude of reflection about experiences and the incorporation of the sense of these experiences in life. This interrelation between self, others and environment makes the learning process 'an ongoing, dialectic and multiform process' (Pineau, 2009, p. 153).

Experiential learning is based on the assumption that individuals learn through experience along with the premise that they assume an active role as well as having the ability to experience and reflect on the situations and events that occur in their daily life (Cavaco, 2009). Experiential learning valorises the work of individuals, their competences and experiences (Lietard, 2007). Dominicé (1991) pointed out that the formative dimension of experience depends largely on the cultural resources that the individual has, which make it possible to assign a meaning to experiences. For an experience to have learning value, it needs to be thought about and reflected on. Adult learning processes should take place in an environment that promotes critical reflection, which involves a critique of the assumptions on which the individuals' beliefs have been built (Mezirow, 1990). According to Mezirow (2000) learning is understood as the process of using a prior interpretation of an experience or situation 'to construe a new or revised interpretation of the meaning of one's experience as a guide to future action' (p. 5).

Learning from experience is part of a concept of education during life, with a character essentially pedagogic and oriented to the individual (Alheit & Dausien, 2006). According to these authors, the 'non-formal, informal, non-institutionalised and self-organised aspects of learning' (p. 180) acquire a crucial role in the development of the individual. Learning arises from the individual's experiences, 'episodes of transition and crisis' (Alheit & Dausien, 2006, p. 190), in formal, non-formal and informal life situations, always linked to the context of a concrete biography.

UNCERTAINTY AS THE ONLY CERTAINTY IN THE PROFESSIONAL FIELD

During the life course, humans spend a significant amount of time working. The way work has been experienced by individuals as well as the role that it has occupying their lives, has been changing over time. In the early twentieth century, work was generally stable, and a worker could carry out his/her professional activity during the course of working life with the same employer, following the evolution of techniques and progressing towards an increased responsibility and specialisation. At this time, when workers began their professional pathways, they had an employment perspective of staying with the same organisation all their working life (Bauman, 2001).

Due to constant social changes, fast technological innovation and the centrality of the economic dimension in current society, professional pathways have changed, both in terms of their beginnings and endings, and in terms of individuals' trajectories. Although work has been considered a means of 'self-realisation and self-expression, the place of a new-found autonomy' (Méda, 1999, p. 143), it is noteworthy that it currently 'can no longer offer a safe axis around which engage and fix self-definitions, identities and life projects' (Bauman, 2001, p. 160).

In the last decades, in the Western world, both professional pathways and learning processes have been characterised by several reorientations and reconfigurations (Monbaron, 2009). Workers are protagonists of 'randomly' (Dominicé, 2006, p. 348) biographical pathways, and non-linear life pathways, punctuated by ruptures and transitions.

Nowadays, many life pathways don't have sequential developmental phases anymore, but are pathways reduced to life slices separated from each other, made of contrasts, and changes of direction (Dominicé, 2006). The professional pathways of adults are marked by 'turbulence, flexibility, impermanence' (Dominicé, 2006, p. 11), where the perspective of a stable routine or an expected career gives way to 'coping with a flexible labour market' (p. 17). Flexibility is, as noted by Bauman (2001), 'the slogan of the day' (p. 169), and has become a common term spread in Western society, linked to 'the beginning of the work by short-term contracts or no contracts, positions without pension coverage' (p. 169), in an environment where the only certainty is permanent uncertainty.

Individuals are always in movement, as they move from one professional activity to another, and because of this permanent change they do not develop a sense of belonging, becoming strangers to organisational cultures (Robin, 2009). In this context, the attachment to work has no longer a central role in the formation of professional identity. In a late-modern society characterised by continuous changes, adult educators have faced the lack of firm anchors for their identity (Filander, 2005). If before a key part of identity was anchored in the professional activity performed by the individual, currently identity is no longer exclusively linked to the job, but is also a result of sociocultural skills that individuals mobilise to deal with the diversity and unpredictability of life situations. The self-development is thus a result of the experience of experiencing a wide range of circumstances and contexts of life (Monbaron, 2009).

Similar to what happens in almost all areas of activity, adult educators have been experiencing this turbulence and instability in their professional pathways. Combined with the uncertainty that exists in professional pathways, we must note the lack of continuity existing in Portugal with respect to adult education policies (Lima, 2008). Between 2012 and the beginning of 2013, all RPL Centres (named New Opportunities Centres) were closed by governmental initiative. In the beginning of 2014, new RPL centres were opened with another name (Centres for Qualification and Vocational Teaching). These centres´ main aims were to develop RPL processes (basic and secondary school education certification) and to inform and guide young people over 15 years and adults over 18 years about education and training offers. Currently a new change is underway in adult education with the implementation of the Qualify Programme (XXI Governo, 2016). This adult education programme has the aim to relaunch the qualification of adults with low level of schooling and to achieve this purpose the number of RPL centres will be increased.

This chapter intends to answer to the following research questions: How did adult educators learn to work as RPL professionals? How are adult educators coping with the uncertainty of their professional pathways in the adult education field?

RESEARCH METHODOLOGY

From a methodological point of view, I used a qualitative approach, as it was considered that this is the kind of research that provides a detailed understanding of the issue to investigate, which can be obtained by speaking directly to people, allowing them to produce a narrative of their life experiences (Creswell, 2007). The research was based on a comprehensive perspective that intended to describe, interpret and analyse critically the learning pathways of adult educators who were working in a changing work context.

The method of data collection used was the biographical interview (Pineau & Le Grand, 1993). The interview began with the following question: 'How did you become an adult educator?' The use of the biographical interview is linked to the need to understand the unique relationship that individuals have with the social and historic world, and also to study the meaning that they give to their experience (Delory-Momberger, 2012). The biographical interview highlights the individual's point of view in the analysis of the social world and the practical knowledge derived from some life experiences (Demazière, 2008).

Empirical data were collected from 32 adult educators who had worked in RPL in adult education centres called New Opportunities Centres. The interviews were recorded on audio support. As a data analysis technique I used thematic content analysis (Bardin, 1995) focused on the four axis that structure this research: professional activity, ways of learning, professional pathways, and professional identity. For this chapter I focused my analysis on the axis named ways of learning. Interview quotations included in this chapter are followed by an identification of the interviewee; however the names of the interviewees are not their names in order to keep anonymity.

WAYS OF LEARNING IN UNCERTAIN PROFESSIONAL CONTEXTS

The sample consisted of 32 adult educators aged 24 to 52; 27 females and 5 males. Adult educators had different educational backgrounds. The majority of adult educators held higher education degrees in social and human sciences, specifically thirteen held degrees in Psychology, four in Education Sciences, three in Sociology, two in Social Services and one in Anthropology. Moreover, nine adult educators held education degrees in teaching.

There were few adult educators who in their initial qualification had studied subjects linked with adult education. This was the case of some adult educators with higher education degrees in Education Sciences, as was referred to by one interviewee:

> I, during my basic degree in Education Sciences, had attended an adult education course…. (Inês)

However, the initial qualification of the majority of the adult educators didn't include the subject of adult education. So, how did adult educators learn to do this job?

The adult educators interviewed have learned through several ways. Experience was the common element to all learning pathways. Experience had a crucial importance in the learning process, as there were only a few interviewees who, in the course of their initial qualification, had contact with adult education. As outlined by one interviewee,

> [I learned] with work, I had nobody who has taught me. I didn't have too much guidance from people, from colleagues. I have learned to do this work alone, daily, with day-to-day experience, always improving, each time more, but it is continuous learning. (Alzira)

Adult educators learned a new professional activity in action, while they were performing the tasks and duties of the job. Experience and reflection about experience was one way of learning how to become an adult educator. The reinterpretation of experience by the individual can transform an experienced action into the appropriation of that action (Clénet, 2012), leading to learning.

Adult educators also learned through attending continuing education courses after they had started working in RPL. These continuing education courses were mostly provided by the national agency responsible for adult education, which at the time was called the National Agency for Qualification and was later called the National Agency for Qualification and Vocational Teaching. As was referred to by one interviewee,

> I started working in early November and I remember that during that year I had received training from the National Agency for Adult Education and Training. Over several days I learned everything about referential competences, balance methodologies, jury sessions and about how jury sessions should take place. All of this really helped me. (Carolina)

The learning process of how to exercise this professional activity was also carried out based on observation, talking with colleagues and sharing information, working processes and procedures. As was told by one interviewee,

> When I first came here I learned as much as I could about all the activities, I had colleagues who supported me and also taught me some of their practical skills. I also observed some of my colleagues' sessions. The whole thing is actually quite intuitive. (Roberta)

Adult educators interviewed had several learning pathways. Experience was the common element to all learning processes. It was through the performing of the professional activity, therefore in action, that all adult educators had learned their new professional activity. Experience had a fundamental importance in the learning process, since there were few adult educators who had contact with adult education in their initial qualification. Individuals can learn a lot through the action, and mainly through the analysis of the action (Pastré, 2007). The reflective and retrospective analysis about the action is a learning tool. The work analysis of a professional activity is a key moment in the building of meaning to the experiences of the individual.

When the interviews were undertaken the majority of adult educators were experiencing a time of big uncertainty. Due to a change of the government, adult educational policies had also changed. But professional uncertainty was a permanent situation for most adult educators because they had temporary employment contracts.

One strategy used by adult educators to cope with uncertainty of the labour market was to diversify their knowledge and competences. Some adult educators achieved vocational or higher education degrees in several subjects, always related to what they thought would offer more employment opportunities in the future. As was mentioned by two interviewees,

> Since I have finished my licenciate degree, my idea was always to diversify my knowledge, having in mind the context in which we are living, in other words to have a wider range of possibilities at the professional level. (Rute)

> Professionally, an area I also like is training management, and so I also want to invest in some training courses, in qualification in this field, because Education Science [that is my area of initial qualification] is not an area with much employability…. (Inês)

Some adult educators had chosen to improve their qualifications in their higher education degree area with the aim to get a job in this field in the future. As was referred to by an interviewee,

> Just now my professional pathway has met adult education due to an opportunity (…) because there was a time when I lived in a situation of unemployment. During this time I had applied here, in this foundation, and there was a vacancy in the New Opportunities Centre. That's how I got here. (Tânia)

Regarding her continuing education, Tânia added,

> I have not invested in the area of adult education. Currently I'm attending a masters' programme in the field of Community Psychology. (…) I'm not investing in technical, practical and theoretical terms in adult education and I do not think I will do it. (…) my initial qualification is the clinical area [Clinical Psychology]. (Tânia)

For these professionals, adult education was only a deviation in their professional pathway, often done to escape unemployment. These adult educators objective is to find a job in their higher education degree field, giving continuity to the investment made in the area of their initial qualification.

FINAL REMARKS

Following the changes that have happened in adult education, there were adult educators working in this field with professional pathways marked by discontinuity and employment instability. Social actors engaged in adult education were hostages of the changes in policies in this field.

With the emergence of new educational practices in adult education as was the case of RPL, there were adult educators who started to work without previous experience and most of them without knowledge and professional competences in this area. The data show us that these adult educators had a variety of initial qualification, and the only common point was the possession of a higher education degree (licenciate degree). Since some adult educators had initial qualification unrelated to adult education, they had learned in several ways, such as learning through experience, i.e., learning by doing, attending continuing education courses, seeing experienced peers working and sharing experiences with colleagues. We can say that adult educators had learned through eco-learning, hetero-learning (Pineau, 2009) and experiential learning, with direct and reflected contact with the learning situations (Josso, 1991).

Another important point to highlight is that, initially, learning dynamics demonstrated by adult educators promoted the acquisition of skills and competences about adult education. However, during their daily working life some adult educators had attended continuing education in some fields that they considered important to strengthen their employment competences, even in areas not related to adult education. They showed adjusted behaviour to cope with the flexibility of the labour market.

Concerning the ways of learning of adult educators and the instability of their working conditions, some questions can be raised. Insofar adult educators do not have an initial qualification in adult education, to what extent would it be important they have it and how does it could be structured? Regarding this issue, Guimarães (2016) pointed out that currently there are no specific formal education pathways directed to adult educators at the level of the initial qualification. A second question is related to continuing education in adult education. Since there is not too much continuing education, would it be pertinent to invest in this way of learning? Should continuing education be organised at national level or should it be structured and implemented by the different actors working in this field, adapting the contents of programmes to their unique work contexts? The lack of continuity of adult education policies in Portugal and the uncertainty of the labour market also leads to some questions regarding the way how adult educators are facing their work and themselves: What effects do the uncertain professional contexts have on the ways adult educators face their work? What are the implications of the instability of work contexts on their professional identity? It is important to note that the instability of working conditions experienced by adult educators can lead them to a process of disinvestment both in terms of attending continuing education programmes and in terms of the involvement with their professional activity (Paulos, 2015). Reflecting on these questions and a subsequent attempt to respond them may contribute to having adult educators better prepared to work in times characterised by instability and uncertainty.

REFERENCES

Alheit, P., & Dausien, B. (2006). Processo de formação e aprendizagens ao longo da vida [Training process and lifelong learning]. *Educação e Pesquisa, 32*(1), 177–197.
Barbier, J.-M. (2009). Voies pour la recherche en formation. *Éducation et didactique, 3*(3), 119–130. Retrieved September 24, 2015, from http://educationdidactique.revues.org/588
Bardin, L. (1995). *Análise de conteúdo* [Content analysis]. Lisboa: Edições 70.
Bauman, Z. (2001). *Modernidade líquida* [Liquid modernity]. Rio de Janeiro: Jorge Zahar Editor.
Bondía, J. L. (2002). Notas sobre a experiência e o saber de experiência [Notes about experience and knowledge experience]. *Revista Brasileira de Educação, 19*, 20–28.
Canário, R. (2008). *Educação de adultos: Um campo e uma problemática* [Adult education: A field and a problematic]. Lisboa: EDUCA.
Castro, R. V., Guimarães, P., & Sancho, A. V. (2007). Mutações no campo da educação de adultos. Sobre os caminhos da formação dos educadores [Mutations in the field of adult education: On the ways of educators training]. *Educar, 29*, 63–81.
Cavaco, C. (2009). Experiência e formação experiencial: a especificidade dos adquiridos experienciais [Experience and experiential learning: The specificity of prior learning]. *Educação Unisinos, 13*(3), 220–227.
Charlier, E., Roussel, J. F., & Boucenna, S. (2013). L'apprentissage par l'expérience: une thématique centrale dans la formation d'adultes. In E. Charlier, J.-F. Roussel, & S. Boucenna (Dirs.), *Expériences des adultes et professionnalités des formateurs* (pp. 9–17). Bruxelles: De Boeck.
Charlot, B. (2000). *Da relação com o saber: Elementos para uma teoria* [The relationship to knowledge: Elements for a theory]. Porto Alegre: Artmed Editora.
Clénet, J. (2012). Se former et se professionnaliser. Le point de vue du sujet. In D. Demazière, P. Roquet, & R. Wittorski (Coords.), *La professionnalisation mise en objet* (pp. 153–172). Paris: L'Harmattan.
Creswell, J. W. (2007). *Qualitative inquiry and research design: Choosing among five approaches*. Thousand Oaks, CA: Sage Publications.
Delory-Momberger, C. (2012). Abordagens metodológicas na pesquisa biográfica [Methodological approaches in biographical research]. *Revista Brasileira de Educação, 17*(51), 523–536.
Demazière, D. (2008). L'entretien biographique comme interaction négociations, contre-interprétations, ajustements de sens. *Langage & Société, 1*(123), 15–35.
Dominicé, P. (1991). La formation expérientielle: un concept importé pour penser la formation. In B. Courtois & G. Pineau (Coords.), *La formation expérientielle des adultes* (pp. 53–58). Paris: La Documentation Française.
Dominicé, P. (2006). A formação de adultos confrontada pelo imperativo biográfico [Adult training confronted by the biographical imperative]. *Educação e Pesquisa, 32*(2), 345–357.
Filander, K. (2005). Experts in uncertainty: Making cultural analysis of identities in adult education. In A. Bron, E. Kurantowicz, H. S. Olesen, & L. West (Orgs.), *'Old' and 'new' worlds of adult learning* (pp. 56–69). Wroclaw: Wydawnictwo Naukowe.
Guimarães, P. (2016). Ocupações da educação de adultos e desafios à profissionalização: tarefas e atividades desenvolvidas em contexto de trabalho [Occupations of adult education and challenges to professionalization: Tasks and activities developed in work context]. *Revista de Estudos Curriculares, 7*(2), 57–81.
Jarvis, P. (2006). *Towards a comprehensive theory of human learning*. London: Routledge.
Josso, M.-C. (1991). L'expérience formatrice: un concept en construction. In B. Courtois & G. Pineau (Coords.), *La formation expérientielle des adultes* (pp. 191–199). Paris: La Documentation Française.
Josso, M.-C. (2002). *Experiências de vida e formação* [Life experiences and training]. Lisboa: EDUCA.
Josso, M.-C. (2008). Formação de adultos: Aprender a viver e a gerir as mudanças [Adult training: Learning to live and to manage changes]. In R. Canário & B. Cabrito (Orgs.), *Educação e formação de adultos: mutações e convergências* (pp. 115–125). Lisboa: EDUCA.
Kolb, D. A. (1984). *Experiential learning: Experience as the source of learning and development*. Englewood Cliffs, NJ: Prentice Hall.

Lietard, B. (2007). Apologie critique de la formation expérientielle. *Vie Sociale, 4*, 11–20. Retrieved December 2, 2015, from https://www.cairn.info/revue-vie-sociale-2007-4-page-11.htm

Lima, L. (2008). A educação de adultos em Portugal (1974–2004): Entre as lógicas da educação popular e da gestão de recursos humanos [Adult education in Portugal (1974–2004): Between the logic of popular education and the human resource management]. In R. Canário & B. Cabrito (Orgs.), *Educação e formação de adultos. Mutações e convergências* (pp. 31–60). Lisboa: EDUCA.

Loureiro, A. P. F. (2012). "Novos" territórios e agentes educativos em sociologia da educação: o caso da educação de adultos ["New" territories and educational agents in sociology of education: The case of adult education]. *Revista Lusófona de Educação, 20*, 123–139.

Méda, D. (1999). *O trabalho. Um valor em vias de extinção* [The work. A value endangered]. Lisboa: Fim de Século.

Mezirow, J. (1990). How critical reflection triggers transformative learning. In J. Mezirow & Associates (Orgs.), *Fostering critical reflection in adulthood: A guide to transformative and emancipatory learning* (pp. 1–20). San Francisco, CA: Jossey-Bass.

Mezirow, J. (2000). Learning to think like an adult: Core concepts of transformation theory. In J. Mezirow & Associates (Orgs.), *Learning as transformation: Critical perspectives on a theory in progress* (pp. 3–33). San Francisco, CA: Jossey-Bass.

Monbaron, J. (2009). Exister dans le labyrinthe de nos parcours: mise en scène de la vie adulte. In J.-P. Boutinet & P. Dominicé (Orgs.), *Où sont passés les adultes? Routes et déroutes d'un âge de la vie* (pp. 85–102). Paris: Téraèdre.

Pastré, P. (2007). Analyse du travail et formation. *Recherches en Education, 4*, 23–28. Retrieved December 4, 2015, from http://www.recherches-en-education.net/IMG/pdf/REE-no4.pdf

Paulos, C. (2015). Qualification of adult educators in Europe: Insights from the Portuguese case. *International Journal for Research in Vocational Education and Training, 2*(1), 25–38.

Pineau, G. (1991). Formation expérientielle et théorie tripolaire de la formation. In B. Courtois & G. Pineau (Coords.), *La formation expérientielle des adultes* (pp. 29–40). Paris: La Documentation Française.

Pineau, G. (2009). L'autoformation dans le cours de la vie: entre l'hétéro et l'écoformation. *Education Permanente, 180*, 141–154.

Pineau, G., & Le Grand, J.-L. (1993). *Les histoires de vie*. Paris: Presses Universitaires de France.

Robin, J.-Y. (2009). Les parcours professionnels: des indicateurs encore pertinents pour penser la vie adulte? In J.-P. Boutinet & P. Dominicé (Orgs.), *Où sont passés les adultes? Routes et déroutes d'un âge de la vie* (pp. 123–144). Paris: Téraèdre.

Rothes, L. A. (2004). A formação de educadores de adultos em Portugal: Trajectos e tendências [The training of adult educators in Portugal: Pathways and tendencies]. In L. C. Lima (Org.), *Educação de adultos – Forum III* (pp. 61–85). Braga: Universidade do Minho.

Villers, G. (1991). L'expérience en formation d'adultes. In B. Courtois & G. Pineau (Coords.), *La formation expérientielle des adultes* (pp. 13–20). Paris: La Documentation Française.

XXI Governo. (2016). *Programa nacional de reformas 2016 – mais crescimento, melhor emprego, maior igualdade – qualificar os portugueses* [National program of reforms 2016 – more growth, better employment, greater equality – qualify the Portuguese]. Retrieved January 2, 2017, from http://www.portugal.gov.pt/media/19012677/20160418-mtsss-pnr-qualificacao.pdf

Zeitler, A., Guérin, J., & Barbier, J.-M. (2012). La construction de l'expérience. *Recherche et formation, 70*, 9–14. Retrieved September 22, 2015, from http://www.cairn.info/revue-recherche-et-formation-2012-2-page-9.htm

Catarina Paulo
University of Lisbon
Portugal

CAROL A. THOMPSON AND PETER J. WOLSTENCROFT

14. NO MORE SUPERHEROES ... ONLY AVATARS? SURVIVAL ROLE PLAY IN ENGLISH POST COMPULSORY EDUCATION

BACKGROUND

Developments such as the incorporation of colleges in England and Wales in 1993[1] had a fundamental influence on the post-compulsory education (PCE) sector by creating a dramatic transformation in culture, ethos and style of management. Prior to this, both managers and tutors had a high degree of autonomy and were given significant freedom in the way they organised their working lives. However, the introduction of data driven efficiency measures and the increased surveillance of professional activity triggered a significant change in both professional role and professional identity and has been referred to as the terrors of performativity (Ball, 2003).

Within the whirlwind of change, many organisations were in a state of flux. They had to contend with new funding mechanisms and subsequent cuts to their budget, as well as prepare for influential judgements on their performance by organisations such as the government's inspectorate of education, commonly known as Ofsted. This presented a range of new challenges which were 'supported' by a plethora of new guidelines, systems and processes and the result was described by Coffield as:

> A sector where the government had to establish a Bureaucracy Reduction Group to deal with the effects of its own hyperactivity in spawning so many new policies, initiatives, qualifications, institutions, partnerships, targets, priorities, ambitions and aspirations that those trying to enact their proposals became overwhelmed with the paperwork. (Coffield, 2008, p. 43)

For a new tutor entering the profession, this presented a somewhat muddled picture of the professional role and identity; on the one hand, there were clear guidelines relating to processes and the 'technical' aspects of the role, on the other, somewhat conflicting information from experienced colleagues who contested the imposed changes.

For teachers, one significant outcome of the changes was the value placed on the skill or craft of teaching above other aspects of the role. This focus created a much narrower professional identity and neglected the wider aspects of the role, potentially leading to a more defined perception of the types of professional development which were considered relevant.

According to the European Commission (2013), a teacher's role should include both teaching and teacher competencies. The former being those things associated with the craft of teaching and the latter encompassing the need to reflect, evaluate and work collaboratively in the wider professional community, recognising this as a body of knowledge which exists beyond the place of work. This view acknowledged teaching as a multifaceted career and provided a systemic view of teacher professionalism which could be likened to the notion of democratic professionalism (Sachs, 2001).

Despite the most significant of these changes having taken place over 20 years ago, there still remains some confusion around the purpose and extent of the PCE tutor's role and this is mirrored in the roles undertaken by middle managers (Thompson & Wolstencroft, 2013). Indeed, there is evidence to suggest that such confusion has led to a sense of conflict between initial perceptions of a particular role and actual practice and has resulted in both tutors and managers leaving the sector or even the profession itself (Chambers & Roper, 2000; Thompson & Wolstencroft, 2013). This illuminates what has been described as the 'disjuncture between official rhetoric of lifelong learning and the experiences of those working and studying in English Further Education' (Avis & Bathmaker, 2005, p. 61).

Although a number of the problems associated with entering the PCE teaching profession and undertaking management roles within it have been documented (Thompson & Wolstencroft, 2012, 2013; Spenceley, 1997; Avis & Bathmaker, 2007), this is not the complete picture. There are many new tutors and managers who had not only survived the process of change but enjoyed the challenge and found specific strategies to overcome the difficulties they were presented with (Thompson & Wolstencroft, 2012, 2013).

Within this chapter, we will explore the challenges and professional identities of new tutors and managers within PCE as well as the strategies they employ to cope with the individual demands of their jobs.

LITERATURE

Attempting to define the roles and responsibilities of either a tutor or a manager within post compulsory education in England is not a simple task. Reece and Walker (2003), writing in one of the most popular textbooks of the early twenty-first century, devoted 15 pages to describing the tutor's role, covering aspects such as facilitating learning, planning teaching, assessment and evaluation and yet, even this exhaustive list does not cover the breadth of tasks encompassed in the role. In addition, this description does not consider the context in which most tutors work or acknowledge the narrative of a sector where key performance indicators (KPIs) are dominant (Elliott, 2012).

The task becomes even more complicated when exploring the role managers within the sector. A role which was traditionally associated with managing curriculum has more recently been defined as being an 'active agent' in facilitating change

(Alexiadou, 2001) in order to 'influence tutors' in a positive manner (Jameson, 2006). Whilst many middle managers maintain that this was one of the main drivers for taking on the role (Thompson & Wolstencroft, 2013), the lived experience did not always concur. The changing nature of the sector driven by the KPI culture established the manager's role in a different light and viewed this as being much more restricted (Elliott, 2012; Briggs, 2006). Alternative evidence suggests that some managers, despite the more restrictive culture do manage to maintain a degree of autonomy (Page, 2015; Thompson & Wolstencroft, 2013) but these managers do appear to be in the minority.

Professional development within PCE is often underpinned by once mandatory (and now 'strongly encouraged') courses such as those leading to the Certificate in Education or Postgraduate Certificate of Education (PGCE). As these qualifications are generic in nature, the complexities of the sector are not always addressed and the accepted norms advocated within the programmes do not necessarily conform with the more instrumental approach demanded by employers (Husband, 2015). Within such programmes, notions such as communities of practice (Lave & Wenger, 1991) bear little resemblance to the practicalities of the job and as a result many new entrants do not always feel fully prepared for their role. This is true of both tutors (Simmons & Thompson, 2008) and managers (Thompson & Wolstencroft, 2013). Indeed, both groups have reported feelings of isolation and a lack of support from both mentors and peers (Spenceley, 1997). Such isolation can manifest itself in many different ways such as feelings of stress, uncertainty and in some cases, a sense of being in the wrong profession (Briggs, 2007; Robson, 1998).

The difficulties identified above have been exacerbated recently due the reduction in funding for the sector. This reduction, estimated at a total of 13.4% over 3 years (Chowdry & Sibieta, 2012), has resulted in a decline in the number of tutors in the sector (LSIS 2013), a decrease in the resources available and as a consequence increased pressure to perform on those who are left, creating a situation whereby 'those running curriculum departments will mainly be judged by student outcomes' (Briggs, 2001, p. 13). Inevitably the necessity to do more with less may take many teaching staff outside of their 'comfort zone' and as described by Jameson (2006) bring to light the 'darker side' of leadership practice when excessive pressure is put on staff, in some cases leading to bullying which impacts on the health and wellbeing of those involved.

Within this context, it is easy to see how many tutors and managers may face a number of dilemmas within their professional activities particularly when asked to undertake activities which challenge their professional values or for which they feel they have had no preparation. Potentially such dilemmas provide an opportunity to reflect on and transform practice (Mezirow, 2003), however, this is not always the case, particularly in environments where staff feel unsupported (Segal, 2006) and indeed in many cases it merely causes increased stress and feelings of being under pressure.

Educational establishments have taken different approaches to interpreting their staff's needs for support (Clandinin, 2008). This has been borne out by this research which illustrated the ways in which support was interpreted by both organisations and the individuals within them. The move to a teaching role from a previous career and subsequently to a management role, is a transition that can entail a significant amount of anxiety and has the potential to impact on a person's life both inside and outside of the workplace. Previous studies (Briggs, 2003, 2006) found that employees felt alienated from their jobs and under extreme pressure from managers. Whilst many find effective coping strategies, a minority turn to ways of coping that might be described as unhealthy, with excessive alcohol consumption and reliance on medication being reported (Jameson, 2006).

The way in which support for employees is implemented is also interpreted differently within establishments. For some establishments, formal mechanisms have been put in place. Within the compulsory sector, the concept of PPA (planning, preparation and assessment time) was introduced to ensure that teachers had a greater work/life balance. Although sometimes viewed as a 'sticking plaster' rather than a solution to deeper problems facing the profession (Hammersley-Fletcher & Lowe, 2013). Within PCE the focus is firmly placed on addressing the consequences of concerns and although access to additional services, such as a college approved counsellor or healthcare programme is sometimes provided, there is little acknowledgement that staff may need assistance in coping with the emotional aspects of their jobs.

METHODOLOGY

A case study approach, combined with semi-structured interviews was used in order to compare two diverse organisations within the post compulsory education sector in England. Organisation A is a military training establishment whilst organisation B is a College of Further Education specialising in the Creative Arts. Both organisations have a reputation for innovation and espoused values which encompass the support and well-being of staff.

A representative cross section of participants was selected using a purposive sampling technique. In each organisation, a senior manager in charge of the training and development of staff was interviewed along with a selection of middle managers. In addition to this tutors were interviewed. To ensure that the article reflected the views of those new to the sector, tutors interviewed were all currently completing their initial teacher training qualification.

Once the results from the initial sample had been examined, follow up forums were carried out to share these findings with a cross section of staff. The main objective of this was to gain insight into what could be done to address the issues highlighted.

The sample contained two managers (one senior) interviewed and six tutors in organisation A, whilst in organisation B there were six tutors and three managers (again one senior manager).

Semi-structured interviews took place in October and November 2015 and the follow up forums were in June 2016. These were used to provide a structure as well as an opportunity to explore specific responses. All interviews were transcribed and analysed to identify common themes. Findings have been structured according to themes drawn from the data for both organisations.

FINDINGS

'Bestowed' Professional Identities

Participants from both organisations described their individual roles in relation to their official job title rather than adopting more generic labels such as 'teacher', 'tutor' or 'manager'. In this sense, professional identity seemed to be something that was bestowed, rather than claimed and was translated into labels such as 'instructor … Lecturer in … or Curriculum Manager for …'. In addition, there appeared to be limited evidence that individuals considered themselves to be part of a wider professional community and reference was not made to the overall profession, indeed some responses deliberately diminished the description of the role, for example: 'I think the perception is it is professional … so I will go with that'.

Tutors in both organisations appeared to operate within small, self-contained units, rather than a broader environment. This was particularly evident in organisation B where tutors operated in discrete departments organised according to subject specialism or whether they were teaching on 'FE' or 'HE' courses. This finding is not unusual and historically is evident in the caricatures associated with certain subject groupings within FE, clearly evident in the 'two cultures' split between practical and academic subjects outlined by Gleeson and Mardle (1980).

Within organisation A, professional identity was even more removed from the overall profession, as most participants described their identity in terms of primary and secondary roles, the primary roles being firmly placed within the organisation rather than the wider profession. 'I am a soldier first of all, then an intelligence officer', although this participant was currently employed within a teaching role, this title was not used in any description. Others referred to themselves as 'subject matter experts' or 'intelligence officers' (titles used within the organisation) with the only concession to the teaching profession being use of the word 'instructor'.

What united both organisations was a general feeling from tutors that their job was being de-professionalised by the introduction of a conformist approach to teaching. This was illustrated by a tutor in organisation B: 'I feel they are telling you how they want you to teach and I want to develop my own way …. I feel like there is a very narrow view of what teaching is'. However, two tutors in organisation B, (both working within the HE section of the organisation), presented an overwhelmingly positive image of the organisation and did not outline any such restrictions on how they approached the teaching role.

Within organisation A, tutors operated within even stricter constraints including the requirement for PowerPoint presentations and resources to be approved before being used for teaching sessions. The process of changing things for individual lessons or groups was viewed as long and laborious and the consequence was that participants tended to complain about the system but go along with it.

The evidence presented in the interview responses did suggest that professional identity was not something that participants felt they had control over. Likewise, notions of professionalism seemed, in both organisations to be intertwined with the approaches advocated at an organisational level. In both cases these approaches leaned towards a competency model with a focus on teaching competencies rather than teacher competencies and did not correspond with more democratic approaches to professionalism. As a result, tutors seemed to view their roles in much more narrow terms. The response from managers corresponded to this by outlining their roles and professional identity as being in line with their roles within the organisation, again evidencing acknowledgement of the constraints imposed by the organisation but not questioning these. One manager, when describing his role, outlined the difficulties but did not question the reasons for them: '… it has become a running joke within the team. Because it is normally a year before someone packs it in'. This participant also showed awareness of the impact of quality assurance measures: 'We have a meeting once a week where we discuss things that are affecting data … sometimes it is bad news that I have to pass down to my team'; but readily accepted this as part of his role and described it as a form of support. The most noticeable difference to this was responses from managers at a more senior level who did raise questions about how systems and processes had created blocks to progress:

> For example, something that winds me up hideously is that we don't offer release to our teacher trainees … and that bothers me because I think they probably need it even if it's not hour for hour … we don't that's kind of the rule and mainly that's because it's so efficient and it's so calculated … so because everyone is doing up to 23 hours a week there's a calculation as to how many staff you need and then if you just say, 'could we just knock an hour off everyone' you are knocking an hour of 60 people and suddenly [financially] that's three members of staff …

Expectation Versus Reality

Previous studies have suggested that tutors do not feel prepared for the realities of working within the post compulsory education sector (Wallace, 2002; Spenceley, 2007; Thompson & Wolstencroft, 2012). In each of these studies, the lived experience of the role was perceived as being less rewarding than the expectations. The data from this research did not replicate previous findings as most participants had a clear insight into the role prior to starting to it. This was particularly evident in organisation A: 'I was already warned that the course was dated so I had the sceptical side of me as well was thinking what can I change when I get there?' and '... I would enjoy the teaching side of it but would be hampered by bureaucracy ...' Yet despite this prior knowledge, most tutors were frustrated by certain aspects of the role, specifically the need to ensure that everything was enshrined in paperwork: 'It can really get me down sometimes, the endless meetings with almost no outcomes and the paperwork filling and all that sort of stuff'. Similarly, tutors expressed concerns about what they saw as a 'no fail' culture within their organisations. These two quotes come from firstly, organisation A, then B:

> Firstly 'Nowadays, the minute I say someone is not good enough I am challenged' then 'If a student isn't doing work, its more work for me rather than for them. You have to do a tutorial and then type it up, phone their parents, write an action plan and I can do all of that and then the students still doesn't do anything, it is frustrating'.

Whilst most participants did have some insight into their roles at the outset, they were often surprised by the extent of the issues they encountered. For tutors these issues were created by college systems and processes. Conversely, for managers the problems associated with staff seemed to present the most concerns including problems with absence and performance management. Accompanying this was the almost constant change most managers had to contend with as outlined by a Senior manager from organisation B: 'My expectation has almost become Heraclitian, I just expect it to be different all the time'. The same manager also had their own particular view on the main causes of stress 'Was it Sartre who said "Hell is other people"'?

Avatars as Agents of Change

The notion of the teacher as an active agent denotes a group of professionals with the ability to make choices and find a balance between personal preferences, student needs and organisational aims. This description suggests that agency is a form of personal power and akin to Bourdieu's notion of 'habitus'. In this sense, agency is something which is not simply free will or a response to structures but an interplay between the two (Bourdieu, 1984). From a pragmatic perspective, agency might be defined as the ability of individuals to 'critically shape their responses to problematic situations' (Biesta & Tedder, 2006, p. 11). Within this research, the concept of agency was explored in relation to tutors and managers' perceptions of professional identity and the ways in which roles were enacted within a given context.

The resistance to the changes imposed on the further education sector post incorporation have been well documented (Ainley & Bailey, 1997; Shain & Gleeson, 1999) and clearly outline the conflicts found between teachers' ideas about their professional roles and the 'ideals' imposed through the adoption of a more marketised approach. As a result, teachers' work is highly controlled through management systems, often in ways which are perceived to have a negative impact on staff. Examples of this were presented in the initial interviews and the follow up forums and were usually recognised in the form of expected outcomes such as targets or performance measurement. The pressures did not appear to have diminished between the two parts of the research and in some cases the situation was viewed more pessimistically, as one participant from organisation B explained:

'I think our situation has actually got worse. Since being asked all of those questions I would have so many more examples to go with that …' This was supported by a colleague: 'The fact of the matter is … challenging is a lot of effort and when you are already really fatigued mentally and physically, that challenge seems like an impossible task …'

Indeed, the examples provided from both organisation A and organisation B represented groups of people who were well aware of their situation and somewhat resigned to it for survival reasons.

If the system doesn't do anything to support you time and again it's like well … why try and beat the system when it's never going to work because there's no other heroes above you.

and: The [organisation] is terrible for it because they don't like 'superheroes' or people who fight back. if you fight back … you won't get promoted … if you don't get promoted you won't get into the managerial positions and the people in the managerial positions are the 'yes men' …

The 'final resignation' came from one of the most experienced tutors in the group:

… people are frightened of losing their jobs so they are therefore conforming to the rules … when you become stressed you revert to a situation where you stick to the rules or a process so that you don't actually feel the stress quite so much. So, if you just keep ticking the boxes then you can keep the stress levels down.

These findings contradict views that teachers are able to be agents of change with an independent ability to act (Priestley et al., 2012), instead they depict a scenario of following orders and 'fitting in' perhaps representative of the accepted culture of conformity present within both organisations. The responses also highlight a one-dimensional view of agency which perhaps reduces the notion to its simplest terms.

Taking Emirbayer and Mische's (1998) view, agency should be seen as three dimensional with *iterational, projective* and *practical-evaluative* dimensions. The iterational taking into account professional histories, in this context the ways in which things have been, or are currently done within the organisations; the projective taking a future orientation, based on the facility to imagine alternative possibilities and the practical-evaluative giving consideration to the context of past history and dealing with the events of the moment. If we examine the data from this perspective, the picture is a little different as illustrated by the following responses; in organisation A, where tutors were often training future colleagues, there was clear appreciation of the underpinning reasons for current processes:

'The management work in their own little silos where they know they have got to get a certain number of people through so that's what they are concerned with. We are not going to be trainers for ever ... we will go back and do our normal jobs ...'. Whilst recognising the data driven reasons underpinning processes and the ways in which staff turnover reinforced norms of practice, there was also acknowledgement of the importance of, and potential for a change: '... and that person who we thought should have failed ... you could end up working with them ... so we should probably take that view and get rid of them because otherwise we are putting them into this trade group'.

In organisation B, where most senior managers did not teach, respondents were also aware of the reasons for current approaches and showed clear appreciation of the potential for change:

'... the reason that happens is that as managers they are not in that everyday routine of what you are experiencing ...' and 'It's a bit like having advice on your career and your love life from your grandparents ... cos (sic) everything they know was relevant like (sic) 40 years ago ...' These responses highlight a shared understanding of the reasons for stagnation in processes and led to suggestions about steps which might be taken to generate greater understandings and potential improvements:

If we turn it around real quick ... instead of love life ... think a war ... which is almost the same thing ... people on the front line, they will have their radios ... (and) can basically explain "this is the path that we have got to take" they have to help the commanders ... and if that's not taking place ... they keep on making the same mistakes.

These responses illustrate that teacher and manager agency cannot simply be seen as personal capacity in the form of the 'superhero' who fights a given cause but is in fact contextually bound and requires recognition of all factors which influence that context. To promote agency for professionals within the post compulsory education sector is not only a matter of professional development or the provision of learning spaces but also requires consideration of the current cultures and structures within which the sector operates.

It was evident that many of the respondents did use their agency in ways which had a positive impact on their colleagues or students; one clear example of this could be described as 'protective mediation' (Osborn et al., 1997), in this case the tutor was well aware of the organisation's 'rules' in relation to student attendance:

My best student is straight distinctions for everything, has attendance of 60 odd percent and everyone else can look at these statistics and go "oh that's pretty awful ... what's being done to punish this one?" ... but they are literally outperforming in every other thing you ask them to do.

By not 'punishing' this student the tutor is acting agentically in order to protect them from aspects of organisation policy which are considered unhelpful or even harmful. The same tutor was aware that these actions were viewed differently by those in more senior positions and interpreted as something akin to wayward, rather than agentic behaviour:

> the problem is I am then being told by 'higher ups' in our organisation that I am taking too much of myself into that room and I am making too much of a personal bond with the students as was pointed out to me earlier in the week … after five years now I am still treated like the unreliable child.

Support Strategies and Coping Strategies

It is clear that the organisations within this study recognise the need to support their staff and there were a number of measures put in place to mitigate against the pressures that tutors and managers experienced. These included additional training and in some cases mentoring. Although these efforts were acknowledged by participants, the general feeling was that the strategies implemented were focussed on organisational, rather than professional aims and as a result were of limited value. Whilst several participants recognised the value of the organisation providing financial support for training, they were also aware that this was overtly directed by more senior managers:

> '… so the hierarchy tell us what we should be doing, how we can develop and give us opportunities to do so'. In some examples there was an element of cynicism which suggested that espoused support strategies may have had more to do with creating the right image than supporting individuals, articulated succinctly by one tutor from organisation A: 'It looks good on paper'.

Within both organisations feedback from participants evidenced the importance of informal support mechanisms which usually revolved around peers. These had some similarities to the concept of communities of practice (Lave & Wenger, 1991) in that all participants had shared common interests usually to do with teaching or managing education. One difference was that, with the exception of teacher training, none of the participants appeared to be involved in communities of practice beyond the organisation.

In some cases, support was linked directly to professional development, for example learning through peer observations or discussing approaches to teaching, opportunities usually facilitated within teacher training programmes. In other examples the support had more to do with managing emotions and colleagues were seen as a sympathetic ear. A minority of respondents did mention the importance of 'individual space' but the majority were enthusiastic about the support they received from their peers, for example:

... just sit in on each other's lessons and sit down now and again with a brew and iron out any problems.

Space to Learn

The concept of learning spaces was interpreted in two distinct ways; firstly, a physical space which was removed from the work environment; secondly, the recognition that space in the work timetable would be the most important learning space. In many cases, the examples given were similar to the more traditional communal 'staffrooms' in effect, a place where people could get away from the stresses of the job. Some participants talked about the practicalities of having a space to get away from the paraphernalia associated with modern teaching: 'A place where I can't be hounded by phone calls', whilst the comments of others were more closely linked to the concept of a community of practice: 'A place with peers to bounce ideas around'. A common theme was that both tutors and managers wanted a 'safe' place where they could discuss things without risk of censure, as outlined by a manager in organisation B '... where you can say the unsayable'.

This final point was reinforced by the differences in the data presented in the separate parts of this research. Within the individual interview transcripts there is evidence of a group of people who felt dominated by the systems and processes in place. Within the group forums, the sharing of thoughts and ideas led to greater clarity in relation to the drivers present for those working within the sector and reference was made to a philosophical, rather than corporate approach: 'There has to be a genuine desire to make a change to see students and think ... they are not numbers and they are not just sheep ... and thinking that "I want these people to become something" ... that drives everything'.

The provision of teacher education was also considered as a possible learning space with the ability to improve professional practice as well as teacher agency, yet this too was questioned in relation to its impact; as highlighted by one participant:

> competence based teacher training programmes breed competence based teachers ... if that's what they think teaching is about .... Jumping through hoops and ticking boxes ... then that's what you're going to get.

The data presented in the forums suggest that that this view might be simplistic. All of the participants were aware of the need to successfully complete teacher training qualifications as part of their professional development but also recognised the opportunity this presented to analyse current processes and practices. When gathered as a collective, participants from both organisations articulated a drive and passion for 'making a difference' to the lives of their students, despite the limitations imposed within the individual organisations. The time and space to share ideas, often encapsulated within a teacher training class was viewed as a vehicle for this and provided the space within which to explore alternative approaches.

CONCLUSIONS

Previous research has suggested that many tutors and managers have fought against the 'terrors of performativity' (Ball, 2003) often through forms of strategic compliance (Shain & Gleeson, 1999). Our own research, conducted 4 years ago, into the roles of curriculum managers in the sector provided a number of examples of this and depicted this group as 'superheroes' driven by their personal values rather than those imposed by the organisation (Thompson & Wolstencroft, 2013). This non-conformist approach was not evident in the data presented here, in fact, whilst tutors and managers in both organisations recognised and often resented, the constraints placed upon them, they did display consistently compliant approaches, albeit 'reluctant compliance'.

This was most apparent in the ways in which participants described their professional identity as something which was 'bestowed' upon them by the organisation, rather than a profession in its own right. It is clear that for the tutors in this study their roles were directed by teaching, rather than teacher competencies (European Commission, 2013) placing an emphasis on the more technical aspects of the role and references made to some of the control measures which had been put into place within both organisations such as prescribed approaches to teaching, checks on data, limited control over resources, did emphasise the role of teaching as a craft rather than a profession. Likewise, managers provided evidence of introjecting the values of the organisation by articulating a need to comply with organisational norms, even to the extent of seeing QA measures such as checks on data, as a form of support.

Most participants in this research took up their roles post incorporation and as a result were not familiar with the professional context prior to the impact of marketisation. The resulting segregation, created by increased competition has increased the power of individual organisations to such an extent that the wider profession does not seem to be recognised. This is particularly apparent for tutors who viewed their professional identities in line with their formal titles or primary roles within the organisation and their agency as being governed by organisational norms. Notions of collegiality beyond the immediate workplace do appear to have become alien and were not considered as a form of personal learning by most of the participants. Despite the more limited view of collegiality, all participants recognised and valued the ways in which their immediate colleagues offered support and sought informal ways of accessing this for professional development and emotional sustenance.

A dominant finding within the interview data is the overall influence of individual organisations to design and dictate professional identity to such an extent that individuals and professional groups appeared to be dominated by given roles. The evidence suggests that the strategic compliance which previously allowed individuals to meet organisational aims whilst guided by their own professional values, appears to have been replaced by high levels of reluctant compliance with complete awareness of how the organisation's management processes were controlling teacher and manager agency.

When talking collectively, as evidenced by the forum data, tutors indicated higher levels of agency and recognised the ways in which they could effect change (Priestley et al., 2012). Although tentative, this did illustrate a willingness to take action which may support personal and professional values over organisational norms.

In the world of computer games, the Avatar is an icon which plays out a particular role, in Hinduism the manifestation of a deity released on earth … in the world of post compulsory education, a reluctant conformer … or an embodiment of potential change?

NOTE

[1] The Incorporation of colleges refers to the FE-HE Act 1992, which released FE institutions from the control of local authorities and gave them responsibilities of self-regulation and independence.

REFERENCES

Alexiadou, N. (2001). Management identities in transition: A case study from further education. *Sociological Review, 49*(3), 412–435.
Avis, J., & Bathmaker, A. (2007). 'How do I cope with that?' The challenge of 'schooling' cultures in further education for trainee FE teachers. *British Educational Research Journal, 33*(4), 509–532.
Ball, S. (2003). The teacher's soul and the terrors of performativity. *Journal of Education Policy, 18*(2), 215–228.
Biesta, G. J. J., & Tedder, M. (2006). *How is agency possible? Towards an ecological understanding of agency-as achievement* (Working Paper 5). Exeter: The Learning Lives project.
Bourdieu, P. (1984). *Distinction: A social critique of the judgement of taste*. London: Routledge.
Briggs, A. (2001). Middle managers in further education: Exploring the role. *Management in Education, 15*(4), 12–16.
Briggs, A. (2006). *Middle management in further education*. London: Continuum.
Briggs, A. (2007). Exploring professional identities: Middle leadership in further education colleges. *School Leadership and Management, 27*(5), 471–485.
Chambers, G., & Roper, T. (2000). Why students withdraw from initial teacher training. *Journal of Education for Teaching: International Research and Pedagogy, 26*(1), 25–43.
Chowdry, H., & Sibieta, L. (2012). *Trends in education and schools spending*. London: IFS.
Clandinin, D. J. (2008). Creating learning spaces for teachers and teacher educators. *Teachers and Teaching: Theory and Practice, 14*(5–6), 385–389.
Coffield, F. (2008). *Just suppose teaching and learning became the first priority*. London: Learning and Skills Network.
Crawley, J. (2012). 'On the brink' or 'designing the future'? Where next for lifelong learning initial teacher education? *Teaching in Lifelong Learning: A Journal to Inform and Improve Practice, 4*(1), 2–12. Retrieved October 27, 2015, from http://dx.doi.org/10.5920/till.2012.412
Department for Business Innovation and Skills. (2012). *Professionalism in further education: Interim report*. London: BIS.
Elliott, G. (2012). Policy, performativity and partnership: An ethical leadership perspective. *Research in Post-Compulsory Education, 17*(4), 423–433.
Emirbayer, M., & Mische, A. (1998). What is agency? *The American Journal of Sociology, 103*, 962–1023.
Etzioni, A. (Ed.). (1969). *The semi-professions and their organization: Teachers, nurses, social workers*. New York, NY: Free Press.
Gleeson, D., & Mardle, G. (1980). *Further education or training? A case study in the theory and practice of day release education*. London: Routledge & Kegan Paul.

Hammersley-Fletcher, L., & Lowe, M. (2013). In K. Safford, M. Stacey, & R. Hancock (Eds.), *Small scale research projects in primary school.* Abingdon: Routledge.

Husband, G. (2015). The impact of tutors' initial teacher training on continuing professional development needs for teaching and learning in post-compulsory education. *Research in Post-Compulsory Education, 20*(2), 227–244.

Jameson, J. (2006). *Leadership in post compulsory education.* Abingdon: David Fulton.

Lave, J., & Wenger, E. (1991). *Situated learning: Legitimate peripheral participation.* Cambridge: Cambridge University Press.

Learning and Skills Improvement Service. (2013). *An analysis of the staff individualised record data, 2011–12.* Coventry: LSIS.

Mezirow, J. (2003). Transformative learning: Theory to practice. *New Directions for Adult and Continuing Education, 74*(1), 5–12.

Orr, K. (2012). Coping, confidence and alienation: The early experience of trainee teachers in English FE'. *Journal of Education for Teaching, 38*(1), 51–65.

Page, D. (2011). Fundamentalists, priests, martyrs and converts: A typology of first tier management in further education. *Research in Post-Compulsory Education, 16*(1), 101–121.

Priestley, M., Biesta, G., & Robinson, S. (2015). *Teachers as agents of change: An exploration of the concept of teacher agency* (Working Paper No. 1). Stirling: Teacher Agency and Curriculum Change, University of Stirling.

Reece, I., & Walker, S. (2003). *Teaching, training and learning a practical guide* (5th ed.). Sunderland: BEP.

Robson, J. (1998). A profession in crisis: Status, culture and identity in the further education college. *Journal of Vocational Education and Training, 50*(4), 585–607.

Sachs, J. (2001). Teacher professional identity: Competing discourses, competing outcomes. *Journal of Education Policy, 16*(2), 149–161.

Segal, S. (2006). The existential conditions of explicitness: An Heideggerian perspective. *Studies in Continuing Education, 21*(1), 73–89.

Shain, F., & Gleeson, D. (1999). Under new management: Changing conceptions of teacher professionalism and policy in the further education sector. *Journal of Education Policy, 14*(4), 445–462.

Simmons, R., & Thompson, R. (2008). Creativity and performativity: The case of further education. *British Educational Research Journal, 34*(5), 601–618.

Spenceley, L. (2007). Walking into a dark room: The initial impressions of learner-educators in further education and training. *Journal of Further and Higher Education, 31*(2), 87–96.

Thompson, C. A., & Wolstencroft, P. (2013). Promises and lies. *Journal of Further and Higher Education, 38*(1), 1–18.

Thompson, C. A., & Wolstencroft, P. (2014). Give 'em the old razzle dazzle: Surviving the lesson observation process in further education. *Research in Post Compulsory Education, 19*(3), 261–275.

Wallace, S. (2002). No good surprises: Intending tutors' preconceptions and initial experiences of further education. *British Educational Research Journal, 28*(1), 79–93.

Williams, J., & Jacobs, J. (2004). Exploring the use of blogs as learning spaces in the higher education sector. *Australasian Journal of Educational Technology, 20*(4), 232–247.

Carol A. Thompson
University of Pennsylvania
Philadelphia, PA, USA

Katy J. Wolstencroft
Leiden University
Leiden, the Netherlands

ANDREA GALIMBERTI, BARBARA MERRILL,
ADRIANNA NIZINSKA AND
JOSE GONZÁLEZ-MONTEAGUDO

CONCLUSIONS

The chapters in this book illustrate the rich ways in which the relationship between continuity and discontinuity in learning careers occur in different learning situations and at different levels. Discontinuities can be easily recognised as a distinctive phenomenon, which is more and more common and widespread in contemporary western countries that witnessed the crisis of linearity in different aspects of human life. A paradigm based on life-lasting jobs and predictable life stages is largely a thing of the past as it no longer reflects people's everyday life. Many authors of reflexive modernisation theory, such as Bauman, Giddens, Beck, describe the progressive uselessness of inherited and consolidated patterns in decision making as well as the possible effects in terms of creativity and emancipation and also of anxiety and fear.

In general we can assume that in contemporary western societies people are facing transitions that involve a discontinuity with previous generations in terms of a variety of socio-economic aspects, but what effect is this having on transformation in the educational system that are historically constructed on the ideas of stability?

> There is a proximity between the ideas of order and continuity. Social order may thus be conceived as an expression of the continuity of institutions and culture. The integrity of the self, as another expression of order, can also be interpreted as a form of continuity, sustained by the capacity to avoid ruptures or the ability to resolve crisis. To some extent, the history of education can be interpreted as a constant research for increasing order, either organizationally (e.g. school's efficiency) or from a social and normative point of view (e.g. equity and justice). (Alhadeff-Jones, 2017, p. 121)

It is possible to consider the continuity/discontinuity dimensions as an interplay of different systemic levels: macro, meso and macro. At the macro level we can retrace the wider socio-economic and cultural assumptions while the meso level is represented by the proximal social contexts that are fundamental for the construction and recognition of one's identity (family, higher education, professional contexts etc). Finally, the micro level is represented by individual lived experiences. In a systemic view (see Formenti et al., 2014) those levels are considered as interdependent and mutual influencing.

The book chapters invite us to reflect on various aspects related to these different levels.

At the macro level the fundamental question is how educational systems are dealing with discontinuities, in terms of educational policies and what are the assumptions underlying this theme. Fenwick highlighted a general lack of metaphors to "appreciate transitions as multiple, complex pathways" and the urgent need for representations of mobility and change, like "oscillating, expanding, returning, stitching" (Fenwick, 2013, p. 363). This possibility of a more complex map has also to do with how we deal with temporality and rhythms' (Alhadeff-Jones, 2017) and how these attitudes shape concepts like "lifelong learning" and "transitions". Roquet's chapter addresses this theme directly, showing how continuity and discontinuity in relation to perceived temporality offers differentiated forms of professional identity construction.

Many of the book chapters can be considered as offering useful insights in order to understand how educational systems in different domains – or "meso levels" (higher education, health systems, social institutions, different professional contexts) are facing challenges related to the continuity/discontinuity issue.

In higher education, for example, one of the most urgent issue is related to non-traditional students and their need to compose the discontinuity of different backgrounds and life worlds (in terms of belonging) in order to construct a learner identity which is able to deal and cope with HE institutions that still hold assumptions, languages, expectations that meet certain middle class habitus (Finnegan et al., 2014). Broadhead's chapter and the chapter authored by King, Eamer and Ammar's give us examples of existing tensions on this theme but also gazes on new possibilities.

The transition between higher education and the market is becoming more and more "non-linear" and needs a resource of imagination in order to create new useful mediations. Non-traditional students represent a category potentially at risk, that may face particular difficulties: Thunborg and Bron's chapter show us how HE can become a means for realising a segregated labour market rather than an arena for equality and social mobility. Paradoxically the market creates difficult conditions not only for those with untraditional learning backgrounds but also for those who have developed key competences for the knowledge economy. This is the case of PhD graduates who are facing more and more difficulties in obtaining a long term career inside the academy and, at the same time, are risking a skill-mismatch in relation to transitions oriented towards non-academic contexts. Galimberti and Ratti's chapter give us an example of an original way to deal with this issue both theoretically and pragmatically.

Another interesting meso level is represented by health systems: Fernando and King's chapter introduces us to learning careers in mental health institutes in relation to previous interrupted educational experiences; an effort to face disruptive disconnections and transform them into social integration with supporting programmes involving different institutions (mental health institutions, hospitals, university campus). Other social institutions where educational processes take place are represented in the book. Pillera's chapter explores the experience of detention in prison: a moment that can be experienced only as a "negative" discontinuity with ordinary life, but at the same time, offering a "liminal" dimension, which has the potential for experiencing differences in lifestyle and possibilities that may trigger generative learning.

Finally at the micro level the single individual trace the continuities and discontinuities of his/her experience and afterwards construct a narration about it. Here there is the space to understand how macro and meso dimensions are interpreted, shaped and performed by individuals in their lives.

At the micro level it is interesting to explore a subject's positioning in relation to their contexts and transitions between them. This experience involves also assuming a personal stance in relation with values, norms, requests that a professional context may require and this means taking a stance also in relation with wider themes related to educational systems (what we called before the "macro" level). Thompson and Wolstencroft's chapter describes subjects positioning in relation to macro-issues like the hegemony of performativity and measurement in education; Paulos's chapter reflects on adult educators' copying strategies in relation to the uncertainty of their professional careers in the adult education field.

Moving attention to the micro level is particularly interesting as individual narratives may open up new points of view on issues raised at the meso and macro levels and that risk to be treated in a too simplistic and generalistic way. For example, Tenorio-Rodriguez, Padilla-Carmona and Gonzàlez-Monteagudo's chapters help us to understand how the status of "non-traditional" student – a status which often reduces employability opportunities – can also become an added value in individuals' narratives. In this case the research participants felt they were better protected in the transition to the market as they have previous career paths and a set of contacts that can facilitate their further insertion. Also their greater life experiences leads them to become more autonomous and to consider themselves as more prepared to open up their own career opportunities by means of self-employment.

An experience of discontinuity can represent for individuals a potential risk but at the same time an opportunity to challenge one's experience and frames of reference, as highlighted by Ted Fleming in the introduction chapter. At this level the question, for educators, becomes: which conditions are useful in order to create leaning contexts that promote transformative processes and support this learning potential? The importance of setting transitional spaces (West & Carlson, 2007) in learning contexts is crucial to sustain people dealing with continuity and discontinuities in their careers. Silva, Dionìso and Cunha's chapter and Leal's chapter are example of how participation in formal learning situations has effects on individual identities and their possibilities to develop critical consciousness. Kastner's chapter helps us to focus also on contexts based on competence assesment that – even not formally – may become places for learning, social inclusion and recognition in crucial transitional moments.

These examples of learning potential in formal and non-formal learning contexts are inspiring and fundamental in order to understand how learning on (and from) transitions may take place in particular contexts. At the same time, as educators, we have to be careful in avoiding the idea that more educational opportunities are always useful in order to trigger better learning processes. Education tends to be accepted as good for helping subjects in transitioning but this must not be accepted in an uncritical way. Ecclestone (2009) warns about the risk of working for a better adaptation in ways that are infantilizing, guiding subjects towards a ready-made idea of "successful transition".

In an interesting study Field and Lynch (2015) highlight how education may be a factor contributing to the sensation of getting "stuck" in the transitions: educational contexts may both become enabling spaces or alienating ones. In order to avoid this risk we have to nurture a complex way of thinking, connecting the interplay of different factors and levels in order to understand which processes are taking place in the learning contexts and how continuity/discontinuity dimensions in learning and professional careers contribute to shape these experiences, and, at the same time, is shaped by them.

REFERENCES

Alhadeff-Jones, M. (2017). *Time and rhytms of emancipatory education: Rethinking the temporal complexity of self and society*. Abingdon: Routledge.

Ecclestone, K. (2009). Lost and found in transition: educational implications of concerns about 'identity', 'agency' and 'structure'. In J. Field, J. Gallagher, & R. Ingram (Eds.), *Researching transitions in lifelong learning* (pp. 9–27). London: Routledge.

Fenwick, T. (2013). Understanding transitions in professional practice and learning: Towards new questions for research. *Journal of Workplace Learning, 25*(6), 352–367.

Field, J., & Lynch, H. (2015). Getting stuck, becoming unstuck: Agency, identity and transition between learning contexts. *Journal of Adult and Continuing Education, 21*, 3–17.

Finnegan, F., Merrill, B., & Thunborg, C. (2014). *Students voices of inequalities in European Higher Education*. Oxon: Routledge.

Formenti, L., West, L., & Horsdal, M. (2014). Introduction: Only connect, the parts and the whole: The role of biographical and narrative research? In L. Formenti, L. West, & M. Horsdal (Eds.), *Embodied narratives. Connecting stories, bodies, cultures and ecologies*. Odense: University Press of Southern Denmark.

West, L., & Carlson, A. (2007). *Claiming space: An indepth auto/biographical study of a local sure start project*. Canterbury: CCCU.

Printed in the United States
By Bookmasters